IF I'M NOT YOURS

If I'm Not Yours

Finding My Father
Through Faith

KAITLIN DAWN THOMSON

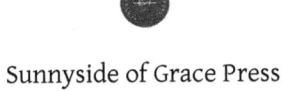

Sunnyside of Grace Press

Contributors: Thank you to those whose memories I relied on to fill in the gaps in mine. To my dad, who helped me word his dialogue, I enjoyed getting to know you. To those who allowed me to divulge the past, despite the hardship or discomfort it might cause you.

Acknowledgements: To my beta readers, your help was immeasurable, especially Mara and Wren who offered hours of their time to help me. I would also like to thank my editor at Black Quill Editing, Reese, who dedicated more than half a year to guiding and teaching me. To Jesus, who held my hand throughout my life and made the positive parts of this story possible. To those of you who prayed for me as I undertook this massive and emotional journey.

Dedication: To my beloved children, may you see the faithfulness of God despite my flaws. To my dad, may God give us many years together. To my mother, who has endured many trials and has somehow maintained a kind heart. To the soldiers who have served our country, I will never forget your sacrifices. To those of my friends and family who did not live to see it written or published. I miss all of you and am blessed to have been a part of your lives, especially my uncle John, Aunt Tary, and my stepdad, Mitchell. To my two friends from youth group, and Martin; they are not on Earth any longer, but I will see them again.

Publisher's Note: This is a work of non-fiction. Names, characters, places, and incidents are a product of the author's memory. Any resemblance to people, living or dead, or to businesses, events, institutions, or locals may be coincidental. The author has tried to write this memoir to the best accuracy possible. Some scenes had to be combined for clarity and ease of narrative. Every effort has been made to respect the privacy of the characters in this memoir.
Library of Congress control number: 2022902999
Book Layout © 2017 BookDesignTemplates.com
Photo stock: Dimedrol, Artist website http://dmkfoto.ru

IF I'M NOT YOURS/ KAITLIN DAWN THOMSON. -- 1st ed.
ISBN *979-8-9857947-4-8*
First Printing, 2022

CONTENTS

vii

~ One ~

I plop onto my bed and sit next to my husband. I'm exhausted from the day I spent chasing after my young children, with their boundless energy. After opening my laptop, I log onto Facebook because I need to unwind and catch up on my social media account. Online, a friend asks me, *Is this your dad?* She is commenting about a picture from 2020 I'd posted from my vacation to Florida.

I don't know how to answer. I lean against my bed's headboard. "Why can't anything be easy?" I ask my husband, Pat, who is sitting beside me.

"What's wrong?" Pat's eyes are full of concern as his gaze lingers on my face.

"I'm okay. My friend asked if Alan was my dad. What should I say?"

Pat rubs my shoulder. "He *is* your dad."

"I suppose you're right." I sit more erect and respond to her question, *He's my biological dad.* I should just say that he's my dad, but it feels like a betrayal to my stepdad and there isn't enough space on Facebook to answer fully.

I could name my fathers, God being one of them, but anytime I mention all of them, it confuses people. Not everyone has five dads as I do. Or like my twin sister does; she has six. I wonder if that's why God made two of us, so someone would understand my situation.

Together, my twin sister Wren and I have been navigating life. Once upon a time in rural Minnesota, we had one dad. It was 1994 then, and I was seven. The days were longer and if someone asked who my dad was; I knew exactly what I'd say.

Wren ran into the kitchen. She moved like lightning. Quicker than I could. Mom said she was born thirty minutes before me, and I could believe it because she was competitive. That's why she was born first. Despite being faster than me, Wren was mine, and she'd always been with me since I'd been alive. I've always seen her as a better part of me.

There were differences. I had a light pink birthmark on my neck where Wren did not, and she had a birthmark that Mom called a beauty mark next to her nose. Wren's face was narrower.

Dad sat in his chair in the room's corner in the worn-in La-Z-Boy chair. Dad's scratchy mustache curled under his nose, which was barely visible over the top of his shiny car magazine. My sister, Sierra, climbed onto his lap. She was a mini-version of Mom, with a fire inside that made her wild like her curly, spring-like hair. Dad winked at me, then continued reading his magazine.

At the end of the couch, Mom read a novel with a shirtless man and a woman on the cover. Mom was prettier than the girl in her icky book. I didn't know why she'd choose to read that kind of story. I preferred princesses.

"Let's take the snowmobiles for a spin," Dad said, rising from his chair, moving Sierra.

Everyone scurried around the room, grabbing their heavy winter gear. It excited me to be doing something fun.

I waddled down the outside steps in my puffy snow pants toward the two snowmobiles idling in the driveway. I became an abominable snowman, stomping my way there, waving my arms to keep my balance. The exhaust floated in the breath-taking cold. The smell of gas hung in the air.

"I'm freezing," Wren said, wrapping her arms around herself, standing midway between the front door and the snowmobiles.

Dad stood with one leg on each side of the snowmobile, so I trudged toward him, hoping I could ride with him because Mom would probably drive too slowly.

Dad raised his voice, "Stop complaining, Wren. Once we get moving, you will be fine." Dad twisted to face me; his breath made a puff of steam in the frigid air. "Hop on, KD."

I climbed on behind him.

"I'm riding with Mommy," Sierra said matter-of-factly as if daring us to argue with her.

I sat behind Dad and wrapped my arms around him as close as I could with my thick jacket. When Dad was near, the world was better. Mom took Wren and Sierra with her on the other snowmobile.

Dad pulled away from the house first, and we traveled along the snowy paths around our house. Mom rode behind us.

After Dad drove a mile through the neighborhood, we hit a bump in a shallow ditch and glided through the brisk air. I knew I could trust Dad to land. The snowmobile skis hit the thick snow with a soft thud, and I hugged him tighter.

Snow burdened the branches of the pine trees along the moonlit road. Snowflakes flew at me, becoming delicate raindrops as they landed on my face.

I wanted the ride to start all over again, but the cold sunk beneath my layers, and I shivered as we pulled into the driveway again. Running to the door as fast as my heavy legs allowed, I followed Dad inside the house.

I lifted the soft rabbit-fur hat off my head, sweat drenched my hair. I let the warm air inside the house fill my lungs. My body became a sauna, and I needed cold air. The urge to take off all the extra layers grew with every passing moment. I stripped off my winter gear and then sat on the couch next to Dad.

Mom left the room and came back a few minutes later carrying steaming mugs of hot chocolate with tiny marshmallows. She handed Sierra and Dad the first two, and returned, handing a cup to Wren and me.

I put my lips on the rim and blew. The sweet brown liquid smelled like chocolate, and I sipped it, even though I knew it might burn my lips.

"Tomorrow we'll visit your grandma Nelly." Dad smiled, then set his cup aside.

"Do we have to?" Sierra asked. "It's such a long drive."

"I can't wait to play with her Barbies," Wren said.

"Go to bed after you finish your cocoa." Dad winked at me. "It'll go fast. We'll split the trip into two days."

I took one more sip, draining the warm liquid down my throat. I set the cup by Dad's and snuggled into his side. "Goodnight, Mom and Dad." I rose and left the room.

My hopes were high; I felt excited about tomorrow. It wasn't often I saw Grandma in Michigan. The trip always took so long, but I loved it because I sang with Wren and Dad in the car.

Mom shook me awake. "Time to go," she whispered. Outside my bedroom window, darkness filled the sky.

I forgot where I should go. Was it time for school? I stood, disoriented, for a moment. After I reached the living room, I searched for my jacket. I buttoned it with stiff fingers. Why wouldn't my hands work? I opened the front door and walked to the car.

The cold air bit my face. The night sky reminded me of a large black stencil, the way the bright stars shone and nothing else did. I wondered if God could see me. A slight line of grayish-blue light came into the sky. Would it be morning soon? Groggy and excited, knots clenched my stomach. It had been seven months since we'd seen Grandma. Mom brought us once a year, and I couldn't wait to return.

Tim McGraw's song, *Don't Take the Girl*, played on the car radio. Dad, Wren, and I sang along.

The back seat shrunk more each hour. Sierra and Wren's arms and legs beaded with sweat, pressing against me on every side. I felt claustrophobic, unable to move more than inches. Sierra shoved her elbow into me. I squirmed to give her more room and ended up jabbing Wren in the arm.

"She looked at me funny," Sierra's voice grated in my ears.

"She touched me!" Wren yelled.

"Don't make me pull this car over." Dad's eyes grew intense.

My heart skip a beat.

His jaw clenched.

The three of us quieted. I didn't want spankings, and I knew Sierra and Wren didn't either. Dad's hands hurt. Mom's spankings weren't so bad.

Sierra's head rested on my shoulder as she drifted to sleep. We pulled into a parking lot in front of a large building with a sign saying *Lodge.*

"Stay in the car with your mom while I make a reservation." Dad parked the car, then got out.

"A reservation? What do you mean?" Wren removed her seatbelt.

"Dad's asking if this hotel has a room we can stay in," Mom said.

"I thought we were going to Grandma's?" Sierra rubbed her eyes, waking from her nap.

"No. Grandma's house is a fourteen-hour drive. We'll be there tomorrow." Mom checked her reflection in her visor mirror.

A few minutes later, Dad returned with a white card in his hand. "We're in room two-oh-four."

"Hooray," Wren, Sierra, and I shouted.

I couldn't wait to swim.

"Follow me, girls. We'll take the elevator," Dad said as he and Mom power-walked toward the elevators at the end of the hall.

Once inside, the four of us faced the elevator doors as they slid shut.

"Press two, Wren," Dad said.

Wren pressed the button with the number two on it.

Sierra pouted, then protested. "No fair."

"You can do it next time," Dad said to Sierra.

Sierra continued whining beside me. She always got her way, so I was surprised when Dad didn't let her push a button.

The elevator doors opened, and we followed Mom and Dad through the hallway until we found the door with 204 on it. Dad slid the card through the slot. A green light blinked, and he turned the handle.

Two beds lined one wall and framed pictures hung above the headboards. Dad dropped the luggage on one bed. I sprawled out on the other, the soft blankets beneath me. The blankets smelled clean. I nuzzled against a pillow.

"Let's dress for swimming," Mom said. "We couped you up in the car all day, so let's have some fun."

Wren, Sierra, and I changed as fast as we could, rummaging through the luggage.

After we changed, we followed Mom and Dad to the pool.

Dad opened the door. Steps with a railing led into the turquoise water. I entered the shallow end because I didn't know how to swim well. The cool liquid touched my feet and legs. I shivered until the water reached my shoulders, then my body adjusted. Dad climbed into the pool with us.

"Dad, can you help me swim better?" I asked.

"Sure." He came and stood next to me, but the water didn't reach as high on him as it did on me. He held onto my midsection. "Kick your feet," he said. "Paddle with your hands; scoop the water."

I moved my arms and legs, sending water into the air behind my motorboat feet.

"Do it at the same time."

I kicked my feet and tried to scoop water in my hands. I wanted to make Dad proud because he believed in me.

"Good, good. Keep your head above the water." He backed away, but his hands reached toward me. "Swim to me, Kaitlin."

"I can't, Dad." I wanted to cry but fought the urge.

"Yes, you can."

The pool wall was slippery as I pushed my feet against it. I paddled and kicked, then paddled and kicked again, over and over until my lungs hurt.

"You're doing it. Keep coming, keep kicking."

He smiled as I reached him, breathless.

"Swim to the other side of the pool." He pointed.

Again? Wasn't once enough? I swam, spitting water out of my mouth. The chlorine stung my nose.

"Come back now."

I swam several more times, growing more confident with each trip.

"Look, you're doing it! You're swimming."

My excitement grew with Dad's praise. I couldn't believe I could do it. I paddled harder; I kicked harder. I wanted to go faster.

"I did it, Dad. I did it!" One more time, I reached him.

"Of course, you did. That's my girl." He held my cheeks in his gigantic hands, then smiled at me.

I knew I'd made him proud.

"You're ready to swim with Wren now."

Wren swam at the deep end of the pool. I swam to her, paddling the way Dad had shown me.

Kids hit beach balls overhead. Wren talked with three kids I didn't know on the side of the pool. I trembled, thinking about the deep end, but if Dad thought I could do it, then I could.

Wren spun in circles in the water, spinning like a corkscrew. Someday I'd swim like her.

"Hey, Kaitlin," she yelled over the echoing pool, the noises bounced off the walls.

"Marco!" someone yelled.

"Polo!" someone responded.

After I reached Wren, she was still chatting with a few girls poolside. She must have forgotten she wasn't leaning on the edge of the pool because she rested her elbows on my shoulders, leaning on me, pushing me under. My body sank more. She didn't notice me struggling. My arms shook as I trod the water. I kicked—nothing happened. Coughing, I paddled. Nothing helped.

Dad told me to kick and paddle together. I kicked harder. Paddling harder, I bobbed in the water. I tried to force the water away. It stayed. She wouldn't let go of me. Help! I'm drowning, I yelled in my head, but I couldn't speak. My arms burned, my legs became lead, pulling me under. I tried to yell out, let me go, but no words formed. I wondered if I'd die this way. Would anyone help me?

She let go, and the weight released. I swam to the ladder as fast as my legs allowed and escaped. My breathing strained, I tried to calm my racing heart. I told myself I'd be safe again soon. After reaching Mom and Dad, I grabbed a towel off a rack behind them. I wrapped it around my body and grabbed another for my hair.

About ten minutes later, we left the pool area. My teeth chattered and they wouldn't stop. We returned to the hotel room; the hallway offered no warmth, and neither did my soaked towel.

In room 204, we rinsed off, sharing a hot shower. After we dried off, we dressed in our pajamas and crawled under the blankets. I warmed again. What happened wasn't Wren's fault, so I couldn't be mad, but I was happy to be away from the pool.

As I closed my eyes in bed, the motion from the pool stayed with me; waves on a calm beach rocked me to sleep.

The next day, we rode in the car, and in the evening; we climbed a steep Michigan hill ending at Grandma Nelly's house.

~ Two ~

My childhood holds precious memories. As a child, my father was one of my greatest treasures.

Fathers are important and needed. Even though my definition of what makes a father has changed, I've always believed in their importance.

Winter left after overstaying its welcome in Minnesota, and at last, spring moved in. The sun shone through the living room of the trailer house. I sat on the plush couch, watching Mom and Dad talking, debating if I should go outside and play. Along the tree line in the backyard, the tire swing sat untouched for too long.

Mom stood by the front door, looking out the window. "Anthony?"

"Yes?" Dad asked.

Mom looked between Wren and me for a moment. I didn't know why people couldn't tell us apart. "It's a good day for a spin on the bike, Anthony. I'm sure you could use a break from sitting at home."

"I'll take KD this time." Dad lifted Sierra off his lap and set her on the chair.

I ran to Dad and hugged him. Dad's new bike was amazing. The chrome shimmered in the sunlight and the leather seats were black and comfy. He'd bought it last week and it would finally be my turn to go for a ride.

"That's not fair. I wanted to go." Sierra stuck out her bottom lip.

Dad told her, "Suck it up, Buttercup."

I giggled. She was his favorite, but today, he was all mine.

"Kaitlin, don't tease your sister," Mom said.

"Dad started it." I crossed my arms.

"Okay, okay." He patted my head. "I have presents for you, girls." Dad grabbed something from the closet behind me.

Sierra ran to Dad, and Wren meandered over.

Dad reached behind me and pulled something out of a shopping bag. When he lifted it out, I caught a whiff of what smelled like leather. It reminded me of a store in the mall that sold fancy biker gear.

"This is for you and Wren." He handed me a leather jacket with silver buckles along one side. I tried not to be offended that we didn't each get one because Wren told me last week she didn't want to ride anymore, so I knew she wouldn't want to use it.

Wren brushed her hand against the material as I held onto it. "It's so smooth."

I hugged it, inhaling a whiff of the leather.

Dad gave Sierra a black jacket, too. "This one's for you, Sierra."

"How come she gets her own?" I asked, kicking the floor.

Dad scoffed. "You and Wren can't ride together, anyway."

Sierra squealed in excitement. Her black curls bounced as she jumped beside me.

I rolled my eyes at her, then tried on the new jacket; the sleeves reached past my fingers, but I liked it. Soon enough, I'd grow, I told myself. I couldn't believe I'd have a jacket like Dad's. I would be a real rider, too. I walked like a runway model, one foot in front of the other, stopping at the end of an invisible platform. I posed, pretending an invisible photographer took my picture. Satisfied, I took the jacket off and handed it to Wren so she could try it on.

She put it on and quickly removed it without modeling it; she didn't even smile. A week ago, Wren took a ride with Dad and accidentally touched the muffler with her leg. Her skin was purple and blistered. It still hadn't healed.

Dad and I walked outside to his Harley motorcycle. Sierra cried behind me.

"I wanted to ride with someone who will stay awake." Dad chuckled, nudging my arm.

I grinned at Dad.

My head bobbed under the helmet's weight as I walked to the bike. It was warm outside, and I hoped I wouldn't get too hot with my new jacket on because I didn't want to take it off.

Dad helped me on the motorcycle first, then he climbed on. "Let's put this on, so you won't fall off." He buckled us into a belt with one loop for him and another one for me, cinching us together. It was how Sierra slept without slipping off.

Dad kicked the stand. The bike rocked like a canoe in shallow water. He pulled out of the driveway; the engine rumbled louder than Dad's truck. Vibrations ran through my legs. He drove down the dirt road next to our house, and pulling onto the asphalt, a cool breeze offset the radiating heat from the bottom of the motorcycle.

"Lean with me on the turns," Dad yelled over his shoulder. The loud engine made his voice sound strange. "Don't fight against the bike."

I nodded, but I didn't know what he meant.

On the next turn, I tried to do what he said. I leaned into his back.

At the stoplights, I straightened. I didn't want to lean wrong and make us tip. I must have done it right because we didn't crash, and Dad didn't yell. A few minutes later, Dad pulled into the lakeside Dairy Queen along the waterfront. He parked the bike and helped me off.

The ice cream shop had outdoor seating. I yanked the helmet off, thankful for a break. The lake air from across the street refreshed my face after being hot and contained inside the helmet. "Sit here, KD." He pointed to a table near his bike. "I'll get the treats." He beamed.

"I want the peanut butter Blizzard, Dad," I yelled at his back. "Not the pieces, the chunky Reese's Peanut Butter." My mouth watered at the mention of the white creamy deliciousness.

He turned to face me. "Sure thing, Kaitlin. You can have whatever you want; it's your day." He moved closer to the order window attached to the shop.

I couldn't believe I got ice cream today and no one else did. I couldn't stop smiling.

He came back, carrying two cups of ice cream. He joined me at the round table, and we ate our treats.

Sierra, Wren, Dad, and I headed into town after Dad, and I returned from eating ice cream. He needed to stop by work, so we got to ride along. The setting sun gleamed through the windshield. Red pines and spruce trees lined the outsides of the wide dirt road. Dad rolled down his window as we rounded a corner. Dad pulled onto a shaded road, my sisters and I had named Roller Coaster Road. The old truck rumbled. The smell of gasoline lingered in the cab, even with fresh air pouring through the window.

Dad slowed, then stopped. He looked at me, then asked, "Want to drive? Come sit on my lap."

I scooted over and he placed my hands on the wheel. Dad shifted into drive, and we eased back onto the road. Before us, the road plunged farther than my eyes could see. As the truck inched forward, it sped faster and faster. For a moment, I had wings. My sisters cheered beside me on the truck's worn bench seat.

My stomach flipped upside down as we climbed the next hill. The terrain blurred.

On the next descent, Dad let go, and I steered without help. The slightest movement veered us to the right or left. I tried to straighten out the wheels. My heart thudded in my chest, and for a second, I couldn't move. Dad slid his warm hands over mine, moving the truck back to the middle of the road. His hands made me feel stronger.

"Good job, KD. I'll take us the rest of the way." His face was peaceful as if he didn't have a care in the world.

I climbed off his lap and sat between him and Wren, relieved to be finished. I rested my back against the worn seat, happy that my dad was once again in control.

It was a late summer day, and my twin sister Wren and I sat together on the couch in the living room. Mom told us we'd be spending the day with Grandma, visiting Grandpa. I enjoyed seeing Grandpa. One place he stayed had a peacock living outside in an enormous cage. When we paid attention to the bird, he'd flaunt his beautiful colors by spreading his feathers like a Chinese fan. I didn't know if this place had a bird or not. Grandpa seemed to move a lot.

Grandma Irene's car pulled into our dirt driveway. She was dad's mom and when we first moved to Minnesota; we stayed at her house until we found a place of our own. The sound of her tires echoed against the gravel.

Sierra yelled, "Shotgun!" She elbowed me in the ribs as she ran past.

Wren and I piled into the backseat. Sierra always took the front. I scoffed at her.

"Buckle up," Grandma said from the front seat.

"Grandpa's memory is worse than when you saw him last," Grandma said. Once, Grandma told us he had "old-timers." We hadn't seen Grandpa for a long time, he didn't remember us then, either.

We arrived at a tall brick building and followed Grandma inside.

The savory smell of crispy potatoes and chicken gravy filled the cafeteria. The smell reminded me of Grandma's tater tot hotdish. I scanned the eating area. Empty food trays sat on top of the round tables in the center of the room. A group of heavy-lidded grandmas and grandpas slumped in wheelchairs along one wall. Their heads sagged to one side, wilted plants in the summer heat. I searched each face, looking for my grandpa. When I found him, I rushed over.

Grandpa's skin wrinkled, marking years of difficulty. He stared out the window, expressionless. Dad said he served in World War II. Maybe that's why he didn't have a memory. War didn't sound like something I'd want to remember. Food crusted at the corners of his mouth. Had the workers forgotten about him?

Grandma approached, but Grandpa didn't smile. She planted a soft kiss on one of his cheeks. "Let's get you cleaned."

I wanted to make him better. If seeing Grandma didn't make him smile, I didn't know what would. As I stared at the bicycle-like wheels of his chair spinning, Grandma pushed him down a hallway with lots of doors. Sierra's shoes squeaked against the shiny floor. Grandma stopped at a door and knocked, but no one answered. Did Grandpa have a roommate, or was he always alone? I didn't enjoy being alone. Grandma stepped around the wheelchair, nudging the door. Grabbing the wheelchair's armrests, she pulled Grandpa inside. We trailed in after.

The room was dimly lit with two empty beds spaced four feet apart, both made neatly. Next to each bed, a nightstand sat; Grandpa's table had a few candy bars. In the room's corner, a box TV sat on a stand. It must be strange for Grandma not to live with Grandpa. If Dad didn't live with us, I don't know what I'd do. I frowned. Everything would be different without my family.

We sat on Grandpa's bed. I kicked my legs, and the bed wobbled. I stared at the candy bars and hoped Grandma would share Grandpa's candy—it looked delicious. Grandma scurried around the room, straightening things that had already looked clean.

"Let's get you moved, honey." Grandma walked toward the edge of the bed. She grabbed a wired remote and pushed a button.

Wren stood, then ran around the room.

"Wren, sit." Grandma's mouth creased into a thin line.

Wren plopped on the bed and frowned. "I'm bored."

Grandma didn't respond. Instead, she went to the sink across from the beds and wet a washcloth. She leaned down in front of Grandpa and wiped the food from the corners of his mouth.

A man dressed in scrubs rapped his knuckles on the door frame, grabbing everyone's attention except Grandpa's.

"Hello," Grandma greeted the man without looking at him. "I'd like to move him to the bed. I know I'm not supposed to do it myself."

The nurse stepped into the room. He wrapped a wide belt around Grandpa's waist, then squatted with his knees against Grandpa's. In one fluid motion, he shifted Grandpa onto the bed.

"Hope that helps, honey." Grandma ran a finger along Grandpa's hairline.

Grandpa groaned and mumbled, but I couldn't understand what he said.

Tears welled in my eyes. I wish I knew what he wanted to say. Wren and I talked baby talk sometimes, and no one understood us. Dad hated it when we did it; the last time he caught us, we got spankings. I cringed. It must be hard to have no one know how you feel. I inched my way to the bedside and looked at Grandpa. Grabbing his hand, I gazed into his eyes and tried to send him love, even though I didn't know how. I searched his face for recognition. The slightest twinkle glimmered in his eye. He must know. He gave my hand a barely felt squeeze. The corner of his mouth twitched upward; his smile was so slight I didn't know if I'd imagined it.

After we watched television, a bell rang like the ones at school.

"Must be dinner already. I lost track of the time." Grandma stood and pushed the button on the remote again.

This time, a female nurse entered the room.

She moved the wheelchair next to the bed and helped Grandpa into it. "Let me know if you need anything else, Irene."

"Thank you." Grandma watched as the nurse exited the room.

Wren, Sierra, and I followed Grandma to the cafeteria room. It wasn't full when we first entered, but now all the chairs had elderly people in them. Grandma parked Grandpa at a round table along the edge of the room. Sierra, Wren, and I sat too.

"How much longer are we staying?" Sierra put her hands on her hips and tapped her shoe.

"We'll leave soon. I want to help Grandpa eat." Grandma narrowed her eyes at Sierra.

"Okay, then can we go?" Sierra persisted.

Grandma opened her mouth as if she might answer, but then a woman with a badge brought a tray with something that resembled a smoothie and set it in front of Grandpa.

"Thank you," Grandma said to the lady, then turned back to Sierra. "Yes, after that we can go."

Grandma moved the straw and placed it between Grandpa's parched lips. He took a sip, then coughed. Grandma wiped the spit from his chin with a cotton napkin and patted his back.

I stood rigidly. Tears welled in my eyes. Was he choking?

"There, there. Easy now." Grandma rubbed his hand where his wedding ring was.

I let out a slow breath, relieved he was okay. I bet he missed Grandma's cooking. At least, if he remembered her cooking, he would miss it. She was the best cook I knew. I wouldn't want to eat that nasty green smoothie.

When he had finished his dinner, we returned him to his room. Wren, Sierra, and I said goodbye first, then waited for Grandma.

Grandma leaned down and kissed his forehead. "I'll see you soon. Someday we'll remember each other. I love you," her voice became quieter, then she said more I couldn't hear.

He stared forward, not acknowledging her or her words. She held his hand, then stood. Her gaze lingered on him before she turned to us, and we left.

A few months after our visit to see Grandpa, Wren, Sierra, Mom, and I sat in the living room of our house. Lightning flashed outside the window. Dad was working, but he'd be home soon. I hoped he'd be okay driving in the downpour. Thunder rumbled, shaking the floor and the walls. I grabbed a pillow off the couch and held it to my chest, wishing Dad would hurry.

The lights in the kitchen flickered and then the microwave turned off before our popcorn finished popping. The room went black.

Mom lit several candles along the shelves in the living room. Their soft, orange glow danced on the walls. I didn't mind the darkness because I was close to Mom and my sisters. "Mom, can you make shadow puppets on the wall?"

"After a while. I need to finish the popcorn. Your dad should be here soon."

"Can we have a sleepover in here, Mom?" Wren asked.

"I suppose." Mom's motions were fluid as she moved toward the kitchen. "I'll get out my Pepperidge Farm cookies. You girls want one?"

"Thanks, Mom!" I shouted after her.

She had the yummiest cookies; they were full of hazelnut and squished between two crunchy wafers. I couldn't wait to lie on the living room floor and pretend I slept under the stars and eat cookies.

Wren, Sierra, and I ran to our rooms, gathered our blankets and pillows, then carried them to the living room. We heaped them into an enormous pile in the middle of the living room floor.

The front door swung open, and Dad walked in. Red hair hung in thick ropes over his eyes; the rain had soaked his clothes. His eyes were red and puffy like Mom's eyes when she cried. Dad said, "Mom wants me at the hospital."

"What? Why?" Mom asked.

"Dad had a stroke, and Mom says I need to say goodbye." He wiped his eyes. "He won't make it." Dad kicked one of my shoes away from the closet.

Mom's face lost its color.

What did he mean? Grandpa wouldn't make it? Grandpa couldn't die. He was a good person, and he loved me, so God would save him, wouldn't he?

"Grandpa's dying? If he dies, I can't see him anymore." I wrapped my arms around Mom.

Couldn't Dad fix him? I wiped my nose on my sleeve and took a step toward the front door. I could tell Grandpa not to die. If no one else would help him, then I would. He might have listened to me, even if he didn't respond. "I want to go with you, Dad." I ran toward the door, sitting in front of it.

"No," Dad said, looking outside, his face scrunched, then he looked at Mom. "I don't want the kids seeing their grandpa like that."

Mom walked over, then kneeled to my level. "Kaitlin, Dad's going alone. It's better that way."

Why wouldn't they let me go? "He's my grandpa, and I don't care if he's sick. I want to see him." It wasn't fair. My chin trembled. He belonged to me, too.

"Don't argue with your mother," Dad ordered, hovering over me.

Mom grabbed my arm gently, pulling me away from the door. "Come here, Kaitlin."

Dad pulled a rain jacket off its hanger, then walked into the storm.

Mom tugged me into her embrace. I stayed there, crying. Wren and Sierra joined us in our huddle.

"Grandpa's going to heaven," Mom whispered, then kissed me on the cheek.

The candles burned, their light danced on the walls until Mom told us to go to sleep, then she blew them out. I closed my eyes and hoped Grandpa wouldn't die, but maybe God didn't love me enough to save him.

The next morning, with tears in his eyes, Dad told us Grandpa died.

~ Three ~

Words can't describe how it feels to lose a father; I've lost two, and I fear the day it happens again. It's an ache in my chest and a void I can't fill. I wonder if Grandpa's dying contributed to Anthony's choices back then.

In 1995, I was eight. Naïve, I thought that people were innately good, and they rarely did wrong. As an adult, I believe the opposite is true; humans are innately bad, but most strive to overcome their faults and become better people.

Where was Mom? I hadn't seen her at all, but the water was running in her bathroom. Maybe she was in the shower.

From down the hall, Dad walked to the fridge. His hair was wet, and I still hadn't gotten used to his new haircut because it was too short. Aluminum snapped and something fizzled.

It must be a soda. I ran to him. "Can I have a drink, Dad?"

"It's too early for you to have a pop."

I crossed my arms. "Then, why do you get one?"

"I don't have time for your attitude, Kaitlin. I have to go to work." He huffed. "Where's your mother?"

I shrugged. "The shower?"

Dad left and returned a few minutes later wearing his blue and white striped shirt with an X company logo on the pocket. "Ugh, I'm going to be late."

I turned to a noise behind me. The front door opened.

Mom walked in and wiggled her fingers at me.

I grabbed Mom's hand, gazing at the deep crimson polish. "Wow, Mom, they're so pretty." I wished my nails looked like hers. "Can I get my nails done too?"

"Maybe someday, sweetie." Mom patted the sides of her tall, curly hair near her ears. "Where's your dad?"

Dad stood at the end of the hallway. His red mustache didn't hide his frown. "Took you long enough."

"Sweetheart, I missed you," Mom said, smiling at Dad.

"I needed to leave fifteen minutes ago, and you were supposed to be here to take care of the kids." Stomping toward the door, he brushed Mom aside.

Mom's smile dropped; her enthusiasm dimmed like the sun being covered by clouds. Closing the front door behind him, Dad left the house.

After Dad left, Wren, Sierra, and I played with Barbies. Mom went to her room. Her crying echoed through the walls.

"Let's play outside," I told Sierra and Wren. I didn't want to hear Mom cry anymore, it made me mad at Dad and I didn't want Sierra upset. Dad shouldn't have treated my beautiful Mom like that; he wasn't being nice.

Outside, we escaped Mom's cries, but her sobs played inside my head.

Wren, Sierra, and I played outside on the tire swing. When we returned inside, Mom said she had a surprise for us, but that we had to change our clothes so we could leave the house. Sometimes she would hide Barbies in our beds, but it couldn't be that, because this time Mom said we were going somewhere. Mom stopped the car at a shop in town, a block from Dad's work. Wren, Sierra, and I trailed behind Mom.

"I can't wait for you to meet my friend," Mom told us. I hadn't met any of Mom's friends before except the ones she played cards with.

Opening the door, a bell jingled. The scent of hairspray and perm solution hung in the air.

A woman said, "Come in."

We walked into her salon. Behind a tall counter, black swivel chairs with silver bars across the bottoms stood in front of several mirrors. Next to the high counter, bottles of nail polish, in at least thirty glittering colors, lined a wooden shelf.

A woman with wide hips sauntered toward us. She might be a fancy lady, but she wasn't as pretty as Mom. "I hear a lot about you, girls." She didn't smile, half-smiled, her voice high-pitched and annoying as if she didn't like us. Her green eyes flashed at us under thick black lashes.

"This is my friend, girls," Mom told us. "She's the lady who did my nails a few weeks ago."

She approached us. "Would you beauties like a haircut? I cut your daddy's hair last week." She laughed. "I cut your mommy's hair, too."

Dad's hair had looked shorter, and I didn't like it, preferring it shaggier. I glanced at the hairstylist's blonde hair. She had cut her own hair in Mom's style, but I liked my hair longer.

My hair hung into my eyes, maybe I could use a haircut, but not short. "Can I?" I asked Mom.

"That's why I brought you here." Mom leaned and kissed my forehead. "While you played outside, I called Ingrid to see if she could fit you in for a haircut."

"Thank you." I beamed at Mom. I climbed into one of the black chairs, setting my feet on the shiny silver bar, then spun around, blowing kisses at myself in the mirror.

"This keeps the hair off you." Mom's friend covered my body with a smooth, black poncho that snapped around my neck. She ran her hands through my hair. When she was finished, I hoped I'd look as pretty as Mom, but Mom wore makeup and she had brown eyes and pearly white teeth. I'd never be that pretty.

There was a gap in my front teeth. Mom's friend pulled my hair straight with her black comb and clipped it across in a straight line with scissors, doing this for several minutes.

Mom moved closer to me, casting a side-long glance at her friend, with an unreadable expression spreading across her face. "Last week, you mentioned you'd gotten into a fight with your ex. Are you doing better?"

Mom's friend stopped cutting my hair for a moment as if considering the question.

Mom continued staring, then sat in a swivel chair beside me. Sierra crawled into her lap and Mom moved a curl out of her eyes. Sierra snuggled into her.

Ingrid fluffed her hair with her fingers, looking pleased with herself. "I'm fine. I found someone new, and Mitchell's in jail as of last week, so. . ."

Mom's eyes went wide. "At least he can't hurt you anymore." Mom spun Sierra in her chair. "Is that fun, Honey?"

Mom's friend watched Mom and Sierra for a minute before continuing. "I'll tell you about it some other time." She reached for the blow drier and brushed my hair as she directed the heat toward my tresses. The noise blared in my ear, and the hot air blasted against my face.

"All finished." Mom's friend unsnapped the black cape and shook my hair onto the white linoleum floor. She glanced toward Mom, then pulled the cape off me. "Who's next?"

"Do you love my hair, Mom?" I spun in my pleather chair. I wished my hair was curly instead of straight because my hair wasn't as pretty as Moms.

Mom glanced at my hair. "It's beautiful, Kaitlin."

"My turn," Wren said.

Mom's friend completed Wren's hair and then Sierra's.

"Thanks, I'll see you in a few weeks. Let me know if you need anything." Mom paid then held the door open for Wren, Sierra, and me.

The bell dinged, and the door closed behind us. We trailed like ducklings following their momma, but we weren't hideous like in the story, *The Ugly Duckling*, we were cute.

At home a few hours later, came the familiar sound of our front door opening. Boots stomped across the carpet then a loud thud reverberated into the floor. Was Dad home already? I ran to see.

"Want to order the best tacos in the world?" Dad wrapped his arms around Mom's waist.

Mom's cheeks flushed. I gave her an emphatic thumbs up, glad Dad was paying attention to her as she deserved.

"Sure. Tacos always sound good." Mom returned my thumbs up and winked at me. "Better get ready, girls. Let's get some dinner."

Dad pulled into the restaurant parking lot. The building sat on stilts at the edge of a lake where we'd once gone fishing.

A server led us to a table near the bar. I bounced across the wide benches to sit next to the wall. Mom left, headed to the tall counter to order a drink, and talked with a young woman I didn't recognize. A few minutes later, she returned.

Dad ordered the food.

I didn't know what happened to Mom at the bar, but her face became pale like she'd eaten something bad. I tried to meet her eyes, but Mom refused to meet mine. I glanced between her and dad, hoping to figure out what was going on, but I didn't know.

After the server brought the food, Mom ate in silence.

The server returned to refill our drinks.

"Thanks," Dad said, then he gave Mom a look of confusion. Maybe he didn't know what was wrong with her, either.

The young woman nodded with a soft smile, then her eyes darted to Mom.

As Mom chewed, tears pooled in the corners of her eyes. Maybe the young woman told her someone died. My stomach tensed into knots like it did on Roller Coaster Road. Black mascara smudged underneath Mom's eyes. Who had died? Why didn't anyone tell me?

Wren, Sierra, and I chatted during the meal, but Mom and Dad stayed quiet. We finished our food.

As Dad looked at Mom, his eyebrows creased. "Time to go."

Maybe Dad knew what was wrong.

"I don't want to leave, Dad." Sierra kicked the pole under the table. "We haven't played Pacman yet."

"I don't care. Get in the car." He pointed toward the door.

Outside the stilt restaurant, the cool night air smelled like dead leaves with a faint scent of fish. We walked toward the car, dragging our feet. I didn't want to leave. I hadn't had a chance to play a song on the jukebox yet. Dad's face wore a scowl, so I knew I'd better listen to him.

Dad squealed the tires as we left the restaurant. The smell of burgers on a hot grill and French fries faded and the smell of burnt rubber filled the car.

"How could you do this to me?" Mom yelled. Her hands shook in the air in front of her face.

"What are you talking about?" Dad demanded.

"You know what I'm talking about. She is my hairdresser, you piece of—" she stopped herself, then turned to look at us in the back seat. Her eyes were bloodshot.

Mom and Dad continued arguing the entire way home. The three of us stayed quiet except for the occasional whimper from Sierra. Wren held her hand and smoothed Sierra's curled locks.

Mom and Dad argued in the kitchen after we got home. Wren and I crept to our door and peeked, searching for Mom.

"Go to your room, Girls." She seethed, hissing through clenched teeth, and moving her hand like she was swatting a fly; but she left our door ajar.

That night, I hid beneath my bunk bed bars. When would the fighting stop? Would it stop? My body shook as I sobbed. Wren cried on the top bunk.

I didn't know if I should help Mom or not. I shook my head. I couldn't make Mom and Dad stop fighting because I wasn't strong enough. It was out of my control, but maybe God could fix it. He could even stop lions. Grandma told me if I talked to Jesus, He would always hear me, no matter where I was. Maybe He could help Mom.

In my prison, I folded my hands and prayed to God. "Please God, make the fighting stop," I whispered. "If you have to, God, make him leave." I squeezed my fingers together as hard as I could until it left a red mark. I squinted my eyes as tears seeped out, so God knew I wasn't peeking and that I needed His help.

Something shattered. A chunk of Mom's white porcelain figurine landed on the floor in front of my bedroom door. Mom had warned us to never touch them because of how easily they broke. I glanced at the arm of one of the broken angels and trembled. I pulled my knees to my chest, hugging myself.

The next morning, I snuck into the living room in case Mom and Dad were fighting somewhere I couldn't see. The hair stood on my arms. Where was Wren? She wasn't in her bed or our room. Silence hummed in the house as I tiptoed. Where was everyone? They wouldn't leave me alone. Mom had never done that. I shook my head. She wouldn't.

I reached Mom's room at the end of the hall. I opened the door.

She sat on her bed, with crossed legs. Mascara-stained tears streaked down Mom's face.

Wren sat at her feet. I sighed. So, this was where Wren and Mom went. Where was Sierra? Mom's red eyes met mine.

I put my hand on her flushed cheek. "What's wrong, Mom? Where's Sierra?"

"Your dad left. He's gone." She sniffled. "He wants to see other people."

"What other people?" I asked.

I didn't know what she meant until an image flashed in my mind. One time, I snuck into their room and found a magazine under their mattress. The shiny pages slipped across my fingertips. My stomach dropped like I might be sick as I saw woman after woman wearing nothing. Married people don't see other people. Do they? Maybe women in the magazines were the ones he wanted.

"Whoever he wants. I don't know." She sniffled.

Mom and Dad always wanted us kids to get along. Why couldn't they do the same? If kids had to be nice, then grown-ups should, too.

"Where did Dad go?" I sat on Mom's bed beside her. Would he change his mind and come back tomorrow? He'd want to get me; I was special to him.

"He took Sierra and left." Mom swallowed hard.

"Why did he take Sierra and not us, Mom?" Wren's eyes welled with tears.

He has to come back for me; I was his favorite. He'd taken me for ice cream, only me.

She paused, then bit her lip. "It's because he's not your dad."

My mouth dropped. I stared at her and stuttered, "W—what?"

Mom stopped for a moment as if thinking about how to respond. "Uh . . . I thought Ingrid told you."

"Why would you think she told us?" Wren moved her hands to her hips.

I continued staring at Mom in disbelief. She was being ridiculous. What did Ingrid know? She was Mom's friend, but that didn't mean she knew.

"I thought she told you. She's the one Anthony wants to be with." She wiped a tear away from her cheek.

I shook my head. Mom must not be thinking straight. Of course, Dad was our dad. Dad would never leave Mom for that girl, Ingrid. She was uglier than mom and she wasn't even nice.

Mom continued, "I met Anthony when you were a year old at a toga party." Mom clenched her teeth. "I should've left him when I had a chance." She glanced at the floor. "I let him take Sierra away. I should have stopped him. She's my little girl." She sobbed, putting her face into her hands.

I did not know what she was talking about. When did she have a chance to leave Dad and why would she? Talking about it, made me mad at Dad. Was he a bad guy? My shoulders drooped. It must be true. I was his. I had his nose. I had Dad's smile. We both like the Steve Miller Band.

"Why did you lie to us?" Wren asked, her eyes full of tears.

My chest heaved. If he wasn't my dad, then my entire life was a lie. Did Mom ever tell the truth? Was Sierra still our sister? It didn't make sense. It couldn't be true.

She looked at me, her eyes red and puffy. "You were young when Anthony became your dad."

I shifted away from Mom. "I suppose you'll tell us next that Sierra isn't our sister."

"Of course, she's your sister. Whether or not you share a dad." Mom straightened. "Look, Anthony became your dad a long time ago, and you didn't remember anyone else," Mom explained. "Your real dad's name is Smith."

"You lied to us!" I left Mom's room and stomped through the house.

I didn't care what she had to say anymore. None of it made sense. Dad would come for me and I wouldn't live here anymore. I was going to tell him I didn't care about my birth father; he was mine no matter what, and then he'd see. Nothing needed to change.

I would pack my bags; he would want me to live with him, just like Sierra. I returned to my room and slammed the door. After Dad returned to get me, I wouldn't have to hear about this Smith guy anymore. He was probably make-believe.

~ Four ~

Learning to be grateful has been a challenge for me, whether I am eight or thirty-five. My tendency to be negative is innate, consuming, and human. It's one of my many faults. Sometimes we have more blessings than we know.

I missed Dad and Sierra. I hadn't seen them in a few weeks. There wasn't anything fun to do. No more snowmobile rides on winter days. We wouldn't be delivering fuel anymore and taking rides on country roads or eating at my favorite restaurant with tacos. And no downhill skiing on the beginner hill. We mostly went with Dad to meet his girlfriends or to go for ice cream. It wasn't the same as before. I sighed, pouting.

It was me, Mom, and Wren living in the trailer now; we were only part of a complete picture. What would we do as a family since we didn't have money? Nothing. I bet Sierra still had fun because Dad was awesome; Mom said he got a new car she called a "chick magnet." I didn't think he was looking for chicks. We were his family, and he would come back. I wished he'd hurry.

As I lay, my head rested on the arm of the couch. I looked at the ceiling. Mom walked past Wren and me in the living room. Mom was wearing a tight black shirt, a leather belt, and slim-fit blue jeans. The smell of Mom's perfume lingered. It was like lilies, earthy and flowery. Her curled bangs made a loop over her eyes. Mom dressed like that when she went somewhere. Where were we going? Mom hadn't mentioned a trip into town. I stood, excited at the prospect of leaving the house.

"I have to run out; I'll see you in a few hours." She fiddled with her necklace.

"We aren't going with you?" I asked, and instantly my excitement dropped, becoming a heavy pit in my stomach. She'd never left us alone before then. Were we old enough? Was she going on another date?

"No. I'll be back in thirty minutes." Mom played with her hair.

Ugh, what would we do? Staying home was all we did; Christmas vacation was lasting forever. How many more days until we returned to school? There had been nothing to do this week except watch movies.

"Fine." I crossed my arms. I couldn't wait to go back to school and see my friends again.

"Sorry, Kaitlin. Money is tight right now. It'll get better soon, promise. I'm going to a job interview right now." She kissed us goodbye on our foreheads. Leaving, she closed the door behind her.

I slumped my shoulders and plodded to the living room window.

In Minnesota, during the winter, if the sunlight was bright enough to hurt your eyes, it was not warm. It was too bright today for playing outside.

Wren stood next to the TV, getting ready to start another movie.

"Wren, wake me if you think of something fun to do." Stretching out, I folded my hands onto my lap.

Wren said nothing.

I closed my eyes and drifted into sleep.

Wren shook my shoulders.

"What—?" I blinked at her.

"Kaitlin, wake up! Wake up! The house is on fire! Help me." She bit her bottom lip.

A few feet from me, flames reached from the entertainment center toward the ceiling. Mom's artificial plant smoked as the fire burned, and a candle burned with a solitary flame. I dashed to the porch outside.

I grabbed a handful of snow from the railing. Sprinting inside, I reached the fire and threw snow into the flames. What else was I supposed to do?

Wren bolted between the sink and the blaze, throwing cupfuls of water into the entertainment center.

The fire kept burning.

I ran outside again, my eyes darted around the snowy landscape. Mom had better hurry. Grabbing another fistful of snow, I ran back inside and threw it into the flames. Then I dashed outside to get more.

The flames ebbed, but the house filled with black, billowing smoke. It was worse than the fire. The stench, like burned plastic, seeped into every corner of the trailer. It was suffocating. The inside of my lungs burned. No place was safe. My nose clogged, forcing me to breathe out of my mouth.

"I'm calling nine-one-one," Wren shouted, grabbing the phone.

"Good idea!" Why I hadn't thought of that?

Wren pushed buttons on the phone, then held it against her ear.

My hands clammed, and sweat beaded my brow as I looked around the room, hoping I'd be able to get the fire out. My eyes moved quickly between Wren and the smoke, which grew denser. How could I breathe in this stench? The smoke surrounded me.

"Our house was on fire, but it's out now. There's a lot of smoke. Can you help us?" Wren looked at me, holding the phone. She shrugged. "No, we're home alone."

I looked outside; Mom wasn't back yet. My breathing quickened. What if Mom got into trouble for leaving us alone?

Wren's eyebrows creased as she listened. Her eyes found mine, and we stared at each other, reflecting panic. We were going to be in trouble.

I paced near the living room window, watching for Mom's car. My pulse raced.

After five minutes, Wren hung up the phone, then sprinted to me. The urgency in her voice was unmistakable. "The cops are on their way. They told me to open all the doors. Then get outside."

"You get the front one, I'll get the back one," I said.

I ran and opened the back door. The cold air rushed in and grazed my face and neck. Wren rushed toward the front door, waving her arms emphatically, as she ran past in the opposite direction as I did.

"Let's open windows," I yelled at her, hoping that would empty the smoke faster.

I opened all the kitchen windows, sliding them upward, so the screen was all that separated us from outside. Wren opened the living room windows.

The smoke escaped outside as cold air billowed in. My breath melded into the thinning black smoke. The smell of burnt plastic still hung in the air. I scanned the entertainment center, and the fire had vanished. I was ready to breathe fresh air again, so I made my way toward the front door.

My eyes burned and watered. "Let's get outta here, Wren." I ran to the closet by the front door and grabbed my coat from inside.

Wren followed me, grabbing her jacket and joining me outside.

I shivered. When would Mom get back? Wherever she'd gone, we hadn't seen her in at least a half-an-hour. Wren's teeth chattered as she and I huddled together. "When will the cops get here?" I asked Wren, as we stood on the porch.

"Soon, I hope. I'm freezing." Wren's teeth chattered.

I debated going inside, but thought better of it; it was too cold. The chilled air made my lungs feel raw. It relieved me to be breathing again, even though it was colder than I liked. I wished Mom were here. If she hadn't left, the whole fire accident wouldn't have happened. My eyes met Wren's. At least we were safe and together, it made it a lot less scary. Wren always made me feel better.

"I hear sirens." Wren leaned forward, draping her arms over the side of the porch railing. "Lights are coming. Do you see them?" She pointed. "Over there."

In the distance, red and blue lights flashed beyond our house. The sirens howled. I covered my ears to silence the noise and warm my ears.

A red fire truck turned the corner and pulled in front of our house. Behind the firetruck, two police cars parked, their lights swirling round and round on the top of their cars. Wearing uniforms, two officers climbed out of one of the squad cars and walked toward the house. A firefighter, carrying a helmet in his hand, walking at a steady pace, joined them. The three of them walked past Wren and me and into the house.

"Stay here," one of the police officers said to us as he passed by.

The two police officers and the firefighter entered our house. Wren and I continued waiting on the porch. The wind outside chapped my face. I hoped we could get warm soon.

I glanced down the driveway as Mom's car turned the corner. I was happy to see her, even if we got into trouble. She parked beyond the driveway and flung the car door open. She ran toward the house. Her black hair blew to the side, her head bobbing. She darted past the cop cars. Past the firetruck. Her face looked pale except for her flushed cheeks. She let out a scream, then her cries turned loud and gut-wrenching. Until she reached Wren and I.

Mom at last made it to the porch. She wrapped her arms around Wren and me, squeezing the breath out of my chest. My sore lungs tightened.

"Oh, my girls, my sweet girls." She rocked us in her arms. "You're safe, you're safe," her voice cracked as she wiped a mascara-stained tear from her cheek.

"We're okay, Mom. I'm so sorry." My body ached. I was happy Mom was back. Everything was going to be okay now.

"When I first pulled up," her body shook against me, "all these lights made me think—" she broke down, hyperventilating. "I thought I lost you, girls." She pulled us into another hug. "I didn't know what to do."

"I'm sorry, Mom." I said.

"It's okay."

"You know how you asked us not to play with matches?" I asked.

Wren frowned, giving me an annoyed stare.

Mom looked at me, then turned and faced Wren. "It's okay. I'm so glad you're safe. That's all that matters." She looked into our eyes, her jaw set and her eyes bloodshot. "Promise me you'll never do that again."

"I promise," Wren whispered.

I wrapped my arms around Mom. "I promise, Mom."

"I better talk to the police."

~ Five ~

When I was nine, life improved for a while.

Dad arrived at our house with Sierra in his "chick magnet" car. He dropped Sierra off without entering our house. I wished he'd come in and talk to Mom, maybe they could still fix their problems.

Sierra sat with Wren and me on our couch, the first piece of furniture we'd bought in our first permanent home when we first moved to Minnesota. It reminded me of us as a family before Dad moved out. This was Mom's week with Sierra—after the divorce was completed, Sierra lived with Dad, and Mom was the one with visitation rights. Dad took Wren and me too, but not very often, and not court-ordered.

The three of us sisters bounced and chatted on the couch. I listened as Sierra gushed details about her life, like the four-wheeler Dad bought her, and her basketball games. I pouted, then remembered that divorce was probably hard on her too. I tried not to be jealous.

Mom sauntered across the living room to the radio and played her country music CD. The singer's soft southern drawl filled the room.

Wren, Sierra, and I danced like ballerinas while Mom moved from room to room. It was nice to see Mom's smile. I didn't know if she was always this happy cleaning because she never let us stay inside while she tidied. Normally she'd kick us outside. She seemed different today. If Mom planned to have company, that would be a reason to clean. I hoped she'd invited Dad for a surprise visit. Maybe he was sick of his girlfriends and wanted Mom back.

The smell of lemons filled the air as Mom mopped the kitchen. I stopped dancing. Mom tiptoed across the wet kitchen floor like a high-rope walker. She didn't appreciate footprints on her clean floors, and she warned us to stay off.

After walking into the living room, Mom pulled the vacuum out of the closet. Dancing behind the vacuum cleaner, Mom sang along with the song.

Wren, Sierra, and I sang Mom's music too—singing always sounded better while the vacuum ran; I wasn't sure why.

After wheeling it one last time across the floor, Mom returned the vacuum to the closet.

She walked over to us, hands resting on her hips. "Girls," she said, out of breath, "be on your best behavior today. I want you to meet someone special."

I huffed. Please don't let it be another one of Mom's boyfriends, please let it be Dad. Didn't we meet a guy a month ago? And another one the month before? Mom and Dad "seeing other people" was annoying. It was hard to keep track of. I didn't know why Mom and Dad couldn't be happy together.

Mom's last guy made us laugh, a football fan who loved all things Dolphins. She'd taken us to meet him at his house. He was nice and made her laugh. I hoped we'd be a family. He acted as if he liked us, tossing his football to us to catch. Then one day, we didn't visit anymore; she didn't tell us why and I didn't ask—sometimes I didn't understand her choices. Maybe Mom didn't love him because he loved football more than her?

The German guy she dated, a month before the football guy, barely spoke English; she'd met him at her airport job. His name was Hans, and he sold Mercedes cars. She told Wren he didn't need to speak English for them to understand each other. What did that mean, and how would they talk about anything? I didn't pretend to know.

Football guy and German car man were better than Dad's last girlfriend. Her name was Bobby, the same as the country song *Bobby Ann Mason*, but she was not cute or cool like the song said. She was a jerk. Well, she was cute, but not cool. Thankfully, she wasn't his girlfriend anymore. She said I was too tall for a gymnast and I should find new dreams. I couldn't believe Dad let her say that. What did she know about my dreams? She was ruining mine by seeing Dad.

Someone knocked at the door. Mom turned the radio off, then rushed to answer it. Before she opened the front door, she glanced back at us. Her face lit up; a broad smile spread across her lips. She opened it. "Hey there," she said, her voice high-pitched, her foot in the air behind her. "Come in. The girls are so excited to meet you."

I rolled my eyes. I wasn't excited. Dad should be standing there, not this guy, whoever he was.

The man moved closer to us. His dark hair was inky like mine, but his thick eyebrows and his skin were darker. He wore a long-sleeved shirt and work boots. "How are you? I'm Mitchell." His wide, green-brown eyes met my eyes.

"Want to watch our cool moves, Mitchell?" Wren asked, hopping off the couch.

"Sure! Let's see them."

Sierra and I leaped off the couch, joining Wren. I ran to the middle of the room and did the splits. After I stood, Wren did a back handspring, flipping through the room.

Mitchell clapped. "Great job. That's impressive."

Sierra waited. Moving her body upside down with her hands on the ground, she kicked her legs over her head. She moved so flaw-lessly, making it look easy, just like a slinky. Back walkovers made my head woozy.

"I got moves, too," Mitchell said.

I looked at him and raised my eyebrows. What moves could he possibly have? He wasn't a gymnast; at least, he didn't look like one.

The three of us moved back to give him space to perform.

He slid into the splits, tipping before he was flush with the floor. He laughed.

Sierra, Wren, and I joined him on the floor, lying next to him, and laughing.

I looked around the room for Mom. She stood behind the couch; a smile adorned her face. I liked Mitchell; how could I not approve of a guy who played gymnast with us? Mom liked him, too.

After our laughter died, Mitchell hoisted himself off the floor and let out an awkward half-laugh. He placed his hands on his lower back and groaned. He shuffled to Mom's side, his lips inches from her ear. I couldn't hear what he whispered.

"I want to talk to Mitchell for a few minutes," Mom told us. "Stay here and practice your moves some more, girls."

She grabbed Mitchell's hand, lacing her fingers through his. Mitchell waved with his other hand as they disappeared into Mom's room.

About a half-hour later, Mom walked Mitchell to the front door.

He kissed her on the cheek. "I need to get back to work; nice meeting you, kids." He waved.

We all waved back.

"See you later," I said.

After he left, I ran to Mom and wrapped my arms around her.

"Did you girls like Mitchell? Did I tell you he's a trucker? He works for his dad. It's a good job, too." Mom's cheeks flushed a crimson shade.

She might want Mitchell to be our new dad and he was great, but I didn't know my real dad, at all. I wanted to know more first. Feel some connection to the one who helped make me. I didn't want to know any more about Mitchell right now. "Mom, can you tell me more about my real dad? Can we meet him?"

She looked down, quiet for a moment. At last, her eyes met mine. "I'm sorry, honey. You can't meet him."

I stared at her. He must be out there somewhere; I hadn't even met him yet. Didn't he want to meet us? "What do you mean?"

Mom sat next to Sierra on the couch. "Come here and sit, girls."

Wren, Sierra, and I sat next to her. I leaned my head on Mom's shoulder.

"Your dad was a firefighter." She winced. "He died years ago."

"What?! How?"

"In a fire; he died a hero." She ran her finger across my cheek. "I'm sorry, girls." She hugged us, then stood and headed toward her room.

I tapped my finger against my lip. What was she hiding? She acted like she didn't care about my real dad dying. A part of me was proud of him for being a hero, but I also felt sad because now I'd never know him.

Mom drove Sierra, Wren, and me to Grandma Irene's house a week after we met Mom's boyfriend, Mitchell. It was the weekend, and that meant Sierra would go home with Dad again. Dad invited us along for the day.

"Bye, girls. Be back in a few hours." Mom kissed Sierra. "See you next week, sweetheart."

She waved at us and left.

Grandma's grass was well-groomed, and she had the lawn furniture and picnic tables set up. Would Grandma have company over today?

Sierra, Wren, and I walked the familiar path in front of Grandma's house.

Dad came outside with his arm wrapped around a woman with blonde hair. "This is my girlfriend," Dad paused. His girlfriend didn't look like she was as nice as Mom. A lanky boy and girl stood in her shadow. "These are her kids." He patted them on their heads; the boy cringed.

The boy looked younger than Sierra. The girl played with me on the playground sometimes at school. My eyes met hers and she stepped out from behind her mom.

His girlfriend smiled as if it hurt her face. "Hello, girls." She looked at Dad and excused herself, returning to Grandma's house.

This was the woman Dad loved instead of Mom? Maybe he loved her kids more than us, too. If I was nice to her kids and if I showed him we could get along, would they ask me to live with them? I didn't know if Mom would let us move in, but I didn't care. I belonged with my dad.

"Want to play red light, green light?" I asked everyone, hoping they'd be my friends.

"I don't want to play." The daughter stared at the ground.

I rolled my eyes. Why would Dad want them and not me? My cheeks burned. He was my dad, not theirs.

"I'll play." Wren jumped to stand beside me.

"Thanks, Wren." I ran to the other end of the yard.

Everyone else stood on the alleyway side, except the girlfriend's daughter.

"Green light," I yelled, my voice carrying across the yard.

The boy, Sierra, and Wren ran toward me. Sierra sprinted into the lead.

"Ugh, she cheated." The boy sat on the ground.

Sierra yelled, "I didn't cheat! You're slow!" She stomped her foot.

"I am not! You aren't nice. I'm going inside to find my mom. I don't want to play anymore." He wiped his nose on his arm sleeve.

I had to agree with Sierra, he was slow.

This was not going how I'd planned. I needed a treat; all the running had made me thirsty. I skipped to the front door, excited at the prospect of a cold soda. Grandma always let us have a pop. She kept it in the basement refrigerator. I opened the front door of her house; it always smelled good. What was Grandma cooking today? I wasn't sure if we'd stay for lunch. Right inside the front door was the basement entrance. I opened the door. My uncle Mitch lived there so he could help Grandma care for the place.

"Mitch!" I yelled. "Are you there?" Usually, I'd call him uncle, but was I supposed to since Dad wasn't my dad? Was Uncle Mitch my uncle? I made a megaphone with my hands. "Mitch?"

I hopped down two steps, closer to the warm basement. I smelled my uncle's cologne, but where was he? Was he in the shower? Something rustled, but there wasn't anyone there. I descended two steps; someone must be there, I'd heard something.

Dad walked into my view. He stood at the bottom of the steps, hands on his hips. "Why would your mom's boyfriend be here?" he asked, his tone flat.

I glanced away from his stare. Why was he mad? I was sure my uncle wouldn't care if I helped myself. My insecurity grew as I eyed Dad suspiciously. How did Dad know Mitchell's name, anyway? Dad never bothered about Mom's boyfriends before, so why did Mitchell bother him?

"Why would Mitchell be here? I was . . ." I looked around the room below, unsure of where my uncle was. "I was—" I bit my lip. "Looking for Uncle."

"Whatever." Dad stared at me with hooded eyes.

"I know you aren't our dad but—" the words came out of my mouth before I could stop them, but I had to tell him that I loved him, and I didn't care about technicalities.

"What? What did you say?" Dad's face turned red; his voice was loud.

"I, um . . ." I hoped he wouldn't yell at me anymore. "I said, I don't care." My lip quivered. "You can still be my dad." I took a step closer to him. "I love you; you'll always be my d—"

"Did your mom say that?" his voice grew louder with every syllable. "Tell me this second. Who?"

I shrugged. I didn't want Mom to be in trouble. Maybe I wasn't supposed to tell him; Mom never told me I couldn't. Besides, maybe he didn't know. Maybe that's why he asked. I was unsure of what to say, without giving Mom away. Would Daddy hate me like he hated Mom? I didn't want him to stop loving me, too.

The basement door creaked behind me.

"Time to go, Kaitlin," Mom said, her voice light. "Let's find your shoes. Did you have fun?"

I had no choice but to leave Dad, never finishing the conversation.

~ Six ~

The conversation that took place on Grandma's stairway with Anthony remained unfinished for the next twenty-five years.

When I was nine, it didn't matter to me whether Anthony was blood-related; he was my dad.

Silent Night played on the radio—my favorite Christmas song. Snowflakes landed on the windshield, the kind that made good snowmen. It reminded me of one year, after a blizzard, when Wren, Sierra, Dad, and I went into the yard and my toes froze, while building the perfect seven-foot-tall snowman. Christmas was magical for me. It was all a dream now. The windshield wiper swished across the glass. The world looked like a snow globe; maybe I could have more magical moments with Dad this year. Even if it was the first Christmas he didn't live with us.

It'd been a few months since the last time I'd visited Grandma Irene or Sierra. Sierra had stopped coming for regular visits to our house. She lived with Dad permanently now. Excitement filled my heart; I couldn't wait to see Grandma and Sierra. Did Grandma make cookies? I hoped so.

Wren and I chatted in the backseat of Mom's beat-down car—the one she could afford. The car's floor rumbled against my feet as Mom turned down the Roller Coaster Road, the road Dad used to let us drive on. We didn't drive with Dad anymore.

After a few more Christmas songs, Mom pulled into Grandma's driveway. Dad's old truck sat parked in front of Grandma Irene's house. Snow covered the tires and windshield. He had driven with his new family and not Wren and me like he used to, but at least I'd see him. I swallowed the lump in my throat.

Wren and I hadn't seen him much lately, probably because he was too busy with his other family.

I asked Mom questions sometimes, like why didn't Dad want us to live with him? Does he love Sierra more? Did we do something wrong? Mom would tell us it didn't matter, he wasn't our dad anyway, but I think it bothered her to see us hurting.

Mom stopped the car. She turned around and looked at us. "I'm going to run some errands while you visit your grandma."

"You don't want to come?" I asked.

"Spend time with Anthony and his new wife? No, thanks. I'll pass," she said, her nose wrinkling like she smelled something gross.

"Love you, Mom," I said.

"Love you too. Be back to pick you up soon."

I squinted as I left the car because the sky was so bright. Wren and I walked toward the house and waved goodbye to Mom.

A light coating of snow covered the sidewalk. The three-story house stood tall, the best-looking house on the block, always tidy and kept—no visible blemishes. Through one of the picture windows, I saw my dad's family laughing and talking. Why hadn't they waited for us to celebrate Christmas?

I pushed the round gray button and the ding, dong, ding, sounded, followed by loud footsteps. The smell of a sweet ham wafted through the door; my stomach groaned. Grandma was a wonderful cook, even though ham wasn't my favorite; hers would be good.

Sierra swung open the door.

Sierra took after Mom, her legs stretched on and on like bean poles. Sierra's bright eyes and rosy cheeks resembled a beautiful flower, waiting to bloom. She'd changed since she moved in with Dad. Her life was mysterious to me now.

"I'm happy you came." Sierra wrapped her arms around Wren, then me.

We followed her into the living room.

"I can't wait for my basketball games, after school starts," she said.

"I hope I can watch you play," I said. It wasn't fair. I'd missed so many things since she moved in with Dad. I hadn't even seen her new house yet.

Wren, Sierra, and I entered Grandma's living room. The faint smell of chimney smoke hung in the air. The fireplace glowed with red and orange embers in the bottom behind thick glass.

When we lived with Grandma, when I was six, I'd stare into the calm flames and feel happy. We didn't have a place of our own, then. Now, I saw her three times a year, and I missed her hugs—she smelled like cookies. I missed being part of one family and knowing where I belonged and to whom.

I looked at the mantle above the fireplace. Mom and Dad's picture had vanished. It was like Grandma had erased their past. Maybe Dad wanted to erase me, too. My eyes watered. The laughter of the others quieted as Wren, Sierra, and I drew closer to the tree.

Dad's wife gave me a stoic stare, and her son looked at the floor. Dad looked at me but didn't smile. I didn't look at Dad's new daughter. We weren't friends anymore. Even though she'd invited me over to a sleepover, her mom wouldn't let me come to her house. It wasn't her fault, but what was the point of trying to be her friend? I tried to smile but my strength wavered; I wanted to cry. They weren't my family. I wiped my nose with my hand. Christmas shouldn't be like this. It was about love.

I moved toward the Balsam Fir tree; cream bulbs hung on thick branches and shiny ivory ribbons hung across. Grandma probably spent hours arranging the ornaments the way she liked. I sat on the soft carpet, running my fingers over it, remembering when we first came to Minnesota. I used to think Grandma's house was like a castle from my fairy tale books when I was young, but not anymore.

Wren scooted beside me. She looked at me but no one spoke. Should I say something, maybe Merry Christmas? I wasn't brave enough so my thoughts tumbled into the air.

Grandma walked over and handed Wren and me each a present to open. Her tight curls looked trimmed, a faint smell of perm solution wafted into the air. Usually, at our Christmases, everyone opened gifts together, but no one besides Grandma joined us at the tree this year. Wren and I must have intruded on their celebration; maybe they didn't want us there. My pulse quickened and my breath felt ragged. I hoped they couldn't tell it hurt for me to breathe. No, I wouldn't cry, I told myself. I wanted to smile. It was Christmas. God's birthday.

I looked at Wren. She raised her eyebrows at me, then reached inside her bag. I reached into my teal polka dot bag, beneath the pink and purple tissue. Behind us, Sierra's family talked again, and I was thankful for the noise.

I pulled out a bottle of purple shampoo and conditioner. Grandma had attached a card to the front of my bag with twenty dollars in it. Maybe Mom could use it to buy us all a treat; we couldn't afford treats much anymore now that we only had Mom's income. "Thanks, Grandma." I grinned at her.

"Now, you take that money and buy yourself something nice," she said, patting me on my shoulder. She gave us money during Christmas every year; she told us the day after Christmas was best for shopping.

I stood and hugged her. I glanced at Dad over Grandma's shoulder; he looked away. What did I do to make him ignore me? Tears brimmed in my eyes.

Wren and I handed our shampoos to each other so we could smell them; I blinked back a tear and pretended to be intrigued by the gifts. Mine was a purple lavender shampoo and conditioner and Wren got a pink peony scented set.

Dad didn't say hi to us; he acted like I wasn't there. Didn't Dad love me anymore?

Sierra had everything—a snowmobile, a nice car, a family, money, and my dad. I fought jealousy every time I thought of her, but I loved her. The conflicting emotions made me queasy in the pit of my stomach.

Grandma crouched next to Wren and me then she spoke quietly, "Girls, would you like to play some cards? The others are visiting, but I'm always game for a round of golf." Grandma grabbed a deck of cards from the cabinet, then headed toward the dining room table.

I followed Grandma, Wren and Sierra came along too. Grandma sat. I pulled out a heavy oak chair and sat, too. Wren and Sierra took seats next to mine. Grandma shuffled the cards, then bridged the deck.

Grandma handed us each eight cards. "Face them down, no peeking," she said. "You remember how to play?"

I nodded.

We'd played many times before. It was a simple game. Each person received eight cards. At the end, the winner had the least amount of points. Pairs canceled each other out, and most cards were at face value. What you had left at the end determined your points.

I tried to laugh and smile like old times, but the rejection from Dad clawed at my heart like a lion. Being at Grandma's house wasn't the same as before. I was losing Dad and nothing I said would change his mind.

We finished the game with Grandma, and the chime rang for the door.

"Must be your mother," Grandma said.

Wren ran past me toward the front door. "Mom's here, KD."

I stood and hugged Grandma. "Love you."

"Mmm," she said. Grandma never said it back. It wasn't something she said, then or before.

"Kaitlin, time to go," Mom said.

It did not surprise me she didn't come in with how Anthony's new family treated Wren and me.

I glanced over my shoulder and said a quick goodbye before putting on my shoes and darting to Mom's car, eager to escape. I didn't want to stay, and even Grandma's ham didn't sound good anymore.

Six months later, in 1997, on a day the sun stood high in the sky—a day good for sprinklers and ice cream—was the day my fears became officially real. Wren and I visited Sierra at her house. She'd been living with her dad for some time then.

Sierra's stepmother opened the door.

Anthony was inside the living room, yet so far away. He couldn't look over his shoulder and nod or wave at Wren and me. It wasn't hard to say hello, so why didn't he say it? I looked at my worn-in clothes and wondered if it was because I wasn't good enough anymore.

He had a twelve-pack of soda sitting on the floor and I remembered the days he used to buy me a pop at his job or at restaurants.

Sierra's stepmother asked us to wait outside and didn't invite us in. On the porch that day, the world crashed around me as reality set in. He was no longer mine and never would be.

~ Seven ~

I texted Anthony, Sierra's dad, last night, as I sat on my living room couch. After not speaking to him for years, I asked him what happened then and why he stopped being our dad. He told me it was never about Wren and me and said he treated us like his own kids until Mom broke the agreement. If Mom hadn't told us, he said, their arrangement would have continued.

Did you ever love us? I texted.

He responded, yes.

The little girl inside me is finding peace with that knowledge. The realization hits me, I hadn't been able to see in my pain: if Anthony loved Wren and me, then he lost someone he loved too.

A new school year began when Wren and I were ten. I was keenly aware of how poor we were now. We'd be attending school with Anthony's new kids, and I felt completely fatherless and hopeless.

The brick building stood beside a wooden, castle-like play-ground. Inside the park were towers, some of which stood taller than the one-story school building. The air smelled like fall; trees dropped the remnants of their orange foliage. Sunlight streamed from the pale blue sky. Fallen leaves on the sidewalk crunched under my feet. My stomach twisted in knots. The first day of school always made me queasy, but this year was worse because I'd be in an unknown part of the building with the bigger kids. Near the red front door, a flag waved in the breeze. Tall, narrow windows hung beside the front entrance of the familiar building.

The chatter of children filled my ears as I shuffled into one of the many school hallways. The building felt smaller to me this year. Maybe I'd grown.

Wren walked behind me, slowly.

As we walked, the school smelled like rubbing alcohol, Elmer's glue, and milk. It made me want to gag. The areas outside the classrooms were full of ruby lockers. The brittle carpet gripped the bottoms of my new tennis shoes. I tried to focus on lifting my feet so I wouldn't trip, not something I wanted kids to remember me for.

Wren headed in a different direction, leaving me on my own.

This was something we did every year since kindergarten. Mom told us we'd find our own interests if we were separated. I didn't like being apart from her, she felt like my main constant in a tide of changes. She was my best friend, but I didn't have a choice. As I entered the section of the school with the other kids, the straps of my backpack dug into my shoulders. I couldn't wait to get it off. Good grief, it was heavy.

I continued walking until I found the door with my teacher's name on it. I hoped my teacher was nice and the kids liked me.

A woman with reddish-brown hair and glasses greeted me at the door. "Hi. I'm Miss Ames," she said and shook my hand.

"I'm Kaitlin," I said, smiling at her.

"Nice to meet you. Your new spot has your name on it. Find your seat and sit when the bell rings."

I entered the room. Several students were already sitting at tables organized in rows. Sierra's new sister was there. Did Sierra like her more than us? I never saw her talking to her new brother or sister.

She waved, then looked around as if to see if anyone noticed.

I waved back. I wasn't sure if I liked her anymore now that she had stolen my dad. Beside her were two kids I'd also played with on the playground. I quickly waved at them, then turned around. Maybe this year wouldn't be so bad.

I found the seat with my name on it, in the first row, on the left. Facing the front of the room, I slid off my boulder-weight backpack and sat. I looked around the room, shifting in my hard plastic seat. Posters covered the walls with maps and pictures of exotic animals. Off to the side of the front was the teacher's wooden desk, a spinnable blue globe sat on top.

"All right, everyone, find your seats. Time for class to begin." Miss Ames stood at the front of the room. Behind her was a whiteboard. She grabbed a red marker and pulled off the cap.

A few kids scurried to their seats, including the girl who slipped into a seat next to me. I didn't recognize her, but I was glad I didn't have to sit alone. I smiled at her and she smiled back. Her cheeks were rosy.

"I've situated you all in pairs." Miss Ames turned to the whiteboard as she spoke. "Meet the person sitting next to you. This will be your partner."

Someone groaned behind me, but I was happy because my partner was friendly.

"You will work together a lot throughout the year, so get acquainted." Miss Ames wrote something on the board with the marker.

"Hi, I'm Kaitlin."

"I'm Bethany. We moved here last week." Her strawberry-blonde hair hung above her eyes, which squinted in the corners when she smiled.

"Okay, okay." Miss Ames giggled. "Sounds like you are all acquainted now. The assignment this week and next week is to invent something." She tapped a finger on what she'd written: Invention. "Draw your design together, as a team. Plan how you will make it, then create it together. This project is due at the end of next week. Get busy."

A boy, two seats from me, had his hand in the air. He was new because I'd never seen him before. He wore thick glasses and was scrawny.

"Yes, um, yes, what is it?" Miss Ames asked.

"What if we can't do it? Can our parents help us?"

"Yes, your parents can help, but try to do as much as you can." Miss Ames walked to her desk and sat. "Get busy."

Bethany leaned in close. "Do you want to come to my house to work on the project?" Her blue eyes were wide.

"Yes, definitely," I said. Inwardly, I felt relieved. Would kids make fun of me if they knew the truth that my parents were divorced? I bet everyone's parents were together except mine.

"Here's my number. Have your mom or dad call my dad." She handed me a piece of lined notebook paper with a number scribbled on it.

Bethany and I worked on a plan for the rest of the day and sketched our design for our project. After the first day of school passed, I talked to Mom about going to Bethany's. She called Bethany's dad and said it sounded like a good idea.

The next day, I rode the bus with Bethany to her house after school. I followed her down a dirt path. At the end of the walkway stood a cozy-looking cottage with a lake behind it. Flower beds stood beneath two windows on both sides of the front door.

I followed Bethany inside. The house was cute and welcoming.

A tall man with light blonde hair stood in the living room. "This is my dad," Bethany said, holding her hand open and gesturing toward the man.

"Hello," I said.

He shook my hand and looked me straight in the eyes. "I'm Kevin." His hands were warm. "It's nice to meet you." He had a sparkle in his eyes that made me think he was nice.

Bethany nudged me. "We better get busy on our project, or we might get in trouble."

"Then, we'd be S.O.L.," I said, grinning.

Bethany's eyes went wide. "What's S.O—"

"None of that language in this house." Kevin lowered his head and his gaze flattened.

"Sorry." I looked at Kevin and wished I could hide. "My dad used to say that. I didn't realize." I looked at my feet.

"It's okay, don't say it again, okay?"

I nodded. I would have to follow the rules at Bethany's house.

"This is Sandy," Bethany said, pointing to a woman with curly red hair in the adjoining kitchen.

Sandy turned and waved at me. "Hi there." She wiped her hands on her jeans, then looked at Bethany. "Sweetie, is this your new friend you told us about?"

Bethany nodded slowly, then turned away, frowning.

Why did she react that way to Sandy's question? It was as if she didn't want to answer. Maybe she didn't think I was her friend. I cocked my head, glancing at Bethany. Was Bethany shy, or was something else going on?

"Hi," I said. "I'm Kaitlin. We're doing a project together." I tapped my fingers on my leg. I hoped she considered us to be friends. Maybe not now that I'd practically sworn in front of her dad.

"Nice to meet you," Sandy said. "Any friend of Bethany's is a friend of mine."

"Follow me into the living room. Right over here," Bethany said, pulling me away.

Safely in the living room, I leaned close to Bethany, and in a low voice said, "You called her Sandy. She's not your mom?"

"No, she's my stepmom." A frown formed on her face. She shifted her foot sideways on the carpet like she might be nervous.

I wanted her to know the truth about me; she probably knew how I felt. "My parents aren't together, either. It's hard, isn't it?"

She nodded, looking at me with a sympathetic smile.

"What do you do for fun?" I asked, hoping the change in subject would cheer her.

"I enjoy singing. Wilson Phillips is my favorite."

"Never heard of them. What do they sing?"

"I'll play some for you. Do you like singing?" she asked.

"I love singing." My pulse quickened—what if she thought I was terrible? Singing with Wren or Sierra was one thing, but I hadn't sung in front of a friend before.

Bethany knelt on the carpet. I sat crossed-legged on the floor in front of the entertainment center. On the bottom shelf of the stand was a cassette player; it made a clicking sound after she pushed a button.

"I know this song!" I said.

We belted out the words to the song together. Bethany and I continued chatting and singing in the living room for another few hours.

"You want to come back tomorrow and do more singing?" Bethany asked, her eyes sparkling.

"Yeah, and we should probably work on our project too," I said, then laughed.

She giggled. "I forgot about that."

"Can my twin sister Wren come too?" I asked. "She's like me." Wren was going to like her.

"Of course, she can come. That sounds fun. I have a sister too. I miss her a lot. She lives with my mom." Her eyes became glassy, and she sniffled.

"I have another sister; she doesn't live with me either. Crazy. We have a lot in common, don't we?" I asked.

"Yeah, it sure seems like it."

I grinned at her; it was nice to share my secrets with someone.

"My dad can help us on our project, too. He knows how to do stuff." She turned and headed through the kitchen where Kevin now stood.

The smile left my face as I thought about my dad. What would it be like if my dad was helping me with this project? He was probably too busy helping his new daughter with her project to be thinking about helping me with mine. I forced a smile onto my face. I was happy being with Bethany and I didn't want to think about Dad.

Bethany gave our drawings from class to her dad to look over. Afterward, Mom picked me up. I couldn't wait to go back to Bethany's house tomorrow.

At home, I told Wren all about my day, and she sounded excited to meet Bethany. I warned Wren not to say any bad words because her dad didn't like them, even if our dad did.

At recess the next day, I introduced Wren to Bethany, and after school the three of us rode the bus to Bethany's house together.

Bethany's dad must have helped her with our project because when we got to her house, she had finished the assignment. So, Bethany, Wren, and I worked on our singing instead.

"Let's break the song into three parts, and then each of us can sing our part. Then we can sing the chorus together," Bethany said, holding a pencil and paper. "I'll write your name next to your part."

"Then tomorrow at recess we can practice," Wren said. "KD, you go first."

"Okay." I cleared my throat. "What if I mess up?"

Bethany patted my forearm. "You'll do great."

After we sang the song, Bethany's dad came into the room, his sandy-blonde hair covering part of his eyes. "I'm not sure if Bethany mentioned it, but I'm a pastor. Would you all like to come with me to a nursing home next week? You'll need to get permission from your mom first."

"Sure. Sounds fun," I said, then looked at Wren. She seemed to be having as much fun as I did.

"Let's do it," Wren said.

Mom would be happy for a night alone. Maybe she'd go on a date with Mitchell or read a book as she used to before Dad left. I wasn't too sure about visiting a nursing home. It might remind me of Grandpa, but I liked Bethany and her dad, and I wanted to visit them again.

The next week, Wren, Bethany, Kevin, and I headed into the cool air outside of the school. Her dad's church van sat parked along the curb. We climbed inside and rode together. On the way, I thought about how much Mom smiled when she went on dates with Mitchell while we hung out with Bethany and Kevin.

I shifted in the seat to listen to what Kevin and Bethany were talking about. "When will you be starting the new youth group, Dad? Can Kaitlin and Wren come to that, too?"

"Of course, you can bring them. We'll start a youth group next week."

I bounced in the seat, excited to see Bethany more. Mom would like it, too, because she'd have even more time with Mitchell. Wren and I hardly saw Mitchell because he didn't come over when Wren and I were home, but Mom said they were still dating. Maybe he didn't want to be around us, but I didn't care. I brushed my hair out of my face. At least Bethany and Kevin wanted Wren and me around.

Kevin turned into a parking lot and parked. He led the way into the nursing home, his long legs making it an effort for me to keep up.

The automatic doors opened, and we all stepped inside. Relieved to be out of the cold, I took off my coat. Right inside the door was a nurses' station. Kevin wrote something in a book on the counter.

White-tiled linoleum floors stretched as far as I could see. Avocado walls contrasted with white wainscotting. I smelled green bean casserole. An image of Grandpa sitting along a wall like a wilted plant in his wheelchair flashed through my mind. I stared at the floor, missing him. When I glanced, my group had gotten ahead of me. I dashed to catch them.

After I reached them. The elderly people looked down, trodden and tired. They had to be sad about their families. I knew I was.

Why didn't people escape this place? Try to run away, or go home? I wouldn't want to stay in this prison; I'd want to be with the people I love. Maybe they didn't have any other choice.

One lady in a wheelchair rolled over with a pile of rubber bands in her lap.

The wheelchair lady laughed, loud and from her belly. I stood, my mouth agape, watching her closely. I didn't know anyone had fun in these places.

She wheeled after Wren, attempting to hit her with the rubber bands. Maybe some people could be happy in a place like this. Wren ran away, laughing.

A terrifying look replaced my puzzled one as the lady changed direction and darted toward Bethany and me. I ran away as her shiny wheelchair raced toward us. I stopped and hid behind Kevin at the other end of the hall. Finally, she relented her pursuit and wheeled after Wren again.

"Why do you come here, Kevin?" I asked, catching my breath. "It isn't most people's idea of a good time."

"I enjoy going to nursing homes because we visit and try to make them smile. They make me smile, too. Plus, I can tell them about God and how much he loves them. God can be anywhere, and they get lonely here. We can be their family, in a way. Everyone needs people that love them and sometimes that's our job as Christians. Something simple, like visiting the sick."

"It's such a depressing place." My face flushed. These people were like Grandpa. Some of them probably didn't recognize their own family, like him.

"They need to be encouraged, as we all do sometimes."

The next summer Bethany, Wren, and I went to a retreat, where we stayed at a cabin along a lake. We did arts and crafts and met lots of other Christians our age. The preacher taught us about how to value ourselves and how God sees us. That we are a treasure to him. It differed from the messages of rejection I'd felt from my dad. Maybe I did matter to God.

Bethany was the first best friend I had besides Wren. The three of us spent a lot of time together throughout the following year. We'd go ice skating, have sleepovers, and take trips together. During the school year, we attended Kevin's youth group every week.

One day, I stopped missing Dad and dwelling on what I had lost.

~ Eight ~

At twelve years old, Wren and I lived with Mom in our trailer house, and we survived on Mom's several part-time jobs and food stamps. Aside from our poverty, we were happy. Then, one day, something happened that pushed our lives in a different direction.

I walked to the front door of the trailer house, pulled out a sweater from the closet, and slipped it on over my T-shirt.

"Come here a minute, girls." Mom stood next to the sofa in the living room, looking concerned.

"What is it, Mom?" Was something wrong again? Mom didn't look like she'd been crying. She seemed happy. Maybe she'd finally won the lottery or something. She did like to buy those tickets sometimes and tell us her dreams about "rich life."

"Mitchell and I are getting married."

I moved closer and stared at where her ring should be. "Don't you have a ring? How are you marrying him when we hardly even know him?" Was she kidding? I didn't want a new dad. My dad needed to come back. I turned away from her, repulsed by the idea of her marrying Mitchell.

"Oh, no, I asked him. I said marry me or it's over." She smirked. "He said, get me a certificate. So tomorrow, we're having the trailer moved so he can live closer to his parents, then we'll get married after that. He's taking us out for pizza tonight; get dressed."

Wren and I dressed quickly, excited to be eating pizza for dinner. It was one of my favorites. I hoped going out to eat would be like when we used to go with Dad. Eating out at Pizza Hut was something we used to do with Mom and Dad. Would we get my favorite? Imagining the deep-dish cheese made my mouth water. I didn't know which kind was Mitchell's favorite.

A half-hour later, Wren, Mom, and I climbed inside Mom's car and drove to the restaurant and Mitchell met us there.

After Mitchell arrived, the four of us headed inside the restaurant.

The smell of fresh pizza filled the warm air. We scooted into a booth near the window overlooking the place where Mitchell parked his fancy blue truck. After sitting, the server came to get our order.

Mitchell handed the stack of menus back to the server. "We'll have a large thin crust five meat pizza, and breadsticks. The girls will have water. Mountain Dew and Diet Coke for us."

That wasn't what I wanted. I balled my fists under the table but didn't say anything because I didn't want to hurt Mom's feelings. Maybe this was what our new family would be like, never getting my way. Didn't he care what we thought? I moved closer to Wren, wondering if she felt like I did.

The server brought our water and their soda. Sierra's dad had always bought me my favorite soda, but not Mitchell. I guessed he didn't love us, either.

"So, girls. How's school going?" Mitchell asked.

"I don't like it," I said, then cleared my throat.

"It's okay." Wren twiddled her thumbs.

"Better pay attention or you'll end up poor." He frowned.

He was blunt. Was money all that mattered to him? Didn't he know we were poor already? Mom worked a lot to make ends meet. Maybe he didn't know. Maybe that was why he never bought us anything, even though Mom said he made a lot of money being a logger.

This had been the first time we'd been able to eat out since Dad left.

The server came and set plates in front of us and breadsticks in the middle of the table. I stared at my appetizer plate.

"Eat." Mitchell gestured toward the steaming breadsticks.

I wasn't hungry anymore. I grabbed a breadstick anyway.

The server brought out our pizza, the gross kind—full of meat and burnt. We ate in silence.

Mitchell paid the bill, and we left the restaurant. "Want to play put-n-go golf?"

The four of us rode together in Mom's car. "I'll leave the truck at Pizza Hut. We can pick it up later."

I wished he'd let us ride in his fancy truck, but maybe he didn't think we were good enough to ride in it.

After golfing, we returned to the Pizza Hut so Mitchell could get his truck. When we arrived, the fancy blue truck was missing. Mitchell called the police, and we rode home with Mom, hoping the cops could find it for him. It didn't seem nice that someone would steal something from someone else.

It had been six months since the truck got stolen and Christmas drew nearer. I loved the colored lights in the windows of the homes. Wren and I shoved our belongings into black garbage bags to move across town.

Mitchell's parents invited Mom, Mitchell, Wren, and me over for dinner. I hoped they liked me, and I hoped our new location would help me make fresh memories.

On the way to Mitchell's parents, we passed an ambulance parked on the side of the road. I hoped the person involved was okay. Minnesota roads were slippery; once Mom had hit a tree during winter, and once she had almost hit another car as we rounded an icy corner.

"I hope no one's hurt," Mom uttered, before blankly staring ahead.

"Yeah. I'm sure the ambulance helped them," Wren said.

"Hmm," Mom mumbled. She seemed off in her own world; was she sad again? Had moving the house made her upset? I didn't mind the new spot much. Some days Mom acted like she didn't have a care in the world, and other days she was present, but distant, preoccupied with adult problems or who knew what.

"You okay, Mom?" I asked.

"Yeah, sorry, I'm thinking about something."

After a few minutes, we arrived at Mitchell's parents.

Following Mom, I walked through the front door and pulled my scarf off my neck. I hung it with my jacket on a hook next to the door.

Wren walked behind me, coming in last. I hoped that Mitchell's parents would like us as much as our other grandparents since we would be a part of their family now.

Mitchell was already inside when I came in. He sat at the table playing cards with his dad. They laughed as they tossed their cards onto the table.

"Want to go again?" Mitchell asked. He gave us a quick wave of his hand, gesturing for us to come in. "Hey, girls." He dealt out a new hand of cards.

Mitchell's mom stood with her back to the door, wearing a blue fair-isle sweater. She spoke over her shoulder, "Come in, come in. Shut the door." She turned back to the stove and stirred the contents of the pot. "Don't want that cold air inside, children."

I stepped farther inside, wanting to clear the path of the door. The smell of a chicken roast hung in the humid kitchen air.

Pulling Wren and me aside, Mom whispered, "I'm going to make a phone call. Sit on the couch upstairs. I'll be there in a minute. I need to talk to you."

I didn't know why she hadn't talked to us when we were all in the car together. What was so important now? I raised my eyebrows at her but said nothing. Mom had warned us that Mitchell and his dad fought sometimes, but they were laughing a minute ago. No one was yelling or arguing, so what else could be wrong? I trudged the steps to the couch on the upper level of the house. I sat on the orange and brown patterned couch with Wren and waited.

Wren twiddled her thumbs.

"Do you know what Mom wants?" I asked Wren.

"No idea."

"Me either. I'm worried, it's not good."

"Yeah."

Mom ascended the carpeted stairs a few minutes later. Her eyes were bloodshot. Even during the divorce with Sierra's dad, she didn't look this sad. I glanced at Wren, as a frown formed on my face. "Mom never looks this way, except—" It couldn't be that because we didn't know anyone that had died.

Mom exhaled loudly then took a labored breath. "Remember on the way here, there was that car sitting on the side of the road?"

"Yeah. The one with the ambulance?"

"So, you know Bethany's daddy?"

I lowered my eyebrows at her. What kind of question was that? "Ugh, Mom, we saw him last week. How could we not know him?" Mom made little sense. I stared at her, my mouth hanging open. What was wrong with her?

Mom was quiet for a minute, tears flowed down her cheeks. "I saw him. I mean, I saw his car. There was a sheet on a stretcher with someone on it." Mom wiped her nose on a tissue. "On the way here, I thought I'd recognized the car. When we pulled in, I called Sandy sh—she said he wasn't home yet, that he was driving to get Christmas lights. I hoped," her voice wavered, "I hoped it wasn't him. I thought . . ." Mom looked at her hands. They were shaking. "Maybe he'd be home already and maybe someone else had the same car. Sandy told me the cops pulled in. She dropped the phone, and I heard her sobbing and then screaming."

"He'll be okay, right?" Wren asked, her eyes were wide and full of fear.

"The cops wouldn't come unless—I'm sorry girls. He didn't make it." Mom sobbed, putting her face into her hands. She took a deep breath and said, "We're the first to know."

My throat clenched; my lungs tightened. Kevin was one of the nicest people I knew. He wasn't even old. Bethany was probably finding out at this very moment, too.

"How could this happen, Mom?" Wren asked, her face red.

"What's going to happen to Bethany now?" I asked. "I'm never going to see her again, am I?" I couldn't breathe. My chest hurt. My ribs ached. It would crush Bethany when she learned what happened. She'd lost her dad like me, only she could never see him again and he didn't choose to go. The tears poured out of my eyes. It wasn't fair. Bethany had already suffered enough.

"She'll probably move in with her mom. She'll be fine," Mom said. "You'll see her again. I promise."

"Are you sure?" I sniffled. This couldn't be happening. It was so abrupt.

"Bethany will be okay, Kaitlin. I promise." Mom hugged me.

~ Nine ~

The loss of another male role model was difficult when I was twelve. After Kevin's death, memories of him flooded my thoughts. I remembered when he shoveled off the lake where Bethany lived so we could skate. I remembered at Bethany's birthday party, he made a campfire and told her not to stay up late and that he loved her. His love restored my faith in fathers.

Like a snowflake touching my hand, beautiful and unique, Kevin was here one day and then gone. His kindness was a reminder of how to treat those less fortunate than ourselves and that good deeds reveal God's love for us.

We saw Bethany again a few years ago, and it was a great time.

Mom talked to Wren. Mom had taken a shower and she smelled like her favorite perfume, a musky, floral scent. "I'm going on a date across the street with Mitchell. Don't start the house on fire this time," Mom said, then laughed light-heartedly.

She stopped in front of a mirror to touch up her hair. "Before I go out, I have something to tell you." She returned to sit with us. The smile left her face. "I want to know more about Mitchell. We need to get settled once we're a married couple."

"That's what people normally do, isn't it?" I rolled my eyes with a heavy sigh. What was she getting at?

"Knock it off, Kaitlin." She gave me a sharp look. "You're going to live at Grandma Nelly's for a while." She pursed her lips.

"What? You're going to leave us there. . . without you?" Wren asked, crossing her arms.

"Don't argue with me. It's for the best," Mom said matter-of-factly.

I glared at Mom and grabbed Wren's hand. I wanted her to know we were in this together. Wouldn't she miss us? Kevin told me we all matter to God. Why didn't Mom think so? She was acting like Dad.

"It won't be forever." She patted our legs, then rose from the couch. "We're leaving tomorrow morning. You better pack," she said with finality like a judge delivering a verdict.

It was Wren and me now; no one loved us anymore. I stood from the couch and moved away from Mom. If she didn't need to be with me, then I didn't want to be with her. Tears blurred my vision as I ran to my room.

Wren ran with me, swinging her rigid arms.

"Kaitlin, Wren, come back," Mom yelled behind us.

I kept running as fast as I could, ignoring her pleas.

I threw myself onto the carpeted floor of my room, the fabric was soft against my face. Mom's decision wasn't fair. Why did Wren and I have to leave? I thought we would finally be a family. I crawled over and grabbed my suitcase from the closet and shoved it across the floor. How could we be a family if we weren't even here?

As I yanked my clothes out of the drawers of my dresser, I heaped them into a pile in the middle of the floor. I stopped what I was doing and turned to see Wren sobbing as she sat on her bed. "Are you okay, Wren?" I asked.

"I don't want to go." She sniffled.

I walked over to the bed and hugged her. "Me either."

The next day, before the sun rose, Mom helped carry our bags to the car. Stars remained in the sky, like when we had taken our fun visit to Michigan, but this time the trip wasn't fun, it was empty and without hope.

We stopped for food and bathroom breaks. Mom drove like she couldn't wait to get rid of us. I tried not to think about it. Didn't she love us? I wiped a tear away as the trees blurred by. The day passed, and night returned. We climbed over the last hill before our new future at Grandma's house. Mom never said how long she was leaving us. How much time did it take to settle into a new marriage?

Mom turned into the driveway and stopped the car in front of Grandma's house. It was smaller than I remembered. The bricked exterior was made of old brown and yellow bricks. Grandma had two large empty flower pots sitting next to her front door. She had probably planted seeds in it that hadn't come up yet. In the summer, Grandma's yard always had plentiful Lilacs growing in the back and tall gladiolas bordering her house. I didn't know why she grew so many flowers when she was allergic to bees; maybe she wanted to keep them happy so they wouldn't sting her.

Grandma walked outside in her pajamas; her wavy gray hair blew everywhere. Her elegant nose held her plastic-framed glasses.

I stepped out of the car and stretched, then shivered.

Mom stood by the car, her hair in a tight ponytail. Wren stared at Grandma's house, then hung her head. Mom folded her arms around Wren.

Grandma rushed to hug me, squeezing me tightly. Maybe living with her wouldn't be so bad. All I had were wonderful memories of her from our visits when we were younger. She kissed my forehead.

Wren left Mom and hugged Grandma.

"I'm happy you're here. I've missed you two," she said, wiping a tear from her eye. "Oh, I love you." She wiggled her body as she squeezed both of us. "We're going to have a blast, don't you worry."

Mom opened the trunk. "Come get your stuff, girls." She crossed her arms as she leaned against the car. "I'm sure your grandmother is tired."

I grabbed my luggage, then heaved it toward Grandma's house.

Wren grabbed her suitcase and dragged it behind her, inside.

"Put the bags on my bed, for now, sweethearts," Grandma said. "I'll sleep on the davenport tonight."

Grandma hugged Mom. They stood outside talking while Wren, and I brought everything inside the house. Inside the room off the kitchen, Grandma Nelly had extensive collections of sewing supplies in tall stacks in the middle of the room. It wasn't a large house; I wondered where Wren and I would sleep and if we'd have our own rooms.

That night, Wren and I slept in the bed next to Mom. Early the next morning, Mom returned to Minnesota without us.

A few months after Mom left, I stood in Grandma's kitchen looking for a snack.

Grandma handed me a white envelope. "Your mother's written." She gave me a half-smile, rubbing my arm.

Inside the envelope was a picture of Mom standing under a white arch, kissing Mitchell. Mom wore a beautiful short-sleeved dress with white lace gathered around her narrow waist. Her fancy dress and hair made her look royal, like Grandma's picture of Princess Diana. Only Mom had dark hair.

My shoulders tensed; my heart pounded in my chest. She looked happy without me. Sierra stood in front of Mom, wearing a dress, and holding a hand-woven basket. When was the last time she wore a dress? Church maybe? I should have been there in my pretty dress —not here, unincluded. Mom should have waited until we came back; we were supposed to be part of the family too. Sierra wasn't her only daughter. The anger built inside me, ready to explode at any moment. Sierra's dad wanted her, and Mom wanted her, but why didn't either of them want us? Tears pooled in my eyes.

I passed the picture to Wren, mostly so I wouldn't tear it to pieces. Didn't Mom know it would hurt us to be left out? I ran to my room, throwing my body across my bed, and sobbed into my bedspread.

An hour later, Grandma yelled, "Your mother is on the phone, girls!"

I ran to the kitchen where the phone was. Wren was already there.

"Can I talk first?" I asked.

Wren nodded. "Sure."

Putting the phone against my ear, I heard nothing. "Mom?"

"Hey, honey." She sniffled into the phone.

There was no way I could give her a piece of my mind while she was crying. "What's wrong, Mom?" Why was she crying? I thought she'd be happy without me.

"I have something to tell you," she said. "Hold the phone so you and Wren can both hear."

"Wren. Mom needs to talk to us both." I held the phone between our ears. "Okay, Mom, we're both here," I said, looking at Wren.

"Okay," her raspy voice echoed on the phone. "Mitchell had a heart attack."

"How did that happen?" My jaw dropped. "Isn't he too young?"

"I guess not," Mom said. "He didn't get in soon enough, so the damage was extensive."

"Is he going to be okay?" Wren asked. She looked at me, her eyes big.

"I don't know."

People weren't supposed to have a heart attack right after they got married; it wasn't fair. "He's alive, right?" I asked.

The silence lasted forever before Mom spoke again, "Yes, he's alive. I would've told you if he wasn't."

I breathed a sigh of relief. "Thank goodness, he's okay. What happened, Mom?" I wrapped one of my arms around Wren's back.

"He was driving, and his arm was hurting. He was delivering wood out of state. Mitchell stopped at a truck stop restaurant. The staff there called an ambulance." Her breath came in heavy sobs.

I didn't know what to say to make her happier. I hated not being able to cheer her up. "It's okay, Mom. We're here."

"Thanks, sweetheart." For a few seconds, there was silence. "They put a pacemaker in his chest."

"What does that mean?" I asked. "What's a pace—"

"It's a machine that shocks his heart into rhythm." She paused. "It's a box in his chest."

"Oh," Wren said, her hands hanging limp at her sides.

"They're giving him five years," Mom said, her voice faltering. "They say he'll be lucky if he's there when you graduate." Mom sobbed again, her breath loud on the phone.

Now, I was going to lose my stepdad, too. How many people were going to die right in front of me? I hadn't even a chance to really know him yet. I fought a sob rising in my chest. "Mom don't cry. It'll be okay," I said, wiping tears from my own eyes. I wished I could help but didn't know how. I glanced at Wren. Tears filled her eyes too.

"I don't know how I'll make it through this," Mom said.

She was too far away for me to hug her.

"Love you, Mom," Wren said.

"Love you too, girls."

I stood in Grandma Nelly's kitchen. Her Blue Willow plates lined the walls on long white shelves. Some had a countryside scene with farms and chickens. A pot of hamburger soup boiled on the stove. I loved Grandma's soup. It was beef, thick Amish-style noodles, and onion soup mix. Amazing.

Being at Grandma's house was a lot different from being with Mom. Grandma didn't boss us around, and we always had plenty to eat. There were no new boyfriends to meet or meals to skip. School and the rich kids were the worst. At least on the reservation, I wasn't the only one who wasn't rich. The kids in Michigan were meaner and school was harder. Everyone here had so much money.

They thought the Indians still lived in Teepees; I couldn't believe it. I set them straight.

I stared at the empty coffee pot, debating whether I should make some. I missed Mom and home more and more. It had been a month since I'd talked to her, so I gave her a call.

"Hey, Mom. Can I talk to you about something?" I wiped the hair from my eyes. "By the way, how's Mitchell?"

"He's good. Taking new medicine and getting his diet straightened out. He probably won't be able to work." She cleared her throat. "Now if I could get him to quit smoking. We finished another round of Scrabble, but he won again."

"Do you know what?" I asked. The smell of coffee filled the kitchen.

"No, but I know his brother, Who," Mom said, then laughed.

I was glad she seemed to be feeling better than the last time we talked, but her joke still wasn't funny. "Can I ask you about my real dad?" I bit my lip. Would she tell me anything she hadn't already said? Maybe if I kept asking, she'd remember more.

"Make your questions quick, I need to fix supper for Mitchell, and he probably doesn't want to hear me talking about Smith."

Next to me, the coffee pot made the bubbling sounds it made when the pot was finished brewing. "I'm glad Mitchell's doing better. But. . . I have a few questions if you have time to talk."

"How did you meet my real dad?" I asked. Maybe knowing more about my real dad would make me miss Sierra's dad less.

"Why? Are you writing a book and don't want to leave out that chapter?" she asked, laughing again. I sat down at the kitchen table.

"Come on, Mom. Seriously? Anything useful?" I stomped my foot. I'd never learn anything when she was so secretive.

"He came from a larger family." She put her hand on her chin. "We met during the Airforce."

"Cool. Have we ever met his family?" I poured myself a cup of coffee in one of Grandma's fancy blue glass cups.

"Yeah, when you were babies," Mom said.

Grandma came into the kitchen and ladled some hot soup into three bowls. "Come eat when you're ready," she whispered.

I nodded. "Anything else? Do we look like him?" I added two teaspoons of sugar, then stirred my coffee.

"He had reddish hair and brown eyes, so no, you don't look like him. You look more like me."

"Why do I have blue eyes if you don't, and he doesn't?" I took a drink of my coffee. It was still too hot, and my mouth watered. I had to admit it, my coffee-making skills were improving. Sometimes the pots I made tasted syrupy. I grabbed a bowl of soup and brought it to the table.

"Grandma has blue eyes, so that must be where you get it from," Mom said nonchalantly.

"I guess that makes sense," I said. I squeezed my eyebrows together. Her explanation made little sense, but maybe it skipped a generation? I knew nothing about genetics, but I wanted to believe her.

"All right, I got to go. I'll tell you more later. Love you," Mom said. "Sorry, Mitchell is really hungry."

"Okay. Don't forget, okay? Love you too, Mom."

It irritated me that she never spoke about my dad; she only talked about Mitchell. Wouldn't she want to know if she was in my situation? I hung up the phone on the receiver and marched from the kitchen to the living room. That conversation didn't help at all. I had more questions and hardly any answers. How do two hazel- and brown-eyed parents have only blue-eyed children? I hunkered down on the couch in the living room.

A half-hour after we ate our soup, Grandma sat in her rocking chair next to me, crocheting. "Girls let's turn on *The Sound of Music*. I'll get the ice cream." Grandma left the room. She always knew when Wren and I needed a treat.

"Are you okay?" Wren asked, leaning toward me, her eyes were full of worry.

I frowned. "Not really. I wish we knew more about our dad. Maybe he'd have wanted us."

Wren glanced at the floor. "Me too."

"I'm not even sure Mom wants us. Wouldn't it be nice to know something about our real dad? Anything at all? We're missing some important part of ourselves."

Grandma handed us each a bowl of Moose Tracks ice cream.

"Thanks, Grandma." Wren took a bite of ice cream.

My eyes met Wren's. "How else can we find out more if Mom won't tell us anything?"

"Find out more about what?" Grandma asked.

"We were talking about Smith." Wren paused before continuing, "Do you know anything about him, Grandma?"

"Let's see." She put her finger onto her lip. "Well, his first name was Josh." She took a bite of ice cream. She set her spoon down. "His siblings' names are Annie, Diane, George, Eden, and a few more. I met him when I visited you girls in the South," Grandma said. "I think your mom might have been engaged to him."

Wren set her ice cream down on the coffee table. She left and returned a minute later with a notepad. "What were their names again?" She ran her fingers through her hair.

"Annie, Eden, George, and Diane. I can't remember the others. He's going to be hard to find with a last name like Smith."

Wren scribbled onto her paper, then scarfed the rest of her treat.

I wondered what it would've been like having Smith as a last name.

"I'm calling four-one-one, Grandma," Wren said.

Four-one-one was like the phone book with an operator for finding out-of-state numbers. Wren walked toward the kitchen where the phone was hanging on the wall above the filing cabinet.

"Try not to run up the phone bill," Grandma said over her shoulder.

Kaitlin Smith, I said in my head. It didn't sound terrible, just incredibly common.

She must have grabbed the phone because a few minutes later, she talked like she was at one end of another conversation, "Is there an Annie Smith in Mississippi?" She paused, looking at me around the corner and shrugging. "Okay. Tell me all the numbers." She wrote for a few minutes. "How about Eden? Okay, what are those numbers? How about Diane? One sec, let me put these down. No, I think I'll try these first. Thanks." There was another pause.

Grandma and I exchanged glances; our eyes wide.

"Hi, this is Wren. I'm looking for someone who knew Tary from the Airforce. If you know her, please call me back." Wren paced into the living room. She shrugged, then returned to the kitchen. "Hi, excuse me, did you know a woman named Tary in the Air Force? No? Okay, thank you." Wren returned to the living room and sank into the couch. "I found a few that fit; I left some messages with the people who didn't answer; hopefully, we'll know something soon."

I hoped someone would call her back, she was so determined to find someone who knew something. How many numbers had she called? It must have been at least twenty or more.

Wren set a pillow behind her head and rested on the couch.

The phone rang a few hours after Wren had called those people. Wren sprinted to it. "This is Wren." Her eyebrows moved higher, and she motioned me to come, waving her arms frantically. "Oh, he is?" She held the phone to her chest. "It's aunt Diane," she whispered. She returned the phone to her ear.

I waited to hear what they said, pacing across the living room. Now and then I glanced at the clock, then at Grandma. I sat, but then I rose and paced. I sat again.

"It's so nice to talk to you; thanks for returning my call. I can't believe we found you," Wren said. She hung up the phone, then skipped into the living room. "Aunt Diane is so nice. She has two kids. Her voice was so cool, she sounded like a country singer. She's living in Mississippi." She stared into my eyes, her smile fading.

"One more thing," Wren said. She looked at me, her eyes wide. "Dad's not dead."

"Mom has got some explaining to do," I said.

~ Ten ~

Mom called a few weeks after we found out Smith wasn't dead. She told us Mitchell's doctors adjusted his medications. In a few weeks, Mom was coming to pick Wren and me up to start our new life.

Wren and I were thirteen when we moved back in with Mom and Mitchell.

The Mackinaw bridge grew closer, a massive bridge, seven miles long. I always hate crossing it because of the way the car shook as Mom drove over the echoing stretched-steel road. From a distance, it was beautiful, especially at night when the lights reflected off the water because it was lit like a Christmas tree. It was too light outside this trip to see the lights.

"Mom, Wren, and I have something to talk to you about." My stomach twisted into knots, wondering if Mom would tell us the truth or not and what she would say. Was Dad a criminal or something? Is that why she didn't tell us about him? I bit my lip. Did Mom know Smith wasn't dead?

"What is it?" Mom asked, glancing at me in the rear-view mirror.

"We talked to Aunt Diane, Smith's sister," I said.

Mom turned her head toward Wren who sat shotgun, then Mom continued looking forward at the road. "What? When did you talk to her?"

"Wren found her."

"How?" Mom asked, shock filling her voice.

"Four-one-one," I said matter-of-factly.

Mom continued, "What did she say? How is she? I always liked her."

Mom had liked her. They must have met like Grandma mentioned. "She told us our dad isn't dead."

"I see," Mom sounded despondent.

When she didn't respond further, I pressed, "Why did you lie, Mom? Did you know he was alive or did you really not know? When we were younger, you said he'd died in a fire a long time ago. Did you make that up? I don't understand, Mom."

Mom stared ahead at the road. "Let's stop and get a drink when we get over the bridge," Mom said as if she wanted to change the subject. Was she going to avoid the questions again? She cleared her throat and then continued, "He called me during the divorce."

"What? What did he say? Did he ask about us?"

"He did ask about you. When Anthony left, I asked Smith if he could take you if an emergency arose and I couldn't take care of you. I didn't know if I could be a single mom."

"What did he say?" Had he wanted to come to get us? Why didn't he ask to talk to us? I looked out the window at the wavy waters beneath the bridge.

"He said he'd have to think about it and get back to me." She sighed loudly. "Look, girls. I don't want anyone else to hurt you. Smith isn't a good person."

"I thought you said he was a hero," Wren said, with sadness in her voice.

"I wanted to spare you from the truth."

I scoffed.

Mom continued, ignoring my reaction. "He cheated on me when we were in the military. I was in love with him, but he left me."

Mom pulled into a gas station so we could get something to drink. Was that all she was going to tell us about him? Where was he now and was she going to reach out to him again? I wanted to meet the man who helped bring me into the world. Didn't Mom understand that?

After the sixteen-hour trip back home from Michigan to Minnesota, Mom pulled into our home behind Mitchell's parents.

As we entered the house, Mitchell looked up from his show. "Hey, girls. Welcome back." He returned to his movie. Maybe Wren and I could pick out the next show; war videos were boring.

"Tary, are you going to cook?" He rolled his eyes. "When you were at the store, did you pick up the jelly I wanted?"

"Yes." Mom sighed loudly.

"None of that knock-off brand, either, I hope."

Mom rolled her eyes. "Nope, it's the right stuff."

I looked at the walls, a different color than before. Maybe the walls had yellowed from Mitchell's cigarette smoke. The stench circulated the room and clung to the furniture.

Mom went to the kitchen and cooked dinner; a burnt smell filled the house.

Twenty minutes later, Mom carried out boiled potatoes and steaks. The steam floated into the air over the pan as she carried the steaks over. Then she brought over the creamed peas, a white slimy mess inside of a pot.

I wrinkled my nose. I'd never eaten creamed peas. Must be something Mitchell liked because Mom had never made them before. I huffed and sat at the table.

Half of my meat landed on the table, as I cut it. Mitchell looked sideways at me and cleared his throat, frowning. I returned the loose steak pieces to my plate. As I ate, the steak crunched in my mouth. I guessed that was the best we had.

With dinner finished, I moved into the living room. I planned to watch television with Wren like we used to do before Mitchell lived with us. I sat on the couch across from the TV, hoping he'd get the hint and let us choose a movie.

Wren moved to sit beside me. Maybe Mitchell could find something else to do besides hog the television.

Mitchell moved in front of us, blocking the TV. "Kids, do those dishes. There's no reason Tary should do them." Mitchell's jaw stuck out, and he looked over toward the kitchen. "Go wash the dishes!" He put his hands on his hips.

"I don't want to wash dishes. You do them, Wren," I said, jabbing her with my elbow.

"It's not my turn, it's yours," she jested, bumping into me.

Mitchell scoffed, his face red.

Mom was the only one who ever washed them. Why should that change now? I didn't even know how to do the dishes. Mom had never taught us. I lifted an eyebrow. Mitchell knew that, didn't he? Hopefully, Mom would straighten out his unreasonable expectations.

Mitchell stormed out of the room. Maybe he'd given up his ridiculous assumptions. Returning, he held out his clenched fist with three toothpicks in it. "Let's play a game. Draw one toothpick and whoever gets the shortest stick has to do the dishes. Here, I'll draw one first." He picked a toothpick that was full length.

I looked at Wren. Was he serious? Wren shrugged. This was not a fun game. Why couldn't Mom do the dishes? This was dumb. Mitchell was out of his mind if he thought Wren and I could do them.

Mitchell had one hand on his hip and the expression in his eyes looked hard. His black eyebrows clung to his eyes. I didn't think he would change his mind.

I reluctantly grabbed a stick and hoped for the longest one. Wren hovered her fingers over the sticks, weighing her options. She drew a stick.

Holding mine next to hers, I had lost. I stomped to the kitchen and then ran water into the sink. I dumped a bunch of soap in, unsure of how much I needed.

Mitchell followed me into the kitchen, then dipped his fingers into my dishwater. "The water isn't hot enough; nothing will get clean with cold water."

"It's not cold." I shrugged.

He splashed a handful of water into my face. "That ain't cold?"

My cheeks burned. He treated me like I wasn't a person. I backed away from him. "No?"

"What did you say?" He pulled my shirt at the neckline, pulling me close to him so his face was directly in mine.

My muscles tightened and I trembled. His breath reeked of stale cigarettes. I looked past him at Mom, trying to avoid his empty eyes. Hopelessness filled my heart. No one was going to save me. I squeezed my eyes tightly, hoping to wake up from this nightmare. Tears seeped into the creases.

"Don't look at your mom! Look at me; you ain't talkin' to her. I'm the one talking to you," his voice drowned my senses until I couldn't think of anything else.

Mom shook her head at me, the expression in her eyes told me she was afraid to move. Mom stared, tears trickling from her eyes. Did I deserve this for not doing the dishes the right way? No one had ever taught me how. It wasn't my fault. I wished Mom wasn't scared so she could stop him.

A scream escaped my throat. Was I the one screaming? It sounded foreign. Mitchell's hands moved from my shirt collar to my throat. His grasp muffled the sound of my scream.

He tightened his grip on my neck, lifting me into the air. My chest tightened. I needed to gasp, but couldn't, so I kicked my legs to get him off. He didn't let go. My vision blurred. I needed to cough, but couldn't. My pulse pounded against his fingers. I stopped fighting, my body weakened from struggling.

He set me down; his breathing was rapid.

After a moment, the world became vivid again. I put my hands on my knees and gasped for air. Blood returned to my face. A new fear crept into my mind: what if he hadn't stopped? Would he have killed me?

My throat throbbed. Did I almost die? I didn't want to die, not like that.

"Finish the dishes, Kaitlin," Mitchell said, standing off to the side of the sink. Having caught his breath, he might be ready to hurt me again. "I don't trust you. I'm standing here and watching until you're done," he said. "Wren, get over here and dry these clean ones."

Wren dried the dishes with a hand towel.

"Tary, get your lazy butt over here and put these away—you ain't doin' nothin'."

I guess it didn't matter that Wren picked the long stick after all. We all got the short stick. Being stuck with Mitchell had cursed us all. Why did Mom let him stay?

He picked up one of the dishes I washed, then held it up. "You're not doing it right. Clean the bottom of the dish too." He then stood behind me, breathing his cigarette smoke down my neck. "You're messy pigs, same as your mom."

"Sorry," I whispered, rubbing underneath the plate with my washcloth.

After I did the dishes, it was time for bed, and I was happy to escape into my room. Mitchell might be worse than the lions in the Bible, the ones God protected Daniel from. I had escaped his grasp, at least for now.

About a month after the dish fight, Mom called us into the kitchen. I hoped it wasn't to do the dishes. She had circles under her eyes like she hadn't slept all night. "Girls, sit. I have something to tell you."

Whatever it was, I was pretty sure it wasn't good news.

"Anthony and I made a financial deal with each other."

Why was she bringing up Sierra's dad? I creased my eyebrows. What did he have to do with anything now? We hadn't heard from him in over a year.

"He promised to pay the mortgage on the trailer during the divorce and then I wouldn't charge him child support." She looked at the floor, shaking her head. "Those payments didn't get made.

We can't live here anymore. I'm sorry." Mom buried her face in her hands. She let out a loud sob, and her chest heaved.

"Can't you call Sierra's dad, I'm sure he meant to pay for it?" I asked, looking at Mom.

"What?" Her face turned red as she looked at me. "No." She clenched her fist. "Anthony is not my husband anymore, Mitchell is. Anthony will not fix this. He doesn't care. He's not the hero you think he is." She rolled her eyes. "He wants nothing to do with us."

She didn't need to put down Sierra's dad. He'd help. He'd never let us be homeless. Would he? "What about our stuff?" Would I be able to keep the things I loved, like my baseball cards? Or the goggles and souvenirs from Metrodome Anthony picked out for me when we went to Uncle Mitch's baseball game? And what about my favorite dolls?

"We don't have any room for anything extra," Mom told us. "I'm sorry."

She wasn't sorry. If she cared, she would have paid the bills, instead of sitting by and letting Mitchell lose our house. I crossed my arms. I was so sick of all these disasters. Why couldn't my life be simple?

"Keep what you have to have," she said. "No toys."

I'd have to get rid of everything I enjoyed. I hated my life. Mom was ruining everything by marrying Mitchell. I crossed my arms across my chest. She should have stayed married to Sierra's dad and none of this would've happened. I gritted my teeth, my fists tight at my side.

Mitchell came into the house from outside.

I glared at him. If he wasn't gambling all the time and worked sometimes, maybe we wouldn't have lost the house.

He sat in a chair nearby. "You told them?" he asked, his voice flat, unconcerned.

"Yes," Mom said, her eyes bloodshot, then she glanced at her feet.

"Pick out what you need to keep." He pointed toward our rooms. "Get moving. Don't stand there like you didn't hear me."

I left the room, stomping to my room. Now I'd have nothing left of my life with Anthony.

Pulling into our aunt's house, where we'd be staying now, my heart felt heavy. I didn't know Mitchell's sister very well, and I didn't know what it would be like to live with her. Would she be nice? Mom and Mitchell would live in my aunt's bus down the hill from us; my aunt had converted it into a two-bed camper and parked it in the middle of her ten-acre parcel.

Wren and I stayed with her in the house.

During lunch, on the second day, my stomach hurt, and I told her I didn't like spaghetti.

"You will eat what I give you," she said, folding her solid arms across her chest. "I gave you clothes yesterday and put a roof over your head. You should be grateful. At least you have dinner."

I pushed my noodles around my plate, unable to eat. She had given Wren and me each a new outfit, and they were the nicest clothes I owned. "You gave me clothes, but I didn't ask for any of that." I pushed the plate away. "I want my house back; not to be stuck here eating spaghetti. I hate spaghetti. I hate living here." Anthony used to make us spaghetti all the time and now I couldn't stand the thought of eating it.

"With that attitude, you can march yourself down to the bus and go live with your parents. You aren't welcome in my house until you can stop acting like that."

I glanced at Wren, who gave me a sympathetic smile. I left the table, then marched out the door and headed toward the bus. My stomach clenched, and I hunched over. I threw up on the ground outside my aunt's house, then continued walking to the bus.

The trek to the bus took a few minutes. I stepped inside the small bus; it wasn't as yucky as I thought it would be. A two-person table with benches sat in the middle of the bus. Next to the table were bunk beds; the top bunk where I would probably sleep was small, and a larger bed was on the bottom. Mom must have folded the itchy fleece blankets that sat in a stack on the bottom bunk.

A small cotton rug covered the floor in front of a small sink and delicate curtains hung before the tiny window. Next to the beds was a medicine cabinet. Mom and Mitchell weren't inside, so I looked outside again to be sure they were still gone; the car wasn't there. Mitchell was going to be so mad when he found out about my fight with his sister, but if they were gone, no one could stop me from leaving this stupid place. It's not like they'd even notice I was gone or even care. They'd have Wren, who was a better version of me, anyway.

Maybe I could run away and find a family to take me in. Anthony wasn't an option anymore; I had no one who wanted me. Maybe no one would take me in. Save me. If I couldn't find someone to keep me, then maybe I could find another way to be free. Going back into the bus, I opened the medicine cabinet and took ten of Mitchell's heart medications, one of each different pill.

Gripping the pills, I ran to the outhouse in between the bus and my aunt's house. Mom told me once that the pills were strong and dangerous. Sitting inside the outhouse, my fingers shook as I clutched the pills. This should be enough, I thought. I didn't want to take too many because Mitchell might notice.

I didn't see any other way. No one wanted me around. Smith didn't want us. Mitchell didn't want us. Anthony didn't want us, either. My aunt hated me now, and so did Mitchell. If no one cared about me, then what was the point of it all? I crossed my arms. Nothing was ever going to get better. We'd probably always be homeless and poor. Hot tears ran down my cheeks. Tossing the pills into my mouth, I swallowed them all.

A moment later, I shivered. Was it the end? What had I done? It was then I realized, I hated my life but I didn't want to die anymore.

~ Eleven ~

Mitchell needed to take those pills to live, and I took them to die. I am so blessed my life did not end there. Unlike on that day, I want to know what God will do with my life story. At the time, I told no one the depths of my depression. However, suicide was not the answer. I know that now.

It looked promising from a hurting perspective because it looked like the end of pain. Here's the truth: suicide is the beginning of pain. The person who commits it releases their pain onto their loved ones and it multiplies. Loved ones blame themselves. They carry that pain in their hearts, perhaps forever.

I lost a special friend to it, and almost lost a loved one.

After an hour, with no reaction to the pills, I snuck to the side of my aunt's house and stole a bike that leaned against the siding.

Riding down the dirt road, I pedaled hard, gliding across the hard sand. After about a mile, the bike wouldn't let me pedal anymore. I hopped off and looked at the chain, which had fallen off. I pulled on the links, then looked over my shoulder. No one was coming yet. I'd better hurry fixing it, in case they noticed I was missing. The grease smelled rotten, and my hands were soon covered in sticky filth. I grunted, frustrated. The chain wouldn't hook back up. I kicked the bike. Nothing in my life worked, not even this stupid bike. I huffed, pushing the bike into the woods. Looking over my shoulder again, still, no one was following me. I knew they wouldn't.

I headed the rest of the way on foot. I'd better hurry if I didn't want to be caught. After walking at a fast pace for another twenty minutes, I stopped outside of my friend's house and hid in the forest.

Tall ferns covered the ground around me as well as moss-covered tree trunks. As I waded through the brush, chickadees chirped in the trees. Why did they have to be happy? I bet if I was gone, Wren would be the only one to miss me. If I was gone, she'd have to face Mitchell alone. I couldn't do that to her. Maybe Grandma Irene and Grandma Nelly would miss me. They'd care. I missed them both.

Maybe if I stopped at my friend's house, I could ask her parents to help me and tell them what was going on. It was useless. I took a deep breath of the countryside air. I couldn't tell them, because then she'd know that I was homeless. If I told her, then the whole school might find out.

Lying next to a fallen oak, I rested, drifting asleep on the ground.

I'd been hiding a while when my cousin rode by on his four-wheeler, hollering for me. I ignored him and continued hiding. He didn't care about me.

Soon, he left.

My stomach rumbled again, and the sky grew dark. I didn't know how I'd survive on the reservation in the middle of the woods. It wasn't safe. Reluctantly, I trekked the two miles back to my aunt's house. Hopefully, she had something to eat, even if it was leftover spaghetti. That evening, she told me I was ungrateful for leaving without telling her where I was going, and that she hoped I'd learned my lesson. That night, on the bus, I shivered in my sleeping bag, crammed into an area above Mom and Mitchell's bed. The next morning, cold sweat stuck to my body as I shivered, and I had already learned my lesson.

Mitchell and Mom chatted, sitting at the table the next morning. Mitchell laughed. How could he be happy sleeping here? I had tossed and turned the entire night.

Michell sipped coffee, and the pleasant smell of it filled the bus until he lit a cigarette. I'd gotten more and more used to the smell of cigarettes; it reminded me of the trailer. Did someone else live in our old trailer now? I couldn't believe I'd be sleeping here from now on. As I moved off the bed, I shivered in my blanket. I grumbled, then climbed out of the small top bunk. I sat at the table next to Mom.

"It's alive," Mom said in her Arnold Schwarzenegger voice.

It was not funny. I rolled my eyes at her joke.

"Morning," Mitchell said.

"Hi," I said, my tone cross. This wasn't where I wanted to live and I refused to live in something so cold, but I didn't know where else to go and so I wouldn't have a choice.

Mitchell opened the door and looked outside. "I'm tired of being stuck inside this bus all the time. Let's take a trip to Yellowstone." He opened the medicine cabinet and pulled out his pills.

I stared as my pulse raced; I hoped he didn't notice the missing pills.

"Let's go today," Mitchell said.

I let out the breath I'd been holding, he hadn't noticed his missing pills.

Mom, Wren, and I climbed into our car and Mitchell drove his Ford Ranger so we could fit all our needed supplies. Two days in the vehicles, one night sleeping in the car in a rest area, and at last, we'd arrived. We made a reservation at a campsite near the middle of the first mountain we found.

After Mitchell and Mom set up the tent, Mitchell pulled out a thick, tarp roll. Were we all sleeping in the big tent? I put my hand on my chin. Mitchell let the thick material plop onto the ground. He stretched it out, shoved two sticks into the ground, then fastened it to them. He finished arranging the two and a half feet tall tent in less than five minutes.

I raised one eyebrow.

As if he could hear my thoughts, he spoke, "It's a pup tent. Used it in the Army. Best kind around. That's where you two are sleeping."

I shook my head, and my mouth dropped. After my recent experience with my aunt and the bus, I decided to bite my tongue, but I still didn't know how Wren and I were supposed to cram into this narrow one-man tent? The Army's best? I'm sure it used to be back in the 1800s.

Mitchell lit a fire and cooked dinner.

After we ate, Wren and I crawled into our tent, too exhausted to argue about it being too small for the two of us.

I awoke the next morning beside Wren, who huddled close to my body. We both shivered under the now-damp blanket. It must have rained last night because water now pooled along the walls of the tent. My body trembled.

The smell of burning wood filled the tent. I sat. It would probably be warmer sitting next to the fire than staying in here covered in water.

I stuck my head out of the pup tent. Mitchell cooked eggs over the campfire and since we hadn't been to the store and had nothing refrigerated, they must be commodity eggs from the food shelf because they smelled funny. Mom sat next to him, wearing a flannel jacket. Her cheeks were rosy and she had a cup of coffee in her hand. I zipped the tent back up, then pulled on some warm clothes on top of my wet ones. After we were dressed, Wren unzipped the tent.

I plopped into one of the chairs around the fire and rubbed my arms to warm them. Mitchell handed me a plate; the eggs were cold already. I didn't realize I had dressed so slowly.

"I can't eat these eggs. Yuck," I stated. They smelled so bad.

"You eat them, now. I ain't kiddin'." His eyes were as cold as the mountain, daring me to disobey.

I didn't think he'd hurt me with other people around, but I would not take that chance. His eyes burned into my flesh. Swallowing my pride and the lump in my throat, I choked on the cool eggs, one icy piece at a time. I tried not to gag and stared into the blazing fire. Another pan sat on the black fire grate. Baby red potatoes steamed in the pan. Mitchell never cooked with onions, which was the best way to eat potatoes. Grandma Irene always cooked potatoes with onions, and she cooked better than anyone I knew. Either way, at least they weren't commodity potatoes. Those smelled like spoiled milk.

"I have to go to the bathroom. Will you come with me, Mom?" I asked.

Mom nodded, setting her coffee cup down. She walked with me along the pathway to the bathroom, there was a small dirt pathway leading to the double outhouses.

"Can I have potatoes when we get back? I didn't want to ask in front of Mitchell since I made him mad with the eggs."

"If there's any left, sure."

We returned a few minutes later, and Mitchell had saved us a few extra potatoes. I was grateful to get the taste of commodity eggs out of my mouth. After I finished, I set my plate down in the hot water Mitchell must have warmed up.

I sat back in my camp chair and then blew warm air into my hands.

Mitchell eyed me suspiciously.

What had I done wrong now? I wondered but didn't ask.

Mitchell cleared his throat. "Do you know, if you rub your hands together, the friction keeps them warmer than hot air will?"

I rubbed my hands together, and they finally warmed. Mitchell was pretty smart, but I didn't tell him.

Early the next morning, Wren and I sat around the campfire. The smell of bacon and campfire smoke filled the air. Thank goodness, he wasn't making those nasty eggs again. Mitchell sat crossed-legged in sweatpants on a camping chair. As he sipped his cowboy coffee, steam rose from his speckled tin cup.

He took another sip of his coffee, then uncrossed his legs, leaned forward, and stirred the sizzling bacon. "Want to hear a joke, kids?"

I nodded. I liked jokes and stories.

"A female and male bear were out in the woods." Mitchell moved his hands like the bear, raising them wide in the air. "One bear eats a Czech traveler. The park ranger hears about this, so he and another man come out to find the bears." Mitchell lights a cigarette. "The Park Ranger walks to the male bear and shoots it." Mitchell laughed, glancing between Wren and me. "The man questions him. He asks the Park Ranger, 'How do you know the male ate the traveler?' The Ranger replies, 'Check is always in the mail.'" Mitchell smiles and takes another drag from his cigarette.

I didn't get it, but I laughed anyway, and so did Wren. Had Wren gotten the joke? I glanced at her. Maybe she could explain it to me later.

The cigarette dangled in Mitchell's mouth. He squeezed the filter between his fingers and blew smoke rings into the cool morning air. The O's vanished. "Bacon is done."

Mom carried over a few logs and dried twigs. Mitchell grabbed plates and served everyone four slices of thick bacon.

"Before you woke, deer and coyotes ran right through the campsite," Mitchell said, exhaling more smoke.

"That's so cool," I said. As I considered the coyotes, it made me think about bears, too. In the west, there were Grizzly bears, not the complacent black bears of Minnesota. My pulse raced as I thought about the unbridled wildlife moving as it pleased, even though our campground. "Do you think a bear will attack us?"

He paused before answering my question, "No, not unless you sneak food into your tent. That's why we cover food at night. Bears like food sitting out in the open." He tilted his head and gave me a look like he was warning me not to feed the bears.

Mom added more wood to the fire and then sat in a camp chair across from Wren and me. The smell of the campfire hung in the air. We sat around it like a family, exploring the West together.

The same day Mitchell told us the story-joke about the bears, we'd spent a lot of the day driving. In the afternoon, we parked the vehicles in a parking lot at the top of an enormous hill with a slope below. After we got out of the car and truck, the four of us descended the steep path. Wren and I walked behind Mom and Mitchell. My calves burned as we hiked down wooden steps. The smell of sulfur was getting stronger the further into Yellowstone we traveled.

A waterfall came into view. The water fell off a cliff above us in a never-ending surge. The water crashed as it hit rocks at the bottom.

A minute later, the four of us reached the bottom. Beneath the falls was a flat patio area with benches and a viewing area with a wooden ledge all around it. Wren and I walked as close as we could to the cascade, stopping at the front of the platform. A mighty river ran off from the waterfall; people took pictures standing in front of it. We didn't bring a camera. Large, white caps crashed into boulders, covering everyone on the platform in a light mist. The water on my face was refreshing.

Wren and I moved away from the waterfall, then sat on a bench, resting. It relieved me to get off my feet for a minute and catch my breath.

Mitchell looked back and said something to me, but I couldn't hear him because of the water. He pointed to the waterfall, then he and Mom moved toward the viewing area. After resting and taking in the view, the four of us hiked back to the parking lot. I groaned as I ascended the steps and couldn't wait to be done hiking. It was not my favorite activity, despite the beautiful destination.

After we reached the top, we took another break, I overheard Mom tell Mitchell that he shouldn't push his heart. He muttered something under his breath, and then as if relenting, he sat for a few minutes. Then we got into the vehicles and continued on our travels.

A few miles down the road and Mitchell pulled into the ditch and parked. Was something wrong? I hoped he wasn't having another heart attack. Mom stopped the car behind him, parallel parking along the road. Mitchell got out, so he must have been okay. The water trickled through boulders on the side of the road. Mitchell walked over to a tiny stream. Bending, he reached his hand into the water, and his eyes narrowed.

I approached him, walking with Mom.

Mitchell grabbed a handful of sand and let the water flow through slowly. "I found a few specks of gold. Nothing big. Better keep moving, Tary." He walked back toward his truck. "I'll find some at the next stop."

Was he searching for gold? Could there be gold in Yellowstone? Is that why they called it yellow stone? If we weren't poor, maybe Mom and Mitchell would be happy. We certainly wouldn't be homeless. We wouldn't have to eat gross food, either.

Ten minutes later, we pulled along the road to check another stream. I wished he'd discovered some gold already. Everywhere we went reeked of sulfur. The smell clung to the inside of my nose. The smell made me ill like the commodity eggs.

Mitchell yelled, "Look for gold, girls! Do what I'm doing. If you find any, bring it to me."

I crouched and gazed into the clear water. There was nothing but regular rocks and sand. We would not be poor anymore if I had found gold and I'd never had to eat commodity food ever again. I began looking with more enthusiasm and determination, hoping I could save our family, but still, I found nothing.

After a few minutes, Mitchell returned to his truck, and we climbed into the car.

Pulling back onto the road, we curved through narrow roads until we parked in another parking lot.

Walking along a planked path, several deep geysers reached into the earth. They were beautiful, haunting. The pools of hot liquid were the colors of emerald, cobalt, and azure.

"If you fall in, you'll melt. Don't get close." Mom shook her finger at me.

I lost my thoughts, gazing into the deep, dangerous pools. I imagined the dinosaurs, wondering if they'd seen the geysers.

The four of us walked farther. We stopped when we reached a sign that said *Old Faithful*.

I stood there with my arms crossed. How long would this take? The sign said that the geyser would go off every forty-five minutes. I leaned against the railing, facing away from the volcanic wonders. Behind me, the geysers hissed. I turned around as steam shot two feet in the air, then it grew to one hundred feet. I was glad to be far away from the danger.

We headed to our vehicles after watching the geyser blow. I slid my hand along the railing, ambling. My hand stung with sharp pain. I grimaced. My hand now held a sliver. It was nothing to worry about. I could carry Yellowstone with me forever and remember the positive memories after painful ones. Sometimes people kept things like slivers, didn't they? Wouldn't the skin eventually heal around it, like a souvenir in your hand? Since we didn't have any pictures, this would work, instead.

We were getting ready to leave, packing the campsite. The fire was out, and the truck was half-filled already. I approached Mom and Mitchell and showed them my palm, which was oozing pus and inflamed.

Grabbing my hand, Mitchell examined my palm. The surrounding skin was puffy and red. "Don't move, hold still," Mitchell said, pulling out his pocket knife. "You should have told me before it got infected." A worried look covered his face.

I clenched my jaw and breathed in deeply. Even having him touch it sent pain shooting through my hand.

He pulled the sliver out by nuzzling the side of his knife against the skin, easing it out.

"I'm sorry," I said. "I should've told you sooner." My palm screamed at me.

After Mitchell got the sliver out, we headed back to camp. Wren and I tried to help Mom and Mitchell cleaned our campsite after Mitchell mentioned we should help.

"We should move here, Tary," Mitchell said as he sat on the tailgate gazing toward the horizon, a smile on his tanned face.

Mom moved next to Mitchell. "Yeah? Sure, we can. I enjoyed it here." She leaned close and kissed him.

"I want to live here, too," Wren said.

"Me too," I said.

Mitchell seemed happier here than in Minnesota, being homeless. Being outdoors came naturally to him as if he were a tree rooted to the earth.

"Why don't you go home and pack our stuff, Tary? We can meet back here in a few days." Mitchell put his arm around Mom.

I loved Montana and Wyoming, the mountains, and the streams. I couldn't believe we'd live here—it was beautiful.

Mom, Wren, and I got into her car. We crossed the flat plains of North Dakota after we left the mountains. There wasn't anything but abandoned railroad towns and no pretty peaks anymore.

Two hours after we got back, as I was watching out my aunt's window, Mitchell pulled in, parking his Ranger outside. We had finished packing up the bus, and Mom had started packing our stuff into my aunt's house. "Mitchell's here," I said.

Mom looked at Wren and me, her mouth opened.

Why had Mitchell come back? Maybe he wanted to help us pack. Mom had been packing since we'd arrived.

He opened the front door before Mom did. Smiling, he said, "For now, maybe we can stay in Minnesota, even if we have to live on the bus. Maybe I can talk to my parents about helping us find some-where better."

Leaving this town behind and all its memories, was all I wanted. I didn't want to live on a bus anymore or with my aunt or think about Anthony anymore. But our adventure and dreams of gold were behind us. I sighed; now Mitchell would never find his treasure.

~ Twelve ~

Wren and I were thirteen in the summer of 2000. Mitchell's parents bought us a new home next to a swamp, so we didn't have to live on a bus anymore. This is the summer I learned about hard work.

"Home sweet home?" Mitchell asked me like it was a question I'd know the answer to.

I shrugged.

His eyes were focused ahead, as we pulled into a circular driveway two miles from the bus and my aunt's house. Mitchell parked in front of a dirty white house. I had been excited to see where we'd be living, but now I wasn't so sure. It looked terrible.

Tall cattails swayed in the wind on the edge bordering the front yard. Tamarack trees and long grass filled the swampy areas along two sides of the four acres. Garbage bags full of who-knows-what sat outside on the rickety porch. It wasn't nearly as nice as our trailer, that was for sure. I walked through the brush and onto a path of wet, gunky newspapers that led to the house. There was a stench in the air that I couldn't identify, something rancid and yet sickly like week-old sweat and rotten, fryer grease that got thrown out from my gas station job.

The mosquitoes swarmed, buzzing endlessly in my ears. I swatted at them, but it didn't help. I opened my mouth and ate one by accident, spitting it onto the newspaper-covered ground.

I stood near the porch watching Mitchell trudge through the ferns and underbrush near the swamp on the front edge of the property. Every few minutes, a twig snapped beneath his boots, and he'd look around more intensely. It was as if he was securing some invisible perimeter, taking slow steps, like he didn't want to awaken anything. I wasn't sure if I'd ever understand the way his mind worked. It wasn't like there were enemies lurking in the brush, but maybe Mitchell thought there were.

Along the opposite side of the front yard, the dark-and-light-green leaves of the quaking aspens flickered. When I walked close to them, the cedars gave off a smell like Christmas. But as I returned to the front porch and approached the door, the smell of news-papers and rot strengthened. If the outside smelled that bad, what would the inside smell like? What would it look like? I was afraid to find out.

Wren and I wandered into the house. The smell of mildew over-whelmed my sense of smell, sticking to the inside of my mouth. What possessions did the old tenants leave for us? A switch. Great. I flipped it on. Nothing happened. This place was such a dump, we didn't even have electricity. I weaved through piles of garbage, random stacks of books with warped covers, and heaps of yellowed papers. Where was the floor? I kicked a phone book into the air. Why would anyone keep this stuff? I was messy, too, but never this bad.

An old, green toilet sat in the middle of the first room I entered. How odd; who would put a toilet there? Was this supposed to be a living room or the bathroom? Maybe the old owner died right in-side this dirty room. I shuddered, hoping some dead person didn't haunt it

More bags of garbage lined the edges of the room I was in, it appeared to be the largest room in the house. I pushed past the garbage, shuffling my feet through it, far into the house. An antique refrigerator sat along one wall; the mold-covered doors being held open by a cinder block. Old food sat inside; flies hovered in the air around the refrigerator. I gagged, trying not to think about the rotting food, but the images of moldy cheese and chunky milk came to mind, anyway.

I tried not to touch anything as I tiptoed through the mess. My skin crawled. Was Mitchell serious about living here? The bus was better than this place.

Mom wore rubber gloves. "It's no good now, girls, but it's going to get better. I promise."

I scrunched my face and looked around trying to imagine all the junk gone and the floors mopped, but I couldn't picture it. In any event, there was no way it would get worse. "Ugh, Mom. Where are we going to sleep?" I asked, glancing at the toilet again and wishing I hadn't.

Mom grabbed a bag of garbage. "I'm not sure." She shrugged. "Let me ask Mitchell." She lifted the bag over her shoulder and hauled it outside.

"Grab some trash bags, girls," Mitchell said. He was somewhere by the front door, maybe right outside of it.

I groaned. Would this place ever be livable? Why didn't Mitchell leave us alone? We'd be happier if he'd find some other broken family to terrorize. I didn't ask for any of this. I grabbed a bag from Mom and a pair of rubber gloves she offered me. Putting them on, I rolled my eyes. We were better off without Mitchell.

Couldn't Mitchell and Mom hire someone to fix it? No, we probably couldn't afford that, either. We couldn't even afford food most of the time. Maybe Mitchell's parents would help us fix it. They had money. They'd bought it, so why not help us fix it? Mom said they'd gotten it for a steal, but thirty-eight hundred dollars was a rip-off for this place. They should have paid us to live there.

Load after load, Wren, Mom, Mitchell, and I moved junk out of the house.

As I carried a heavy garbage bag to the front porch, I walked past Mitchell to set the bag into Mitchell's truck bed for a dump run later.

"Burnable here, start carrying those out next," Mitchell said, pointing to a spot to his left next to a burning barrel. "Wood or supplies for fixing the house, go right here." He pointed to a pile with three or four scraps of wood. "If you don't know where to put something, ask Tary." He walked toward the back of the house.

After several hours of cleaning, I was exhausted. I thought I might collapse at any moment, but my body was resilient. Wiping my sweaty face on my shirt, I realized the four of us were going to have to do everything. No one else would come to help. Wren and I were slaves—unpaid workers of our new tyrannical king. I grabbed another armload of burnable stuff and carried it out.

On the side of the house was the pile of wood Mitchell had started. He must have found a lot of lumber because earlier the pile had little on it. Past the pile, on the same side of the yard, Mitchell and Mom had set up our tents from our Yellowstone trip. Mitchell and Mom laid bricks in a circle, five feet in front of our tents. Around the fire pit sat four foldable chairs.

"Girls, run and grab some twigs," Mitchell said, shooing us away.

I knew better than to argue and I wanted to explore more of the property. Wren and I headed toward the tree line to search for kindling where Mitchell had secured it earlier.

After we returned and handed him the twigs, he stacked them like a teepee and lit them with a match. Watching him make a fire was intriguing, he was so meticulous. Not like Wren with the trailer fire. I sat down. Every muscle would hurt tomorrow. I rubbed my neck, not looking forward to sleeping on the ground tonight.

Over the fire, Mitchell cooked hotdogs and brats on sticks we'd found. They sizzled and browned. The smell made my mouth water.

After dinner, Mitchell held onto a branch, narrow enough to wrap his hand around. He pulled out his pocketknife and scraped it along the outside of the rough bark. The bark fell on the ground in thin strips. As he worked, the movement of his knife revealed elegant, dark knots in the otherwise light-wooden color.

"What are you making?" I asked, surprised he could make something so beautiful since he was so cruel.

"Probably a walking stick. Not sure yet," he said, brushing the loose wood off.

The flames of the fire danced against the shadows of the evening. The mosquitos' buzzing stopped, and the only sounds were the fire crackling and the crickets chirping a song about summer.

Early the next morning, Mitchell scrambled eggs over the fire. This time, I ate them as fast as I could before they got cold and was relieved to discover they weren't commodity eggs. Then the four of us worked on the house again.

Mitchell held a shovel. What was he going to do? I raised my eyebrows at him. I saw nothing that required a shovel. Maybe he'd dig a hole to put the endless trash in. "Grab the wood by the side of the house and stack it behind the house. We'll use that lumber later to make your rooms. So, be careful with it."

Wren and I moved the pile of wood from the side of the house, one piece at a time, to the backyard. Alone, we'd each carry smaller pieces. The longer or heavier wood, we carried together. As the day went on, my shoulders ached from the weight; the hard edges of the wood pressed into my skin. One by one, our pile of wood grew. We moved all the wood from the side of the house, soon it was to my waist.

I set the two-by-four Wren and I had been carrying down, and I wiped the sweat from my forehead. The dirt clung to my shirt sleeve and made my forehead itchy. While our friends enjoyed summer, probably swimming at the beach, we didn't take a break until lunch. Thinking about water made me hotter.

After several more armloads, sweat stung my eyes. I walked across the pile of boards, and my platform shoe got stuck on a nail.

Great. What else was going to go wrong? I hopped over to an even spot on the pile and pulled my shoe off the rusty nail. That could have been my foot—I hated my life.

Mitchell carried a piece of wood to us and then joined us at the pile. "Let's take a break." He handed Wren and me a jug of luke-warm water to share. "Sorry, warm water is all we have."

I swallowed a big gulp. Wren laid on a clean grass patch next to the pile and acted like she might take a nap.

I glanced to the side of the yard. A mountain of metal scraps, old broken junk, someone had piled taller than me sat there. I sighed. I knew we'd have to sort through it someday. It must be where the awful smell came from the day before. It was a far cry from the pristine smell of the Montana mountains, although it wasn't as bad as the sulfur from the geysers. The metal blinded my eyes as it reflected the sun, which was in the middle of the sky now. How long had Wren, and I been at this?

"What is that pile of stuff there?" I asked Mitchell, looking in his direction but avoiding his eyes.

"The previous owner worked at a recycling center before he died. We'll sort that, too, and see if there's anything we can sell."

I nodded. I wanted to ask Mitchell if the man who used to live here died in his house, but I decided I didn't want to know; I'd never be able to sleep inside. In the pile, I could see broken bikes, lawn-mowers, and lots of metal pieces of small items. I doubted there was anything valuable in that rusty mess.

The heat made the smell worse.

"Well, better get movin'," Mitchell said, then left. If we stayed busy, he'd leave us alone, and that was good to know.

I sighed. "We better get started," I said to Wren.

She continued to lay on the grass for a minute, then dramatically pulled herself off the ground. "Ugh." She grunted.

We got back to work, and Mitchell let Wren and me work alone—what a relief.

About an hour later, Mitchell shouted. I couldn't understand what he yelled. Because I thought someone hurt themselves, I dropped my lumber on the woodpile and ran toward Mitchell and Mom.

"Everyone! Come here!" Mitchell shouted. "Come here!" He looked okay, but warm because sweat left dark spots on his gray T-shirt near his armpits and collar.

Mom, Wren, and I stood facing Mitchell. He pushed the red lever on the top of a thick metal pole the size and shape of a PVC pipe. Water shot out from the spigot. He must have dug for water all morning. I'd never seen anyone pull water from the earth before.

Wren and I cheered.

Mom kissed Mitchell's cheek. "Good job," she said to him.

Mitchell wore a rare smile. He waved us to come closer. Seeing everyone happy made me excited. I couldn't believe we finally had water. I hopped closer to the pump. It had been the longest day of drinking warm water from a jug. Mom left for a minute, returning with cups, a radiance covering her face. We each took turns trying the pump.

When it was my turn, I filled my cup to the rim with ice-cold water and gulped it. My hot, sticky throat drank in the sweet relief. I was more thankful for that cup of water than I had ever been for any drink.

~ Thirteen ~

In the fall of 2001, when Wren and I were fifteen, Wren stayed in the house at the swamp, but I returned to Michigan and lived with Grandma. It was the first time I'd lived without my Wren. She hated Michigan, and I hated it, too. At the time, I hated Mitchell more.

Out of Grandma's Nelly's living room window, and across the street was a spacious lawn—soon to be a golf course. The gray skies and trees were empty. I imagined Mom's car ascending the hill any minute, bringing Wren back, but my imagination was running wild. Wren wasn't coming back. We'd been apart for six months now. As much as I missed her, I wasn't ready to return to Minnesota and Mitchell.

"Cheer up, Kaitlin," Grandma said. "We'll have fun. Wait and see."

At school the next day, I walked through the cafeteria. Even though I'd been attending for a while, I had made no friends. Off to the side of the cafeteria, someone talked to me. I didn't recognize their voice. I slowed my pace to hear them.

"You're so fat," a boy said. I turned toward him. He was leaning against a wall, chewing on his pen. He was the same dumb boy cussing in class earlier that day.

I quickened my pace toward class. I didn't want him to know he'd hurt me, so I forced myself to stare ahead. His words echoed in my mind: Fat, fat, fat. A tear formed in the corner of my eye. I arrived at my next class.

The woodshop classroom next door made the hallway smell like sawdust. Walking through the doorway, I crept toward the back of the room and found a spot along the back wall. I propped my face onto my hands and listened as the teacher taught us our lesson.

After the bell rang at the end of class, a girl from my homeroom approached me. Her thick braids draped down her shoulders. She peered at me through her thick glasses. What was it she wanted? Hopefully, she wouldn't be mean like the guy earlier.

"Do you want to come to a concert with me tonight?" She shrugged. "They have pizza, and games, too. It's in the cafeteria after school. I thought maybe it could be fun to listen to some Christian music."

I cocked my head to the side. She wanted me to hang out with her? "Sure. Sounds cool," I said.

She had friends, unlike me. It could be enjoyable. I used to have fun at the youth group with Kevin and Bethany in Minnesota, like when we visited the nursing home; maybe this would be good, too. Why not? She walked away and I couldn't help but smile. It felt nice to be included.

The rest of the day went by fast as I looked forward to the concert more and more. Finally, the last bell rang, ending the school day. I made my way toward the office through the narrow halls lined with lockers. I called Grandma and asked permission for the concert and she said yes. My heart might jump into the air or do a cartwheel. I had finally made a new friend and there would be pizza and music.

I headed toward the cafeteria, which was connected to the auditorium. The cafeteria, normally full of tables, was half-empty. Lots of kids filed into the chairs in front of the stage inside of the auditorium, and soon the room filled. I stayed in the cafeteria and looked around.

At last, I saw my new friend. I put my hands in my pockets and shuffled my feet, walking toward her. I hoped she hadn't changed her mind about liking me.

She was standing with two girls; one was tall with thick brown hair and the other had a short haircut.

She greeted me. "These are my friends."

The tall one with brown hair was in my science class.

"Hey," the blonde girl said.

"What's up?" I pulled my hands out of my pockets.

A guitar sounded, and the noise reverberated through my feet. "I hope it starts soon," my new friend said, waving her hands.

"Me, too," the one from my science class said.

"Mic check, one, two, three."

A vinyl sign hung over the stage. It said, *Red Cord*.

A woman with thick red streaks in her brown hair approached the microphone. The band members tinkered with their equipment and the room filled with the chatter of excited teenagers and middle-schoolers. "Hello everyone. We're so glad you made it. Let's sing praises for Jesus tonight," the young woman said.

Loud music echoed through the auditorium and cafeteria. It was an upbeat song I didn't recognize.

My new friend spotted a row of seats and pointed to it, enough for all of us to fit. As we reached our seats, the band changed songs. A slow, melodic song filled the auditorium with peacefulness. The hands of the students in the room swayed. They sang words like redeemed and hope, but I didn't recognize the songs.

As the band played, there was a stirring in my soul. A deep hunger ached inside me, a hunger for something missing. It was like how I missed Sierra, Wren, and Bethany. The faces of my new friends looked happy as they raised their hands into the air as if to touch their invisible God. It was the same expression Kevin had, a kindness, and inner peace, like a sense of community, acceptance, and reckless abandonment—not the kind in which parents leave you, but the kind where you can do anything, and someone would still love you. I swayed along with the other kids; maybe God hadn't forgotten about me.

Soon the school year ended. Summer days became longer, and the perfect Michigan heat radiated into each beautiful day. I was eating breakfast when Grandma jumped into the room, a smile warming her face. Grandma had been on the phone, so maybe that was why she was happy. "Guess what, Kaitlin?" She spread out her fingers and waved them around. "Ooh, ooh, ooh." She danced, shaking her butt.

"What? What's going on, Grandma?"

"Your aunt has to go to Alabama to get costumes for the theater she works at."

"Uh, okay?" I furrowed my brows, unsure of what that meant.

Grandma stared at me as if waiting for my reaction, but when I only showed confusion, she continued, "Can you believe it? She wants us to come with her!"

"Really?" My mouth dropped open. I jumped away from the table and joined her, dancing around the kitchen. "Going on a trip, going on a trip," I sang.

Grandma and I hugged. I couldn't believe I could be so lucky.

Grandma, my aunt, and I arrived in Alabama a few weeks after Grandma had gotten the invitation. The sky grew darker as we drew closer to the coast. Palm trees swayed near stop signs on quiet streets lit by city lights. It was so close to where I was born. What would it be like to live in a place like this? I wished I could remember my dad. Mom said we used to live next to the ocean when we were babies.

"Guess what, Kaitlin?" Grandma squealed as we pulled into our destination.

"What is it, Grandma?" I wasn't sure what Grandma was so excited about. Outside the window stood a house on a side street with pineapple trees in the yard. Shadows covered the lawn.

"Aunt Diane is going to pick you up tonight and return you tomorrow. She'll be here any minute."

"What?" I was going to meet my dad's actual sister. It was the best news I'd heard since Grandma told us we were taking the trip; I could hardly believe it. Butterflies filled my stomach. What a great Grandma I had.

"I called her after I found out we were coming," Grandma said.

"That's amazing. Thank you. I can't believe you'd do that for me. Thank you, Grandma."

"I'm sorry, Kaitlin, it'll be a brief visit. You'll leave tonight and come back tomorrow."

"Oh, it's perfect. Thank you, Grandma." I hoped my aunt would like me. She sounded nice on the phone. I'd talked to her two or three times in the past year, even after Wren left. "Wait, I thought she lived in Mississippi, not Alabama." I creased my eyebrows. I hoped it wasn't far away.

"She lives in Mississippi, but it's a forty-five-minute drive from here."

"That's so cool." That wasn't far at all. We climbed out of the car, the air was dense and warm like it might rain. I glanced around at the dark yard, then entered the house. Before I took my shoes off, headlights reflected on the living room wall of the house.

"Your ride is here. I'll walk you out," Grandma said. She walked me to my aunt's two-door car idling in the driveway.

A woman leaned against the car, waiting. "Hi, sweetheart. I'm your aunt Diane, I'm so glad to finally meet you," the woman said, leaning on her driver's side door. She had a heavy, southern drawl, shoulder-length brown hair, and resembled Sandra Bullock. Would I be that beautiful when I grew up? I wasn't beautiful now, that was for sure.

"Hi," I said, nervously.

I smelled the gas exhaust of the engine and looked at my aunt for a moment longer. The car was low to the ground, and the muffler sounded like it needed to be fixed. I climbed into the two-door car.

My aunt broke the silence, "Let's get you to my house. We've got so much to catch up on. And not a lot of time."

The humid air blew against my face. She waved at Grandma from the driver's side of the car.

"See y'all soon, thanks, Nelly. I'll get her back to ya real soon."

"Love you, Grandma. See you tomorrow." I sat in the front passenger seat, beaming at Grandma through the windshield. Jitters flitted in my stomach. Nothing this exciting had ever happened to me before." I waved at Grandma emphatically.

After closing the door, my aunt Diane pulled the car out onto the open road as the air conditioner blared against my face. Soon we arrived at Aunt Diane's house. We stayed up most of the night chatting until we couldn't fight off our sleep anymore.

Early the next morning, I sat on Aunt Diane's couch. The cushions were soft and smelled like leather. Her house was like a modular home. Aunt Diane paced in front of me. "We don't have enough time together. I wish you could stay longer." She sat beside me, resting her hands on her knees. "Would you like to stay longer?"

I nodded. "Of course, I want to, but how will I get home? Grandma is leaving tomorrow."

"I'll get you a plane ticket, sweetheart. I have some frequent-flier miles; it won't cost me a thing. Sweetheart, don't you worry about it at all." She patted my arm, then stood again. "Why don't you call your grandma and ask if it's okay if you stay longer?" She scrambled over to the counter. "I have the number where your grandma is right here." She returned, handing me a phone and a piece of scrap paper with a number on it.

It sounded too good to be true, like most things in my recent history, but I called Grandma anyway. Maybe a miracle would happen, and I could stay with this amazing lady longer. No one had ever bought me a plane ticket. I sighed. I wish Wren were here, too. "Hey, Grandma."

"How are you? Is everything going well?"

"Aunt Diane and I are having fun. I'm calling to ask if I can stay longer? Please? Aunt Diane says she'll pay to fly me home."

"That's great! Yes, yes, of course, you can stay. That's perfect. Your time was so short, now you'll have lots of time to visit. I love you. Have fun, okay?"

I couldn't believe it! I was so excited, I hopped up and down. "Thank you, thank you!"

"Call me back later so I know you'll arrive at the airport," Grandma said.

"Okay, Grandma, I will. Love you." I hung up the phone. My eyes met Diane's. "Grandma says I can stay," I said.

"We're gonna have fun. Let me call the airline, Okay? It shouldn't take long." Diane talked to the airline and figured out the details of my flights and she hired someone to escort me from one plane to the next since they didn't offer a direct flight. She was going to let me stay with her for two entire weeks. She motioned for me to sit with her on the couch. "I'll be back in one second." She walked to a shelf and grabbed a leather photo album and brought it to me.

We sat leg to leg on the couch. She turned to the album's middle section. "This is your dad here. This is your brother and sister."

"I have a brother and sister?" I asked, shocked. It wasn't what I expected.

"Yup. Your brother is a couple of years younger than you." She turned the page. "Here's your sister. She's two years younger than your brother."

"My little sister, Sierra, is two years younger than me, too." I glanced at the pictures again. Looking for similarities in our features. "What are they like?" For the first time, I saw my siblings' faces. I wanted to take in every detail. I'd missed too much.

"They're talented kids. Your sister is creative and bright. Your brother is funny. He's a whiz at math like his daddy. They'd like you."

"Will my dad want to meet me since I'm here?" I asked. Maybe he would like me like my aunt Diane. "I'm not sure, honey." She grabbed my hand. "I know he would love you if he got to know you. Honey, your daddy is stubborn. He isn't ready for a relationship with you. At least not now." Aunt Diane frowned. "He's missing out." She hugged me.

I stared at the carpet. I wished my dad loved me, this dad or Anthony. Someday, some dad would. Wouldn't they? I didn't know, but I couldn't give up hope.

She stood and returned the photo album to the shelf. "Speaking of daddies, I have something for you." Aunt Diane grabbed a book and walked back over to me, then handed me a hard-covered book.

The cover said *Study Bible*.

"There are so many wonderful stories in here, and advice for anything you will go through. Jesus is like a daddy to me. I lost my daddy many years ago." She gave me a sympathetic smile. Her sweet, southern voice soothed my pain, somehow.

"Did he die or leave you?" I asked.

"Oh honey, he died in a car accident," she said.

Sadness for her loss swept over me. "I'm so sorry. It's hard not having a dad." I wouldn't mind if Jesus would be my new daddy like he became hers, but I didn't know how any of that worked.

That night, I did some baking with Aunt Diane, then we had dinner. She showed me to the room where I'd be staying for the next fourteen days; I hadn't slept in a room the first night. We talked the whole first evening and when I did finally close my eyes; I had fallen asleep on the couch.

On the second night, I lay in bed and closed my eyes. I breathed a sigh of relief. My body sunk into the soft mattress. I listened to the quiet hum of a fish tank on the shelf next to the bed.

Holding my brand-new Bible in the nook of my arm, I imagined God sitting in the heavens, and I imagined He could hear me. Quietly, I asked Him, "Jesus, if you love me, please be my daddy. I don't want to feel alone anymore." I felt warmth in my heart in that southern heat, like I'd found strength I didn't know I could find.

~ Fourteen ~

Snow covered the swamp in the winter when I was sixteen. After I visited my Aunt Diane in the South and encountered Jesus, I wasn't afraid to return to Minnesota. Maybe it was like Daniel in the Lion's Den, and my newfound faith made me braver.

On Mitchell's hard days, Wren and I kept to ourselves, disappearing into our rooms in the back of the house.

On the good days, Mitchell left us alone and did his own thing, which was mainly watching war movies. Maybe staying in Michigan would have been a safer place, but looking back, I can see God's hand moving through these struggles.

Wren opened the front door of the swamp house, and I followed her inside after school.

Wren held her finger to her lips and said, "Shh."

Nodding, I moved farther inside the new porch as quietly as a mouse, unsure if the lion would pounce on me. My face brushed against the musky jackets. Cigarette smoke welcomed us home.

Wren and I waited. If we could determine what kind of mood Mitchell was in, we would know whether to come in or wait outside. A scrabble board sat between Mom and Mitchell; it was one of his favorite games. Sometimes Mitchell sat and read the dictionary, too. Once, he tried to convince Wren and me to read it, but I didn't get past the first page of As.

"Why didn't I die, Tary?" Mitchell's voice was full of angst, but he wasn't yelling.

I raised my eyebrows at Wren.

She shook her head and shrugged.

"Does God have a sick sense of humor? What's His point of keeping me here, suffering like this? It's not fair that I get to live when they all died."

Who had died? He'd never mentioned that before. I accidentally bumped into the shoe rack, knocking over one of Mom's winter boots.

"Kids are home. You won again, I guess," Mom said, kissing Mitchell's cheek. "Hello, girls."

We slipped off our shoes and entered. There was no point in hiding anymore.

"Hey, Mom," I said.

Mitchell rubbed his arm.

Mom said when he'd had a heart attack, his arm was where it hurt, so maybe he wasn't well today. In the living room, Mitchell played a movie and plopped onto the couch across from it.

I took a deep breath. Clint Eastwood yelled on the TV. I hovered behind Mitchell; I wanted to see my favorite part. It was when Clint Eastwood's character told his platoon their shirts had to match. They huffed and puffed. Then they stripped their shirts off. The next day, his platoon tried to outsmart him. They entered the scene all wearing the same green shirts. I giggled every time I watched it. Clint Eastwood's character then informed them they were supposed to match him, not each other. Once again, they're forced to remove their shirts, losing this mental battle with Clint yet again. It reminded me of Mitchell. He had rules we had to follow—and we didn't know what they were.

With my favorite part of the movie over, I wanted to talk to Mom about her secret conversation with Mitchell earlier.

Mom was in the kitchen making Spanish rice. The spices filled the air: garlic and peppers.

I walked over to her and pulled on her arm. "Can I talk to you for a minute?"

She looked around the kitchen as if to make sure no one could hear me. "Let's talk in my room. I'll turn supper on low and cover it. It needs to simmer."

I followed her into her bedroom.

"What is it, Kaitlin?"

"What were you and Mitchell talking about?" I stood square in front of her. "I heard him blaming himself for someone dying."

"What do you mean?" she asked, looking everywhere but at me.

Great, she was going to act like she didn't know what I was talking about. "Come on, Mom." What wasn't she telling me? "When we came home, what were you and Mitchell talking about?" I said. I crossed my arms across my chest. "He's my stepdad. I should know what's going on."

"Fine." She pursed her lips. "His best friend died in the war. Mitchell saw him blow up. He couldn't do anything to stop it."

My mouth dropped. "What?"

Her face grew pale. "He has nightmares and wakes in a cold sweat a few nights. That is all I can say." She moved closer to the door. "He wouldn't want me talking about it." Quickly, she left the room. She seemed as scared of Mitchell as I was.

Whatever scars he had were invisible to me, but maybe now I'd understand why he was the way he was. I did not know what I'd do if my best friend died—it was hard enough to be far away from the people I cared about. I stared at the floor. "Sorry Mom, I wish he felt better."

"Me too. You know when he is the meanest, that is when he is the sickest. Try to remember that. I love you, Kaitlin." Mom hugged me.

"Love you, too."

"I have to finish dinner. We can talk later, okay?"

"Okay." I knew it wouldn't come up again.

That night, Wren, Mitchell, Mom, and I sat around the kitchen table. Mom served us the Spanish rice and baked chicken. We ate in silence.

Mitchell's gaze landed on Wren, and his face grew red as if irritated with her. "Put that fork in your mouth the right way," Mitchell said, a scowl forming on his face.

"What? I am." Wren looked at her tilted fork as if she didn't know she had it, then she took another bite.

Mitchell slammed his tin cup against the table. "Stop turning your fork sideways." Mitchell's jaw clenched. "Hold it straight."

"W—we don't have to listen to you, you're not our dad," Wren said, stammering.

The vein on his head pulsed and sweat beaded his hairline. "Don't talk back to me. Get over there, both of you." He pointed to the wall. "Put your noses on the wall." He pushed his chair hard, and it squealed as it scraped across the floor.

I stood rigidly, his beaming voice forcing me to face the new sheetrock wall. If I took too long, his anger would grow.

"Hold your arms out," he said, his arms folded behind him like the men in his army movies. "Don't touch each other."

I wished I had warned Wren about what Mom had said earlier. If I'd told her to be nice, I might have prevented this whole situation.

Wren and I moved away from each other, but I wished I didn't have to stand away from her. Being close to her would have made the punishment more bearable. I gritted my teeth. Why couldn't he learn to control his anger? Hurting us would not make him better. I stood there, arms extended, like a faithful soldier.

As the minutes wore on, my arms became heavy, like they were holding anchors. I didn't have the strength to hold them any longer. My heart pounded in my chest. Black and purple spots blotted my vision. My stomach tensed. The colors in my peripheral crowded out the white sheetrock until I couldn't see the wall anymore. I cried out, then collapsed onto the hard floor, sobbing. I couldn't stop.

Wren collapsed on the floor beside me, wailing and writhing.

I couldn't move for a few minutes. Where was I? I didn't know. Was Wren okay? I couldn't be sure.

Mitchell hovered over us as we lay there. I stared at his Army boots, unable to move.

Mom sat on the chair near the window, refusing to make eye contact with anyone. It looked like she had a bruise on her cheek.

"You can sit on the couch now," Mitchell's voice drew me back to reality.

It took a minute to gain composure and rise from the floor. Once I could stand without dizziness, I slowly trudged to the couch. I plopped on the sofa cushions.

He sat on the couch on the other end of Wren and me, smoking his cigarettes, and he didn't yell anymore.

I didn't move out of fear I'd offend him; I didn't know what might set him off. The rest of the night, no one said anything.

It was lunchtime at school. Thank goodness. The night before, I had eaten little and my stomach groaned as the bell rang, releasing us from our fourth-period class. I saw my friend Delilah in the hall. She had her hair pulled back into a twist braid. I met her on the first day of school in art class. She had transferred from a school about forty minutes away. Delilah was beautiful. She had a tall, lean figure, medium brown skin, and a pearly smile. I dashed through the crowded hallway to catch up to her. With her as a friend, the boys left me alone, and I was thankful.

She waved when she saw me. She greeted me once I reached her.

"How's it going?" I asked.

"Ugh, I hate math." Delilah rolled her eyes. "I wonder what's for lunch."

As we walked toward the cafeteria, I smelled pizza. My mouth watered. Pizza was one of my favorites. We joined the lunch line and, after grabbing our trays, we left the queue, food in hand. We headed to our round table on the edge of the spacious cafeteria, which was half the size of a football field. An older man sat at our table, about Mom's age, but none of our friends were there yet.

I looked at Delilah, eyebrows furrowed. She shrugged. Adults didn't normally sit with us. Why was this gray-haired man at our table? I did not know who he was or why he was there. It didn't surprise me when Delilah sat next to him. With several brothers, she was fearless and not a pushover. I sat on the other side of Delilah.

"I'm Steve," the man sounded excited to see us.

"I'm Kaitlin. This is Delilah."

"Nice to meet you. I work for Campus Life Youth for Christ Ministries."

I took a bite of my pizza, keeping eye contact with the man. His glasses sat low on his nose. He was wiry, similar in size to Mitchell, but less muscular.

"What's campus life?" I asked, tilting my head to the side.

"It's a youth group for teenagers who want a relationship with Christ." He pulled out a pamphlet. "This is who I work for. If you come to the youth group tonight, I'm bringing candy bars and soda."

Delilah wrinkled her nose. "You aren't one of those people our parents warn us about, are you?"

He laughed. "No, I only work in ministry, before that I was a realtor. Your principal, Mr. Sabre, knows I'm here. See, here's my visitor badge." He held out a pass attached to the lanyard around his neck. "If you want to come, bring along anyone you want. Friends, family, whoever." He turned to look at two of our friends as they sat. "Hello."

"Oh, hey," Delilah's friend said. She gave him a dismissive wave.

"I'm a pastor, and I've invited your friends to a youth group tonight. You're invited, too. Hope you can all make it." He set his hands on the table, palms down.

Man, I bet this guy could cut through a tree with dental floss if he put his mind to it. "That sounds fun. Maybe we'll see you then," I said.

I hoped Wren and Delilah wanted to go because I didn't want to go alone. I used to have fun when I was younger and attended the youth group with Kevin and besides, pop and candy sounded amazing. The only time I had soda was when the art teacher snuck it for Delilah and me from the teacher's lounge.

"I'll pick you up in a van at three forty-five in front of the school. After the youth group, I'll bring everyone home." He rose from the table. "Nice to meet you all."

That same night after school, Steve picked us like he said he would.

At Delilah's invitation, four or five boys had shown for the youth group. Most of the other kids at our lunch table came as well. I told Wren about the youth group because she sat with her friends at lunch and not with me. She wanted to come, too. Anything to get away from Mitchell, she had said.

The group of us followed Steve, descending stairs into a room with a group of chairs set in a circle. "All right, icebreaker time," Steve said.

What did he mean by icebreaker? I glanced at the others to see if they had any reactions. Everyone else looked as confused as I was.

"It means getting to know each other better. Everyone, tell us something about yourself."

One girl's cheeks flushed, and she giggled. "I like science class best of all, even though I pretend I don't."

"I have seven brothers and sisters," Delilah said.

"'Sup? I'm from California, just moved here," the new boy said, who I'd seen earlier this week in the lunch line. He was cute but short and the waist of his pants rested far too low.

"Hi," a boy with light-blond eyebrows said. "Steve's my dad, and my sister and I homeschool." He pointed at the girl with red hair.

A few girls murmured amongst themselves, but I couldn't make out what they said. Maybe they'd never met a homeschooler before. I hadn't.

Steve's daughter said, "I love animals and I want to make more friends."

The rest of the students said interesting things about themselves and then Steve asked us to stand while he moved the chairs into a circle. The group of five boys stood after we'd shared our ice-breaking information.

"Now that you've introduced yourselves, it's time for musical chairs."

I laughed at the silliness. I hadn't played musical chairs since I was a child at a birthday party.

Steve pushed a button on a portable cd player and a song I didn't recognize played.

The group of us sauntered around the folding chairs until Steve hit a button and the music stopped.

Laughing and giggling, we shoved into fewer chairs than there were people. One girl lost.

In the next round, I lost. Then the new cool kid lost. Then Wren lost, then Steve's daughter lost. The tall boy won. He always had something funny to say at school. I was pretty sure he had a crush on Delilah, but who didn't?

He bowed, and a smile stretched across his face. Steve's son probably would have won, but he gave his chair to a girl.

We sat and Steve talked about the Bible and how it related to us. I thought a lot about how cute the boys were sitting across from me. What would it be like to have a boyfriend? I'd never had one before.

The group climbed into the van to go home. First, he dropped off Delilah, her house was on the other side of town. From her house, he dropped everyone else off next, traveling through town. Steve's two kids, Wren and I would be the last to get dropped off.

He pulled into our driveway. Wren and I climbed out and were halfway to the house when Steve hopped out of the van.

"Hold on, girls," Steve said.

What did he want? Maybe to tell us when the next meeting was. I raised my eyebrows, waiting to hear what he had to say.

"I'd like to come in for a second and introduce myself to your parents, so they know who is taking you to the youth group."

"I'm not sure that's a great idea." I hoped he wouldn't come in because I did not know what mood Mitchell was in. I didn't know if Mitchell liked Christians, either.

"Oh, no. I'm sure it's no big deal. It'll take two seconds."

Steve did not give up easily, so I didn't stop him when he trailed in behind us. I hoped Mitchell wouldn't toss him into the swamp. I gritted my teeth. Poor Steve didn't know what he was getting himself into.

"Hello," Steve said, proudly planting himself right in front of Mom and Mitchell, offering his hand. "I'm the new youth pastor. I wanted to meet these girls' parents. Thought I should stop in and say hello."

Mitchell stood, then shook his hand. He gave Wren and me a sideways glance. I didn't like the expression on Mitchell's face, it said, you better hope this Steve guy leaves soon.

Mitchell moved his hands to his hips. "Thanks for bringing them back," his statement sounded more like a question.

"Are you familiar with Jesus?" Steve asked.

My mouth opened as I stared at Steve. That was unexpected. I held my breath. Surely, Mitchell would lose his composure at any moment.

Mom glanced at me, her jaw was set, then her eyes got big.

I shook my head. I didn't know what to say or do. I did not know he'd ask that. How was I going to get this guy out of here before Mitchell overreacted? I'd never be able to go to a youth group again.

Wren sat on the couch, biting her fingernails.

Mom cleared her throat. "Yes. We know Jesus well. Growing up, I went to a Christian school." Mom looked at Wren and me, giving us a sympathetic smile.

Mitchell sat, returning to his computer desk, and lit a cigarette. "I got a Bible, so if I want to know more, I know where to look," Mitchell said.

"Oh, good. Reach out if you have questions. Okay?" Steve turned back toward the front door. "Nice to meet you, girls." He waved at us. "See you next week?"

I nodded, hoping we would, but doubting it. He left unscathed, so I was relieved. I glanced at Wren, she let out a deep breath as her shoulders dropped.

After school the next week, as we sat at the dining room table, Mitchell gave us one of his 'talks' as Wren and I called them. Once he began these talks, I knew I'd be sitting for two hours while he complained about anything from toilet paper, to dish soap, to the dirty laundry pile, or not having enough money. Most of the talks were about toilet paper, which in his mind was why we had no money. It had nothing to do with the casino. Nothing at all. I held my tongue.

"How many sheets of toilet paper could you possibly need?" Mitchell asked, holding an empty cardboard roll. "It's a butt. It cannot be that dirty."

What a micromanager. How would he know what we needed? Girls weren't the same as boys.

"You only need four sheets."

I rolled my eyes, careful to look in a different direction so he wouldn't see.

Mom snapped a haughty stare at me.

Wren and I sat waiting for him to finish. I shifted in my seat as he blew cigarette smoke in our direction. What did Mom expect me to do? Never speak my mind? I stared at the floor. Mom was probably right. There was no point in getting Mitchell riled. It would be better to say nothing and let him calm down.

"Any gripes? Communication is important." He chuckled, and for a moment it made me think he could be nice.

I wanted so badly to gripe, but I didn't. Opening my mouth was not advisable. He didn't care what I had to say, despite his insistence. It was a trap.

Wren was biting her lip, probably thinking the same things as me.

"No gripes, huh?"

Wren and I shook our heads.

"I got another gripe." He stood, then paced. "Is that Jehovah's Witness coming by the house again?"

"He's not a Jehovah, he's a Christian. His name is Steve," I said, folding my hands across my chest.

"He's knocking on our door like a Jehovah."

"Ugh. No, he's a youth pastor." I sighed.

"Whatever you say. I think he's a Jehovah," Mitchell said. He put his cigarette out in a black ashtray on his computer desk. "Is he coming today?"

"Yeah," Wren answered above a whisper.

Mitchell didn't respond.

A honk sounded outside. It must be Steve.

Inwardly, I prayed Mitchell wouldn't stop us from going. The youth group was the best part of each week, and I didn't want to give it up. Wren and I looked at Mitchell. He said nothing, so Wren and I left.

Sometimes our youth group took place at Steve's house, instead of in the basement of the travel agency. Steve's house was two stories and sat on the backside of his property. A spacious open area of vibrant grass spanned the front of the house. Underneath a walk-out deck, decorative bricks, and stones wrapped around flower beds.

Inside the living room, I sat on the carpeted floor. Steve's daughter and Wren and I sang *Shine, Jesus, Shine*. Steve's college helper played guitar as we sat.

I sang my part first. My cheeks were rosy, I was nervous to sing in front of the others.

Steve's daughter sang second, smoothly, and quietly. Wren sang her part, then the three of us finished together.

"Good job." I nudged Steve's daughter and smiled. I knew she was shyer about singing than I was.

"Thanks." She glanced at her feet, her red hair falling into her eyes. "It's nice to have friends. I always wonder if people like me."

"Me too. Feeling rejected is hard. It's nice of your dad to invite us here. You have a beautiful house."

"Yeah, I like it. I wish I had more pets, though. I love animals."

"Me too."

Rain pounded on the roof. Condensation glistened on the window, it made the evening feel cozier.

I rose from the couch and asked Steve, "Can we go outside?" I loved rainstorms. They reminded me of camping in the living room when the power went out.

"I suppose," he said, shrugging.

All the youth group ran outside through the patio doors, then down the steps and into the yard.

The warm rain trailed down my face. I spun around. The others danced and ran around. The freedom of being under the wide, open sky released me from the tension at home.

White electricity shot across the black expanse of the sky and made me jump. It was probably safer inside. I walked through the front door, taking off my soaked sweatshirt.

Steve set his espresso machine out on the counter. He pulled out the fancy syrup and added milk to a frother. He handed us each a cup as he finished making them. "This should warm you."

"Is this espresso?" Delilah's friend asked, her mouth agape.

"Yes, don't have too much though. You'll be awake all night with that caffeine content."

"We're teenagers. We'll be awake, anyway." She laughed, then walked toward Delilah.

Wren's teeth chattered as she stood in the kitchen.

Steve's son poked Wren's arm. "Let me get you a sweatshirt."

After we finished our drinks, Steve drove everyone home. This time, he didn't come to talk to Mitchell.

The members of the youth group sat in a circle in chairs in the basement of the travel agency. It was the last Tuesday of the school year.

"Steve, are we going to have a youth group this summer?" I hoped he'd say yes, then I could see my friends and be away from home.

"I want to talk to all of you about that. Everyone—sit for a minute, please." Once everyone sat, Steve plopped into a chair on the opposite side of the circle. "Instead of the usual meetings, I thought we could take a trip together."

"A trip? To where?" Glancing around, everyone looked as stunned as I was, except his kids. They must have known already. I hoped it would be somewhere exciting. I loved trips and couldn't wait to hear what he had in mind.

"There's a rally where hundreds of Christians congregate and camp. It's in Colorado at Estes Park."

The boys whooped and hollered.

"This is going to be great. No parents," the new boy said.

"I'll be there. I'm a parent." Steve straightened in his chair.

"Yeah, but not mine," the new boy said, then laughed.

Steve's eyebrows creased. "All right, boys, easy. This is a trip to fellowship with other Christians, not to get away from rules. There will be rules."

"Fine. I'm joshing. Relax, Steve," the new boy said.

My excitement faded. Mitchell would never let Wren and me go. I guessed I could go to the youth group fundraisers, but the camping trip would never happen. "I don't know if we can make enough money for this trip," I said. Mom and Mitchell were always broke.

"You will make enough money," Steve's voice was firm. "Work hard and God will provide for your needs."

Even if we came up with the money, God would have to convince Mitchell. I sighed. It might be too big of a job even for God.

"I've got some odd jobs lined up on the weekends at the beginning of the summer." Steve rose from his seat. "Let me know if you're interested. I'll pick you up next Saturday morning at nine."

The new guy groaned. "Ugh Steve, nine is too early. I don't wake until ten."

"If you want to take part, you'll need to follow the rules."

As we were leaving, I shuffled closer to Steve and said, "If I don't make enough, you could give my money to someone else, right?"

"You'll make enough, don't worry. It's going to work out." He put his hand on my shoulder. "If it's God's will, He always provides."

What if it wasn't God's will? I didn't know how to tell.

That afternoon, I sat by Mom and Mitchell at home. "So, Steve wants to take us to a place in Colorado to go camping. If it won't cost anything, can we go?"

"No." Mitchell took out a cigarette and lit it. "Why would I allow you, girls, to go with that Jehovah?"

"Yeah. I told Steve you wouldn't." I looked at Wren. "Nothing good ever happens to me."

"Don't say that," Mom whispered then she frowned as her gaze drifted to Mitchell. She had to know it was pointless to try.

I shook my head. It wasn't fair. Maybe if I kept pestering Mitchell, he'd change his mind. "Well, you love camping, Mitchell. I know you'd love a trip like this. Don't you trust us? His wife and kids are coming, and all my friends." I stood. "It's not fair they can all go, but we can't. Want to know my gripes? This is my gripe." I stormed to my room, laid across my bed, and cried. Maybe my life would be miserable forever.

~ Fifteen ~

As an adult I've noticed we like to put limits on what God can accomplish. In hardships, we are given a chance to see God moving in ways we don't expect.

After school let out for the year, Steve picked us up in the van, then after he picked everyone up, we headed to the lake. He parked. Everyone stood to get out of the van and outside. "Time for our first odd job. We should make some good money for our trip here. Make sure you work hard," Steve said.

"Yeah, yeah," the new guy said.

Following behind Steve, I trudged toward a boat sitting on choppy water at the edge of the boat landing. Why did I come today? Oh yeah, it was to help someone else go on this trip with the money I earned. At least my efforts wouldn't be in vain. I debated who should get my money. Probably Delilah. I doubted Mitchell would ever let us go to Estes Park, but Steve seemed so confident that God would make it work out.

"Climb in, everyone. I'll push us off." I grabbed onto the side of the boat and maneuvered myself inside, throwing one leg over at a time. The other nine kids climbed in, too.

Steve shoved the boat deep enough so he wouldn't hurt the motor after he dropped it. He waded into the water and then climbed in.

Steve sat in the back and drove. Once we got out of the shallow water, the boat picked up speed. The wind blew my hair in my face as we skidded across the water. I shivered. We hit a wave, and the boat made tiny jumps over the water. At last, the land came into view. Ahead, quiet waters lapped against the sand. Steve stopped the boat, jumped out, and pulled us ashore. I climbed out and plodded over the smooth shore. The water smelled like fish. I wrapped my arms around my body, trying to warm up. I hoped that the sun would be high in the sky soon so I wouldn't be so cold.

"When do we eat?" the tall boy asked.

Delilah and I giggled. The tall boy was always hungry.

"Didn't you eat at home?" Steve asked.

The tall boy's sister nudged him. "Dork. You skipped breakfast, didn't you?"

Steve headed away from the shore, and we followed him. The sand became dirt as we walked toward a cedar-sided house. The air smelled like rotting leaves. The brush covered the ground in a thick, wet layer. We all grabbed rakes from a large pile. I drug my rake across the ground in long swipes, scraping leaves together into clumps.

"Good job, everyone. Keep going. We'll take a break in a bit," Steve said a few hours after we began.

I looked down at my hands. Blisters were forming on my palms. Something about the exercise made me feel better and happier.

As we worked through the yard, the ten of us pushed our leaves into piles. I had jumped in the leaves as a child, but those days were gone. Still, it looked fun.

Steve handed out black garbage bags, and we each stuffed them with wet leaves. The cool foliage soothed my hot achy hands. I wiped the sweat off my face with my arm sleeve.

"Lunchtime," Steve called out.

A thin woman with white-blonde hair came out of the house carrying a platter of sandwiches, cookies, and lemonade.

I sat on the porch and took a swig of the bittersweet lemonade. The cool drink felt amazing running down my parched throat. I admired the work we had accomplished. A few more trash bags and we'd be done. It looked like a different yard, groomed and neat.

"The generous occupants paid our group three hundred dollars," Steve told us on the way back.

Wow. That lady was incredibly kind. Maybe this trip would be possible.

The new boy and the tall boy whooped.

"We divide how much we make by the people that come," Steve said.

"So that's what? A hund-o each?" tallboy jested.

"Where'd you learn math?" Delilah asked, hitting him on the arm.

The joke was funny, but I didn't laugh because my heart felt heavy. If only I'd be able to convince Mitchell to let us go. It would take a miracle.

The money trickled in with each odd job we completed. Steve kept a notebook and after each job, he'd pull it out and show us how much we'd earned. After the three or four raking jobs and two cook-offs, we earned more than enough money for the trip. We even earned enough funds for food. After the last job, he pulled out the notebook for everyone to see.

"You did it. All of you." Steve clapped a few of the guys on the back. "All of you have worked so hard. Congratulations. Your hard work has entirely paid for this trip. You'll need money if you want souvenirs, snacks, or extra things."

I hoped Mitchell would let us go, but so far, he hadn't changed his mind. Mom promised she'd help convince him, but even she didn't stand a chance against Mitchell's willpower.

The day of our trip arrived, and Steve pulled into the driveway and honked. We hadn't gotten Mitchell to agree, but Steve convinced himself if he showed, God would make it work. Mom had told us to pack. What was the point? It wasn't going to happen.

My hands shook as we waited to hear what Mitchell would say.

Mom stood in the living room and Mitchell was by his computer in the dining room. Mom approached Mitchell. "Mitchell, the girls want to go today."

"I told those girls no, Tary." Mitchell moved closer to Mom, his hand in the air as if he might hit her.

A second later, a knock sounded behind Wren and me.

"Come in," Mom hollered, shrugging at Mitchell.

Steve walked into our house.

"What are you doing here?" Mitchell asked, his voice loud.

"I'm here to pick up the girls. I thought you knew."

"For one, I never said they could go. Second, why are you in my house?" Mitchell poked Steve in the chest.

"Look, let them go." Steve gestured toward the van. "They've worked hard all summer. You'd be proud. They flipped burgers, raked yards—"

"I don't give a crap what they did. They aren't going. Get out now." Mitchell crossed his arms.

Oh, no, I hoped Mitchell didn't hit Steve. Then my days of youth group would end forever.

"Honey, let them go. Please." Mom hugged him. "We can have the house to ourselves. No kids for an entire week."

"Ugh. Go, before I change my mind." Mitchell turned away, his fists clenched at his sides. "Get that Jehovah out of my house."

As we rode in the van, leaving town, Steve played Christian music.

"Can't we listen to country music, Steve?" I asked.

"Sure." He turned the dial to the country radio station. Strawberry Wine played through the speakers, and a few of us girls sang along. Halfway through the song, he turned the station off. "You know what that song is about ladies? He waited. "Only Christian music on this trip."

"Yeah, how about rap?" the new boy asked.

Steve didn't reply, just turned up the Christian song.

"Whatever," one girl said behind me.

A song about Daniel and the lion's den played. That was something I could relate to. Always living in fear and waiting for unseen danger to claw me at any moment. Someday, I hoped God would save me from him. At least I was free for the week.

"Did someone let one rip?" the new boy asked. "It smells awful back here. Was it you?"

The tall boy shrugged. "Not me."

"Yuck," Delilah said, rolling her eyes at the new boy. "Boys are dumb."

I nodded. "You can say that again."

We'd driven past North Dakota and South Dakota when a smell filled the van like burnt rubber. Smoke wafted into the air from beneath the floor. The carpet under my feet was hot, and the smell made me cough. If the van broke down, would we have to turn around and go home? I couldn't go home now; Mitchell had barely let me leave. I stared out the window. This would all be gone soon.

Wren lifted a melted key chain that had stuck to the side of her backpack. "Steve, the floor is awfully toasty back here," Wren called out.

"One second," Steve called back. He pulled over. "Everyone, take fifteen minutes, go for a short walk or stretch."

Everyone hopped out. Some of the others explored while Steve crouched beside the van. I sat near the van under a tree.

Steve's son walked over to him. "Think we'll be able to keep going?"

Steve crossed his arms. "Yeah. It'll work out." Turning toward us, Steve said, "We'd better camp for the night and give the van a rest. There's a lot of heat coming off the exhaust. Everyone back in."

After getting back on the road, we passed winding roads, and eventually, Steve found a campsite.

At least we weren't going back home yet.

The next morning, we packed the campsite and kept driving. Tall mountains cut into the sky; a rosy glow hovered around the peaks. Why would God make something as large and beautiful as a mountain and waste time making someone insignificant like me? I rested my face in my hands. I imagined Moses descending the mountains. He had been so near to God. Was God in heaven just above the mountain tops? I couldn't wait to find out.

The van turned sharply as Steve wove through the valleys. Steve drove next to the edge. I clutched the seat, unsure of Steve's driving skills. My stomach tensed. A sign read *Watch for Falling Rock.* I sucked in a sharp breath.

"We're here," Steve shouted.

I exhaled slowly, excited to be off the narrow, winding roads.

We passed a National Park sign and then pulled into some type of driveway that led to an open, expansive campground. Some campers had set up their tents already. There were people everywhere. Trees grew around the camping areas like a natural border. Campfires smoked in many of the campsites. Steve had said there would be hundreds of people.

Steve stopped, and we climbed out. In front of our campsites were signs that identified our specific youth for Christ group. We had two designated spots, presumably one for boys and one for girls. Outside the van, I closed my eyes, and the warm sun beamed on my face. It was nice to be out of the van and the stench. Birds chirped in trees behind us, and squirrels scurried branch to branch. Soon, we'd have to set up our tents.

Early the next morning, I woke to the smell of mountain air, like rain and fresh flowers. Outside my tent, I stretched my arms over my head. Steve was heating water over the campfire. "Tomorrow, after breakfast, we're going into town." He laughed. "And guess what, girls? You can take showers while we're there."

Some girls cheered, high-fiving each other. Steve had been so kind as to boil water for them. Every. Single. Morning. Poor guy, not like he had nothing better to do. They were such ninnies. Camping was about being grimy and smelling like campfires, not perfume. I rolled my eyes at their high-maintenance mumbo jumbo. They'd probably attract a bear with all their fruity stench and kill us all. Mitchell had warned me about those dangers at Yellowstone. I guessed no one told the girls.

"First, we go rock climbing." Steve reclined in his chair. "After rock climbing, we'll go mountain climbing, and then we'll take showers and go swimming."

"So, we have to work hard first?" I asked.

"Yup." Steve nodded. "I think a few of you ladies could use something productive to do instead of fawning over boys."

We pulled into a dirt driveway and parked, then we climbed out of the van. Steve parked next to three white vans with their logo, Este's Climbing Co., printed on the side.

Fifteen feet from the van stood a one-hundred-foot stone wall with a rope connected to the top. Were we supposed to climb the entire thing? Next to that wall was another climbing wall, shorter than the other one. This one was wider.

All of us crowded around the instructor, a college-aged kid wearing khaki cargo pants. He pulled out a harness. Holding it out in front of himself, he stepped through the straps on the leather device. "This is how you put the harness on. Once it's on, I'll help you lace the rope through." He moved closer to the rock wall and climbed a few feet. "When you're ready, say belay is on. I'll attach the rope to myself. If you fall, the person holding the rope will stop the fall, but hold your hands out and keep your face off the rock."

The new boy went first. He grabbed a rock with one hand, then pushed off another lower rock with his left foot, lifting himself higher with each push. Once he reached the top, he rang a bell attached to the highest point of the rock wall.

The new boy wasn't even athletic. If he could do it, I could.

"Kaitlin, you're up," Steve said.

I strapped on the awkward straps around my butt. When the belayer tied the rope through my harness, I looked away, embarrassed. Standing too close to the worker, body heat radiated off him; he was a few years older than me and cute. This contraption was not attractive. It looked like I was wearing a diaper. After he finished, I approached the high wall.

"On belay!" I shouted as he'd instructed us.

"Belay is on," the guide said, his voice monotone. He looked bored.

My arms shook. My hands clung to the scratchy rocks. I lifted my right foot but couldn't feel notches in the stone. My heart pounded in my chest. Glancing around, I saw no rocks I could reach. I clung to the rocks; my arms shook. I was stuck. Would I have to start over again, since I hadn't reached the top? Hoping there was a place to move my hand, I reached running my fingers over the jagged stone, searching. There was nothing. My arms couldn't hold me much longer. My face rested against the rock. I grunted. "I can't do this!" I yelled in frustration.

"If you glance to your right, there is a rock with a groove five inches above your foot. Slide your toes onto it," Steve said. "You might have to jump."

To the right, I looked. I lifted my leg, but it wouldn't stretch enough. "I can't reach it," I cried out, my face hot.

"Try bounding off your foot," Steve said.

I jumped and searched for the jutted-out rock with my foot. My face brushed the rough stone. "I want to come down. It's too hard. I can't do it." I hoped no one laughed at me.

"You can do it, Kaitlin," Delilah and Wren cheered behind me.

I came down, embarrassed. I hated being a quitter because it made me look weak.

"It's okay, Kaitlin. You did great," Steve said.

"Thanks." The other members of our group climbed, one by one. The bell rang when someone made it to the top. I rolled my eyes. Why was everyone better at things than me?

The group walked toward the second rock wall. Behind it, a path wound around the back, so we didn't have to scale the front like the other wall. We hiked until we reached the top.

On the ground, a man stood on a patch of grass next to the parking area. "It's so far down," I said. This wall wasn't as high as the climbing wall in front of me, but it was high enough to get hurt. My hands ached, sore from trying to climb the first wall. I grabbed the harness off the ground and stepped into it.

The instructor attached the rope. "Push off the rock and keep your feet out in front of you. Once your feet hit the rock, push off again until you reach the bottom."

I hovered at the top, my back to the ground. The taut rope pulled against my waist. Pushing my toes against the rock, I bounced away from the wall. I was floating through the air. Was this what space was like, moving through the world without gravity?

Landing, I kicked my feet against the stone, then dropped more. This was something I could get used to. I took a deep breath. The air in the mountains was so clean and fresh.

After we all finished, we stood by the van, drinking water.

"Want to go on a hike?" Steve asked.

"Why don't you take a hike?" the tall boy asked. "Ha-ha. A hike. Get it?"

"Leave the guy alone; we wouldn't be here if he hadn't brought us," Delilah said.

"Sorry," the tall boy said, looking sheepish.

Wearing my heavy bag, I stepped onto the narrow four-mile-long trail. Pine trees and juniper shrubs grew along the path. The smell of sap filled the air. My calves burned with each step and my feet felt hot. What was the point of all this trudging uphill? I took off my shoes and knocked out the pebbles. I wanted to be done. "I'm tired." After rolling my eyes, I put my shoes back on.

"One foot in front of the other, one step at a time. That's all you need to climb a mountain," Steve said.

He always saw the best in situations, didn't he? Couldn't he admit this was hopeless? I huffed, annoyed.

"Kaitlin, let me carry your bag. It should help," Steve said.

I handed it to him, then stretched my arms across my body and sighed. "I wish I had water. I'm so thirsty," I said, noticing Steve's canteen.

"Here, Kaitlin, drink my water." Wren handed me her bottle.

I grabbed the bottle and took a swig. "Thanks."

I handed Wren's water back to her and climbed higher into the thinning mountain air. Tall, white-topped mountains covered the skyline. The air smelled like Christmas trees and sap. Refreshed, I took strides.

Boulders sat on top of a wide, flat area.

"This is the top of the plateau. Let's rest and have lunch," Steve said, then took a swig of water.

Across from us, mountains reached higher than ours. A vast valley separated our peak from the next. Puffy cumulus clouds covered the tops of the tallest mountains. I could almost reach out and touch God.

~ Sixteen ~

The story of Jonah running from God might be a good way to describe the turns my life would take in 2003. On the cusp of being an "adult" by American standards, I wasn't ready for a world of temptations and expectations.

On June first, Mom dropped Wren and me off at the local university. We'd have a college-like experience by living on campus, auditing one college class, and attending several high-school-level classes with HS teachers from around the area. The state-funded program helped underprivileged youth increase their likelihood of attending college.

A plastic welcome banner rippled in the wind. Kids sat on the lawn and at picnic tables in front of a brick building that contained the dorms. Wren and I grabbed our bags out of the trunk, then made our way toward the building.

I couldn't believe I'd live here, on a real college campus, away from home and Mitchell for five days a week.

Wren and I entered the building. I stopped a few feet inside where a woman stood holding a clipboard.

"Hi. Welcome to Upward Bound. What are your names?" she asked.

"I'm Kaitlin and this is Wren."

She glanced between Wren and me. "Wait, are you twins?"

I nodded. I hadn't been asked that in a long time.

"That's so cool." She looked at her clipboard. "Wren, you're in room seven-oh-seven, and Kaitlin, you're in seven-oh-one. Take the elevator to the seventh floor. It's over there." She pointed across the lobby.

A group of boys played hacky sack in front of the elevator. I sighed, and my stomach fluttered. Being around those boys five days a week, all summer, what a dream. I could have squealed.

The elevator doors opened, and Wren and I entered. As we moved, the elevator creaked. I looked at Wren and shrugged. "Maybe we should take the stairs next time."

"Yeah." She nodded.

Wren and I headed down a hallway, our luggage in tow.

Wren reached her room first. I kept walking.

I reached my room near the end of the hall. Inside were two beds on opposite walls. Inside the room, a window stretched over a desk underneath. The RA had mentioned I didn't have a roommate, and I didn't mind. I sat on the bed on the right. Could this be real? I kicked off my shoes.

After I unpacked and settled in, Wren and I walked to the cafeteria with the other fifty students who had also arrived.

A girl named Sarah sat at the table with Wren and me. Her eyes met mine. "Have you seen any cute boys yet?"

"I did. There's a few," I said, then giggled. "Did you see any?"

"Well—"

"I like Jim," another girl with a pointed nose, who reminded me of a peacock, interrupted Sarah.

"Yeah. He goes to our school." I shrugged. "He's nice."

Wren rolled her eyes. Jim had liked Wren last year, but Wren told me she wished he'd stop trying to be her boyfriend. He had not taken the hint, and last week, he'd been insistent. Maybe this long-nosed girl would convince him to give up on Wren.

After we all finished our food, we returned to the dorms to call it a night. I couldn't wait to see what tomorrow brought.

I followed the crowd to my next class. High school teachers from each school taught us different subjects. First, we had Spanish with a teacher from my school.

She stood in front of a classroom. Her black hair reminded me of Sierra's the way it curled. The teacher's thick black glasses were like frames around a photograph, her dark eyes stark against her skin. "Hola!" She waved. "Me llama, Trish." She held her hand to her chest. "Boys say, *me llamo*, ladies say *me llama*. You try now."

"*Me llama*, Kaitlin," I said, along with my class of fifteen.

"*Muy bien*." She clapped. "Very good!"

During the rest of the class, she taught us colors and numbers, which I had learned in her class at school.

I sauntered down the hall to my first class. No, Mitchell or drama and surrounded by new friends. The halls were about the same size as at school, minus the missing lockers. I entered the first room marked *Composition/English*. The teacher had pushed the desks against the wall in a semicircle. I moved through the wide room and picked a seat toward the back, so I could see everyone coming in. I shifted in the seat, and my hands brushed against the cold desk.

An older man stood in front of the group. A sparkle glimmered in his eyes like a comedian thinking of their next punchline or like Santa Claus, ready to share a loud belly laugh and hand out presents. Everyone sat.

"Hi. I'm Mr. Carter, but you can call me Marty." He paced the front of the room. "So, you all want to be writers, right?" His eyes flitted across the student's desks. "Why wouldn't you? It's the best job in the world." He threw his arms into the air, then laughed.

The English teacher at my regular school had a monotone voice and gave boring assignments. This guy wouldn't be like that; I could already tell.

"There's nothing more fun than writing." He put his hand on his chin. "If there is, I'll put it out of your mind. I want to convince you all there is nothing in the world quite like it." As he smiled, lines crinkled near the corners of his eyes.

What would he teach us? I sat forward in my seat. Hopefully, something amazing.

"Let's begin. Sean, can you sharpen the dull ones?"

A boy with shiny, straight black hair rose upon hearing his name. Mr. Carter held out a stack of pencils to him. Sean walked over to the pencil sharpener, turning the handle with finesse.

The way he sharpened pencils was a beautiful thing. I stifled a giggle.

Martin told us about his love of the theatre, acting, and the written word. As he talked, my attention flitted to Sean walking through the room, and I didn't hear Martin anymore.

Sean finished sharpening the pencils.

"Everyone, take a pencil from Sean," Martin said.

Sean walked through the room, handing them out. I'd gladly accept anything from him. When he handed me one, I blushed, then held onto my pencil.

Mr. Martin wrote on the whiteboard behind him, *Perspective.* "Your first assignment is to write about an experience from the last school year." His face brightened. "Imagine you are someone else. Make it fun by choosing someone you don't like. I want you to write a story from their perspective." He smiled. "I'm not grading you. I'll be here reading." He walked over and sat in a chair at the side of the room. Martin pulled out a book and read while we wrote our papers.

I glanced at the back of Sean's head between scribbling words on my notebook paper. I thought about an annoying boy at school. He believed himself to be the greatest thing since money, but I knew better.

Would Wren ever notice me? He thought to himself. He spun in his chair and whispered to his best pal, Jim. "Did you ask her out yet?" He nodded toward Wren. He hoped his friend, Jim hadn't asked her out because he liked her. But it was a game and they both knew it and he was determined to win.

Little did he know, he wouldn't win. Neither of them would because Wren was too good for either of them.

Martin stood. "All right, you can put your pencils down; you're excused. Please put your papers on my desk. I can't wait to read them. I'll see you all tomorrow."

The next night, we headed past fields where the football teams practiced in the spring. We stopped at the baseball field. An RA sent half of the people to the outfield and the rest sat in the dugout.

By some miracle, Sean, the pencil sharpener, was on my team.

"Hi," I said, moving to stand next to him in the dugout area. Dirt and dust flew into the air as the outfielders headed onto the field. I watched them, hoping I'd remember something from the little league when it was my turn. Of course, when I played kid league, they never put me in.

"Hi." Sean looked at his shoes, which were full of dirt and worn on the toes.

"Where are you from?" I asked him.

"Park Rapids." He put his hands in his pockets.

"Sean, you're up," the team captain said.

Sean put on his baseball cap. "Talk to you later, okay?"

"Okay. I'd like that."

He walked toward home plate, a bounce in his step. I knew I could get lost in that smile. He had perfect teeth and dreamy eyes.

Sean bat, hitting the ball with a loud ting sound. The ball soared between the left base and pitcher.

I was next. I walked to home base, then grabbed a bat, and rounded the plate. The pitcher flung the ball toward the catcher. I imagined myself hitting the ball to the fence as I swung hard. I hit myself in the back of the head. "Ouch," I whispered, cowering. I was such a klutz. I bet Sean had seen, but I hoped not. He was going to think I was an idiot. My ears turned red. A few people laughed behind me.

The pitcher threw the ball a second time. I hit the ball this time. It landed to the left of the pitcher. I sprinted to first base; my foot scraped against its soft leather. It wasn't a great hit. I didn't make it home, but I was right behind Sean now. I put my hands on my knees and caught my breath.

He turned from second base and waved at me.

The team captain approached the home plate to bat. He swung the bat a few times like he was practicing. I hoped he was better than me; but who could be worse?

He hit the ball past the pitcher and into the outfield. Yes, he was better.

I ran from second base to third and then slid into home. I stood and brushed the dirt off my pant legs. Sean and I high-fived.

After the game, Sean walked fifteen feet ahead of me by himself.

I ran and caught him. "Mind if I walk with you?"

"Company would be nice." He grinned, his pearly teeth showing.

"You did great out there," I said.

"Thanks," Sean said.

"I love baseball. When we watched my uncle play, my dad and I would go to the store, then collect the player cards. I paused before continuing. "I have a stepdad now, but he doesn't watch baseball. He watches war movies."

We talked more on the way back to the dorms.

"I'll see you later, Kaitlin."

"I'll see you tomorrow in English." Oh, no, I glanced away, embarrassed. Now he'd know I'd noticed him earlier. I didn't want him to think I was a stalker.

"I thought I'd seen you before." He smiled.

I felt less embarrassed but now that feeling was replaced with flutters in my stomach; he had noticed me, too. "Want to eat lunch with us?" I tucked in a loose strand of hair.

"I eat with a few of my friends; you can join us if you want to."

"Great. I'll find you." We separated at the elevator doors. I liked that boy.

That night I went and told Wren all that had happened. "Where were you? I don't remember seeing you?" I asked.

"I snuck away to help out at blind camp. I needed to get away for a while."

"Blind camp?" I asked. "What's that?"

"On the other side of campus, there are blind students here, they're a lot younger than we are, but they are a ton of fun."

"Does anyone know you went?"

"The RAs know. They were okay with it. I've been thinking about leaving Upward Bound, but I don't really want to talk about it."

"Oh, no. Leave? Please don't leave. I hope you stay."

I glanced around the lunchroom. Sean wore the same worn-out, red ball cap and maroon T-shirt. Yesterday when Sean mentioned his friends, I didn't know one was from my school. I breathed a sigh of relief; it was nice to see a familiar face.

"Mind if I join?"

His thick eyebrows rose when he saw me. "Hey, Kaitlin." He shuffled over to make room for me.

"Hey, Kaitlin," the boy from my school said, giving me a slight wave. "What's up?"

"Not much." I sat, then took a bite of my pizza. The warm, salty cheese and thick crust filled my taste buds with joy. It was amazing.

"We're taking a walk after lunch if you want to come," the girl said.

"Sounds fun," I said. On our walk, I discovered that Sean was a smoker like me.

That night after lights-out, I wiggled into my blankets. What would it be like to be near Sean all the time? I closed my eyes. Could he be "the one" for me? I'd had a boyfriend before, one boy from Steve's youth group, and I dated him for six months, but that was ridiculous. He was nothing like Sean. Sean's rich brown eyes and lightly freckled face filled my mind. How would it feel to kiss him? Maybe someday I'd know.

That night, Wren told me she was leaving Upward Bound and going home again, but she didn't say why.

Students from Upward Bound filed into a lecture hall for a weekly morning meeting. The stale-smelling auditorium quieted as the RA walked to the front of the room. "You know, every year we take a trip as a group. Next week," she paused, "we're taking a trip to Chicago. We'll do some educational things like visiting the Chicago Museum and a Broadway play. Expenses are all paid. You have worked so hard this summer and you deserve some fun."

We hadn't worked that hard—but Chicago! I couldn't believe it. I hadn't been there since I was young. I only wished Wren could come with. Was she doing okay at home?

The room erupted in applause.

I stood and joined in the clapping.

One morning, a few days before our trip to Chicago, Mom dropped Wren back off at the college campus. After speaking with the RAs, she was allowed to come back, on the condition of the head RA, that she "act happy." It was ludicrous. How was she supposed to *act* happy if she wasn't? I didn't know what they expected her to do, but I was so happy she had returned. I gave her half of the money I'd earned during Upward Bound so she could have fun on the trip, too. And not just pretend to.

I took a deep breath, grabbed my bags, and headed outside to the parking lot. Soon we'd be in Chicago. The sun peeked above the horizon. The air was brisk and the excited chatter of the students made it hard to hear anything else. Reaching the parking lot, all the students huddled together in a group. The bus pulled in as I bounced on my toes to keep warm.

The bus stopped, and the door opened. I couldn't wait to get out of the chilly air. Sean stood in front of me in line, behind two people.

I stepped into the fancy charter bus behind him and saw five other students. There must have been thirty rows. I made my way toward the back, where I saw Sean sitting. "Mind if I sit with you?" I asked him.

He shook his head. "I don't mind."

I moved in beside him before anyone else could. I hadn't seen him as much as I'd wanted because of classes. Now was the perfect opportunity to get to know him better. The engine rumbled, and we began our journey to Chicago.

"What do you like to do for fun?" I asked Sean.

"I want to play guitar, but I can't afford one because my parents don't make a lot of money. My mom is the only one that can work." Sean shifted uncomfortably.

"My stepdad can't work. He had PTSD from the Gulf war and heart complications."

He lifted the brim of his hat, then rubbed his forehead. "My dad and brother served, too. I'm sorry your parents are divorced. Mine are together, but sometimes my dad's hard to be around."

"Why is that?" I asked, and my eyebrows rose.

"Well, he drinks a lot, and he isn't always nice."

"Oh. I get that. My stepdad isn't nice, either. He doesn't drink often because of his heart, but my mom does. She used to drink a lot after the divorce."

"Yeah, it's rough." Sean bit his lip.

"Sorry about your dad. Someday we won't have to live with our parents anymore." I grinned at him and nudged his arm, attempting to cheer him. "You okay?"

"Yeah." Sean shrugged. "I can hardly wait to move. But my sister lives with my parents and I don't want to leave her there."

What a sweet guy. I didn't know any boys that loved their sister enough to sacrifice their own happiness. He truly was special.

An hour later, I leaned on his shoulder and the soft rising and falling of his chest, along with the vibration of the large bus, put me to sleep.

We arrived in Chicago. The lights shimmered in the dark sky against the backdrop of skyscrapers. The bus pulled into a tall building with cream-colored stone in the center of downtown. They did not make buildings like this where I lived.

Once inside the hotel, I found Wren in the lobby. I couldn't wait to tell her all about the day I spent getting to know Sean. I spun around slowly with my arms open and glanced at the expansive ceilings with crystal chandeliers and gasped. How did anyone afford to stay here? I imagined a queen descending the grand staircase behind the front desk.

The excited chatter of the other teens filled the eating area. As I ate breakfast, I couldn't help thinking about how great it would be to see more of Chicago. The taste of warm syrup filled my mouth as I took a bite of French toast.

Someone tapped me on the shoulder. I turned my head and my eyes met Sean's.

"Can you believe it? A real baseball game." He wore his red baseball cap and smiled ear to ear.

"Seeing the Cubs play is going to be awesome. I'm so excited about the play, too. I can't believe we get to do all of this."

Sean rubbed his hands together like he was warming them. "Kaitlin, I forgot. I wanted to ask you a question about the play."

"What is it?"

"Do you want to be my date tonight?"

I set my fork on my plate. "Of course, I'd love to." Once I'd gone on a date with the cool, new guy from a youth group to a movie, but that was nothing compared to a Broadway play. I brushed the hair out of my eyes. Could this moment be real? I wanted to pinch myself, to be sure.

I applied light makeup, blush on my cheekbones, champagne-colored eyeshadow, and mascara. I hoped I didn't mess up my first date with Sean. The girls in my room did a delicate job on my makeup. I grinned at myself in the mirror. Perfect.

Sarah, Wren, and the long-nosed girl helped me style my hair until every strand was in place. It was in a loose bun, with wisps of curls escaping near the sides of my face.

"Girl, you look hot," the long-nosed girl said.

I laughed. "Thanks. I hope Sean thinks so, too." A wide smile spread across my face. I hoped the night was perfect.

That evening, I sat beside Sean in our group's van. Every bump on the paved road moved our bodies closer together. The heat of his leg warmed mine. I let out a slow breath.

The van parked and Sean and I walked arm in arm across the sidewalk.

"Are you warm enough?" Sean asked.

"I'm a bit cold."

Sean put his sweatshirt over my shoulders, and then he wrapped his arm around me. Having him so close warmed me more than the sweatshirt. There were no rules with Sean, nothing I couldn't say—not like at home. He accepted me the way I was. I couldn't believe I'd been lucky enough to find love. We might be together forever. I savored the moment as the tall historical theater came into view.

A neon sign sat on top of tall pillars at the front of the building. Under the pillars, Sean opened a glass door with a golden handle. How many famous people had been there? The theater smelled like a museum: stale and old.

A man with a tailored suit stood near the doors. "Your tickets, please." He held out his palm.

We handed him our tickets.

"Ready?" Sean asked.

"Yes."

Inside the theater room, the ushers handed us each a playbill. Sean and I walked the steep stairs and sat near the back. No photos allowed; a sign read. We scooted into the back row. I glanced at the patterned ceiling. The chatter of the excited students echoed in the enormous room. My hands were clammy, and my stomach had butterflies as Sean and I sat. I couldn't believe I was here with him. Golden lights hovered above the stage in a semi-circle. A heavy maroon curtain stretched across the front of the stage until someone drew the curtains and the lights dimmed.

The RA in our row leaned forward and put her fingers to her lips. "Shh."

The spotlight shone on the side of the stage. A person holding a staff and wearing blue-and-white-striped face paint sang. He held out his hands like he was telling a story.

"Sean, it's a monkey." I squealed.

An orange light rose on the back of the stage, like a sun. Actors walking on stilts, dressed as giraffes, meandered across the stage. The crowd gasped as an elephant waddled down the theater aisle. Actors ran onto the stage, wearing grass skirts. Some held birds on top of tall sticks. Some dressed as gazelles, moving gracefully across the stage like ballerinas. They were so talented. Their voices thundered as the acoustics carried the sound through the theater. I sat in awe, staring at the men and women dancing in their grass skirts, their movements in sync.

I nudged Sean's arm, pointing at the lions, who had become parents, as part of the stage rose into the air on a spiral staircase. How did the stage move like that? I sat forward in my seat. The monkey held the baby lion in the air. The animals beneath him looked on adoringly. What would it be like to have everyone love you?

The actors sang a romantic song.

I snuggled into Sean.

My jaw dropped in awe of their raw talent. I leaned my head on Sean's shoulder. So, this was what love was like? I never saw Mom and Mitchell smiling and holding hands. This moment was perfect, but what about next week when Upward Bound ended? I might never see Sean again. A hollowness ached in my stomach.

At the end of the play, blue light flooded the stage, reminding me of rain. Animals on stilts and birds on tall sticks grazed across the stage as they had in the beginning of the play. A red sun rose behind the monkey as he returned to the stage.

The actors bowed, and the curtain closed.

Everyone in the auditorium stood and clapped.

"Students from Upward Bound, make your way outside," an RA shouted.

Sean and I, along with the rest of our group, walked back to the van.

~ Seventeen ~

When I was seventeen, my focus was on Sean and nothing else mattered. I was wrong.

It was my senior year of high school, and I was in love. Things were perfect, and I couldn't wait to spend forever with Sean. He hadn't asked me to marry him, but I knew he would, maybe if I moved in with him after school. I told myself we'd be strong enough to resist temptation until marriage. I'd stay pure no matter what. Sean understood.

In October, Wren told the counselor at school about her depression. She always seemed kind of happy, unless we were at home, but I had been hanging out with Delilah and my other friends more lately, maybe I missed her being depressed. Was she upset because of how Mitchell treated us or because of school? She'd had some issues with a boy a few weeks ago, but I wasn't sure if that was the cause. I wished I could make her happy.

Mom, Wren, and I rode in the car, to an office building in the next town over, to see what they could do about Wren's situation. I sat next to Wren in the backseat of Mom's car. What could this social worker possibly do to help? I fidgeted. Would they take her away from me? I didn't want to be home without her. How would I survive alone with Mitchell and Mom and no one to understand me?

Mom surfed through the radio channels until she landed on a country station. *Check Yes or No*, by George Strait played.

Wren stared out the window, saying nothing. Rain trickled down outside. She finally spoke to me in a quiet voice, "They might ask me to move away from home."

"You think they will?" I asked, sad that it might come to that.

Wren shrugged.

We arrived at a one-level building on a side street. We walked through the front door and into a waiting-type room like in a hospital The fan whirred overhead, and the vending machine hummed. A stout woman with smart eyes and dull, fire-truck-colored hair came out of an office and then escorted Wren into her office. On the front of the office was a large window with shades drawn all the way open. Something about the lady intimidated me as I watched Wren sitting across from her. Maybe she made me nervous because she held Wren's future in her hands.

I sat in a chair next to Mom. What were they saying? I couldn't tell. I stood and paced. How long was this going to take? Mom picked up a magazine off a side table and flipped through its pages.

Wren exited the room, then Mom went in and sat where Wren had sat.

Wren saw me and then sat in the chair next to mine.

"You, okay?" I asked.

She shrugged, then glanced away.

Did they know what Mitchell was like? Had Wren told them? No, she hadn't mentioned me moving. I frowned. "What did that lady say?"

"They want me to go into foster care."

"Foster care?" I raised my voice. "Will I ever see you?" I wished I could go with her but was afraid to ask; it might pull me farther away from Sean.

"It'll be okay. They'll let you visit me whenever you want. The guardian ad litem, the lady in that room, says you'll be able to come once I'm settled." She sighed. "I know it's hard for you, but it'll be better for me. She told me there's a friendly couple interested in taking me." She patted my shoulder.

My eyes watered. What would it be like at home without my Wren? I couldn't be home with Mitchell and Mom all by myself.

Mom exited the room, and the woman came with her. "See you in a few days," Mom said to the lady. They shook hands. Mom's eyes looked red and puffy.

In the car, Mom told us the social worker recommended Wren live in a healthier environment until she was doing better. It was all settled.

I sniffled. Why did she have to leave? Couldn't I go with her? I hugged Wren tightly. I didn't know when I'd see her again. Where was she going? I had so many questions and no answers. What if she got put with bad people who would hurt her?

Wren entered foster care two days after the meeting. I continued living with Mom and Mitchell. The school was different without Wren around. I didn't hear what my teachers said for the first week because my thoughts were elsewhere. Tears clouded my vision as I stared at the whiteboard, in science class. Delilah moved in to sit next to me, taking Wren's old spot.

A boy, the one I'd written about during Upward Bound's Day in the Life of essay, leaned over the desk close to my ear. "Your sister's crazy."

My face grew hot. I balled my hands into fists. "No, she's not," I said, my voice strained, as I tried to control my hatred.

That guy had better hope I didn't see him after class. If I had to, I'd find Sierra to teach him some manners. She wasn't scared of confrontation. I crossed my arms.

Delilah leaned close to me and whispered, "Ignore him; he's stupid."

"Thanks." My face cooled at her words. He didn't know what had made Wren so depressed. Her life was hard, and he had no idea about any of it. I fought tears until the bell rang.

I took a deep breath in the hallway, then dragged my feet as I wandered past the rows of lockers, avoiding eye contact with the crowd all around me. No one understood the world Wren and I lived in it every day. No one understood me, except Wren.

I saw Wren about once a month after that, and her foster family always let me stay if I wanted. We talked on the phone often, too, when Wren wasn't busy.

Wren had been in foster care for a semester now, and she was doing well in her new environment. She had lots of friends and good grades. I sat in the study hall, resting my head on the table at my school. I didn't enjoy being alone. The beginning of the year was great, but now it was dragging, as I became more aware of the distance from the two people I cared about the most.

I had six months left of school, and I didn't know how I'd survive, but one day, during the second half of the school year, Wren moved back in with me and Mom and Mitchell. Finally, the world seemed brighter.

It was the day after I graduated high school, when I grabbed all the money I'd received from my graduation party, packed my bags, and waited for Sean to pick me up so I could move in with him. As soon as Sean arrived, I'd leave the swamp and its nightmares behind. In the fall, I'd attend school for nursing. Sean would drive me to my Nursing classes.

I didn't want to leave Wren behind, but she planned to move to another city three hours away for college and she'd be leaving soon, too.

Wren and I stood in the living room, with my bags on the floor beside the couch. I gave her a hug, and a lump rose in my throat because once again we'd be apart. "Love you. Hope everything works out for you." I took a deep breath; she'd be fine, I told myself.

"See you soon. Love you too," Wren said.

"Sean's here. I'll see you." I grabbed my bags and bolted outside.

I sucked in fresh summer air then glanced at the swamp house one last time, hoping I wouldn't return. "Good riddance," I said to no one in particular.

I climbed into Sean's dad's car, and we left. I felt a weight lift off me. There would be no more listening to Mom or Mitchell or toilet paper lectures. The rules we would live by were mine and Sean's now. My heart warmed, thinking about my future with him. Life would be great.

The cool breeze drifted across my face as Sean and I stood outside of his house, which sat in a trailer park court. My new home was falling apart on the bottom, but it was home now. It wasn't as nice as the trailer I lived in when I was young. My stomach tightened. I'd never lived with a boy before and didn't know what to expect, but it had to be better than living with Mom and Mitchell. Sean and I carried my bags into Sean's house.

Thick blankets covered the walls behind two sofas, and the cigarette smoke hung in the air. Home, sweet, home: I didn't mind the scent of smoking anymore.

Sean's dad sat on the couch. He nodded in our direction. "Hey." Sean had warned me he wasn't friendly, so I decided I would keep my distance.

I didn't want to live with another Mitchell. "Hi." I gave him a wave.

"You'll be in Sean's room," he said without making eye contact.

I nodded then walked down the hall, following Sean. My stomach tightened into a knot. Was this day real? I couldn't believe we'd be sharing a room, like a married couple.

His room had two beds shoved together. On one entire wall of his room were the poems I'd written to him throughout the year. I couldn't believe he'd saved them all. He must have loved me.

Sean sat on his bed next to me. "Welcome home," he said, grabbing my hand.

"Thank you for letting me stay with you. I couldn't live at home. I couldn't do it anymore."

"I know." He patted my leg. "We'll find our own place once I get a job."

I leaned over and kissed him. "I know."

Sean drove us in his dad's car, a classic white beetle. After a few brief minutes on the highway, he pulled into the boat access. The beetle's wheels rumbled over the loose dirt and rocks. Sean parked the car, and we made our way toward the water. At the end of a gravel hill, a dock floated on shallow water.

I sat at the end.

Sean carried the poles, bait, and a five-gallon bucket. Once he was at the end of the dock, Sean put bait on the hooks, then cast out two lines, one for me and one for him. He handed me a pole. "Do you ever want more out of life? Sometimes I'm so stuck."

"I don't know. I want to do mission trips. Maybe I will write a book about what happens on the trip. I shrugged, then said, "Or something like that." I stood, reeled in the line, and recast. "Is there something you want to do?" I hoped his future would always include me.

"I'm not sure. Maybe I should join the service like my brother." He reeled in his line and then cast again.

My heart sank. "I hope you don't join the military. It doesn't end well, look at my stepdad." I paused, fearing to imagine Sean being as mean as Mitchell. "What if there's a war?" I imagined him fighting in a foreign country, far from me and home. Anyone I'd ever met who served in war suffered after returning home. It wasn't a future I'd ever want for him. The water lapped gently against the dock. "Please don't. I don't know what I'd do without you."

Sean shrugged. "I probably won't. Don't worry."

I leaned my head against his shoulder, then recast my line. I hoped I'd catch a lot of fish so we could feed everyone at Sean's house.

Something tugged my line. I spun the reel. Pulling in the unyielding Sunny. I took it off the hook and plopped it into our five-gallon bucket half-full of lake water. I caught a whiff of fish scent and crinkled my nose. Moving away, I kissed Sean's tanned cheek.

That day we caught a lot of Sunnies and Large-Mouth Bass.

After the day grew darker, we hopped into the car, and Sean drove us to his house. That night we ate delicious fish, and my stomach was as full as my heart.

That weekend, like most weekends, Sean and I got drunk. Sean's two friends from Upward Bound came over. They were kissing in the corner of Sean's living room. My face grew hot, embarrassed by their public display and ashamed of my inexperience. Those two weren't even a couple, and they were probably sleeping together. For a year and a half, I had fought temptation because I wanted to honor God, but I didn't want to fight it anymore. No one else was. We already lived together, so we were practically married.

I confessed my feelings to Sean.

"Are you sure you want to?" Sean asked me, touching my shoulder. "I know you have your God."

"Oh, he'll understand," my words slurred, and I got lost in his dreamy brown eyes. "I'm ready as I'll ever be." Sean was the only person I'd ever be with, so why did it matter if we did it now instead of waiting, marriage was just a piece of paper, I told myself.

People said it would hurt, but I felt numb and brave from the alcohol.

The event wasn't what I'd hoped, not that Sean did anything wrong. It felt like I'd given Sean the last remaining thing I had left to give and now there was nothing else I could offer him. It didn't make me closer to Sean or make our love more real. Our love had now diminished into something less.

Ashamed, I covered my body with the blanket, then after a few minutes, I dressed, wishing I could undo it. I wanted to marry him; but would that make this shame go away? I loved Sean, so that's how it was supposed to be, right? Something wasn't right, but I didn't know what. I touched the doorknob, then hesitated. I didn't want to see anyone. Why wouldn't they go home? I didn't even want to see Sean. Maybe God had been right about saving this stuff for a proper marriage. Cringing, I returned to the living room.

One night after fishing, Sean and I sat in the living room. Sean's dad watched the news while Sean and I chatted quietly on the couch. During the week, we'd fish almost every day. One night after fishing, someone knocked on the door.

"Answer the door, Sean," his dad said, waving his hand.

Sean opened the door and talked to whoever stood outside. "I'll get her." Sean turned and looked over his shoulder at me, then motioned for me to come over.

I walked to Sean's front door and peered outside. The sheriff stood on the porch, his posture stiff and his expression was stern. Maybe he knew we'd been drinking underage. I wasn't drinking now, so hopefully, I wasn't in trouble. Sean returned to the couch, but I wished he'd stayed with me.

"Are you Kaitlin?" the sheriff asked, looking at his clipboard.

"Yes." The police car was behind him, but his lights weren't on. I hoped he wasn't arresting me for underage drinking. Did someone tell him?

"Your mother didn't know how to get a hold of you." He frowned.

My mother? What did she have to do with anything? I gave the officer a confused look, my eyebrows furrowed.

"Your sister, Wren, tried to take her own life," the sheriff's voice deepened. "You need to call your mom."

I couldn't breathe. The air suddenly felt thick. "Is my sister— is she okay?" I asked, frightened by what his answer might be. I couldn't find the strength to ask if Wren was still alive.

"From what your mom said, she's at the hospital. Your mom will know more. Do you need a phone?" the officer asked, holding out his cell phone.

"No, my boyfriend's dad has one. Thanks." I motioned toward the couch where Sean's dad sat.

"Have a good night," the officer said. "I hope your sister is well."

Sean and I closed the door.

My heart pounded, the sound reverberating in my ears. "Can I borrow your phone?" I asked Sean's dad, my throat tight, tears streaming down my face. Why didn't the Sheriff tell me how she was doing? He should've known more or brought me to her. Something. I needed to see her now.

Sean's dad reached into his pocket and handed me his phone. "Is everything okay?"

"It's my sister. She's in the hospital."

"Keep the phone as long as you need," he said.

I dialed Mom, then put the phone to my ear. "Hey, it's Kaitlin," I choked out the words. "The sheriff gave me your message." I held my hand over my mouth, trying not to scream or cry.

"Wren tried to kill herself today." Mom whimpered. "Mitchell and I left to go to the cities. On the way, we got sick and had to turn around," Mom sounded scratchy over the phone.

I waited for her to continue, eager to know what else happened, and if my sister would make it. Without her, I couldn't live. I couldn't. She was my Wren.

Mom sniffled, then continued, "Mitchell found her at home and forced her to the car; we sped to the hospital. She mumbled and dozed in and out of consciousness." Mom cleared her throat. "I yelled at her, 'What did you take? What did you take?' I shook her and tried to keep her awake. Mitchell sped the entire way to the hospital. She almost died. It was lucky, or maybe even God, that we got sick and turned around. We were supposed to be gone a few days. We would've been too late."

"Where is she now?" I sucked the air into my lungs.

"She's stable at the ICU."

"Is she going to be, okay?" I swallowed hard, then cleared my throat.

"We don't know yet, but stable is good. It means her condition isn't fluctuating, and her vitals are within range. I'll call you on this number when I hear from the hospital. I love you."

"Love you too, Mom." I hung up the phone and returned it to Sean's dad.

"Everything okay with your sister?" he asked.

I nodded, then went to my room to be alone. How had Wren gotten so sad, and how didn't I know? I loved her more than anyone. Why hadn't I helped her? I was so selfish. I was so blind to everyone's pain, except my own. I sprawled face-down on the bed.

Sean came in after me, rubbing my back.

"This is all my fault," I said. "I should've done more to help her."

"It's not your fault. We can go see her," Sean said in a soft tone.

"We can?" I wiped my eyes on my sleeve and sniffled. "I knew you'd understand."

That night I couldn't sleep. I didn't know what I'd do without her. I cried quietly as Sean slept next to me. *Please God, help her. If you're still there, I know you probably hate me for my choices, but please help Wren.*

It was the morning, and I was groggy after a night of restless sleep. I curled up on the couch under a blanket and stared at the television.

Sean's dad's cell phone rang. "Hello?" he answered. "Yup, she's right here." Sean's dad handed me the phone.

"Hello?" I asked.

"It's Mom. The hospital transferred Wren to a long-term facility. It's the state institution." Mom whimpered into the phone. "She's old enough now. They can treat her as an adult."

"What does that mean?" I asked, biting my lip. It sounded bad.

"They want her to stay for a mandatory six months in the adult ward."

My mouth dropped open. First, she'd almost died, and now this. What if there were murderers in there? I put my head in my hands; it was such a long time for her to be locked away. Why did she want to die so badly? Was it my fault because I hadn't been there for her? What if they never let her leave?

"Can Sean and I visit her?" I asked.

"They have rules so make sure you listen. You can visit after her seventy-two-hour watch is over in two days." She added, "She's in Brainerd. I'll give Sean directions." That was only an hour away.

I handed Sean the phone and he wrote down the directions.

Sean and I drove to visit Wren at the state facility. Surrounding the cold historical buildings was barbed wire above chain-linked fences. I trembled at the towering prison. Sean parked.

Inside the building, was an office area to the side and a hallway that was like a hospital's, with robin-egg blue walls and white wainscot. A nurse led us through a locked door. She shielded her hand and typed in a code. "Follow me," she said. Her ponytail bounced as she walked down the hallway with stoic gray walls.

A girl with disheveled hair hugged the wall. Two people talked in an animated conversation. Why were they there? They weren't the straight-jacket-wearing murderers I'd feared.

The nurse led us to another locked room, then let us inside. "Your sister will be right in, she's with the doctor and is almost finished," the nurse said, closing the door behind her.

Wren entered with the nurse a few minutes later. Tight cornrows weaved around her head in swirls. It must have hurt, having her hair wound so tight.

"I'll leave you to visit, Wren. You have group sessions next, I'll come and get you when it's time." The nurse left.

"Wow, your hair is crazy cool," I said as I stared at her braids.

"Yeah, my roommate braided it. She taught me how to do a crypt walk, too. Want to see?"

I nodded. "I didn't know you could do that." I felt out of place in this muted room in the middle of the psych ward. What was I supposed to say? It was like some scene out of a horror movie.

She danced around the room like she didn't have a care in the world. "Did you sneak me a smoggy one?"

"I thought you might want one," I said, then reached into my bra, taking out a Ziploc with a cigarette hidden in it. She took it from me, then stuck it in her bra.

"Thanks." She straightened up her shirt. Wren bit her lip. "Sean, can Kaitlin and I trade spots so I can leave, then you can give me a ride to McDonald's?"

My eyes widened and inwardly I cringed, wishing she had asked before we had come. "I would trade places with you, but if they caught us . . . I don't think they'd believe me telling them they had the wrong person."

Wren laughed. "That's a good point. I wouldn't want you stuck in here."

I breathed a sigh of relief. The idea of being stuck there terrified me. "I don't even like you here." I looked at the floor.

"It's not exactly where anyone would want to be. All these rules, making you take pills. It's annoying. But my friends and I sneak into the bathrooms and smoke. We don't care that we aren't supposed to. We need something to pass the time." She ran her fingers through the ends of her hair. "One girl had a pack and shared it with all of us."

The nurse knocked, then popped her head in. "Time to go. We're starting the group sessions in five minutes. Say goodbye."

I hugged her and didn't want to let go. Tears filled my eyes. I missed her so much. Would she be here forever? I shuddered.

"Love you too. Thank you for coming and for the smoggy one." She winked at me. "I'm going to get out, don't worry."

She must have gotten phone privileges because a few days after my visit with Wren, she called. "Can I tell you, my testimony?"

I sat on my bed in my room. "Is that your story about God?" What did He have to do with any of this?

"Yeah. He found me."

"What do you mean He found you?" I creased my eyebrows.

"My friend in treatment asked me if I wanted to go to church with her yesterday. We walked to a room where a preacher waited. He read us Psalm thirty-seven. Afterward, I prayed to God to rescue me and told Him I'd follow Him. Guess what happened then, Kaitlin?" She sounded so excited.

Bewildered, I asked, "What?" I did not know where this was going. Since I'd been intimate with Sean, I hadn't prayed because I was ashamed that I'd let God down.

"I had court earlier today for a pre-hearing. Mom, my lawyer, and my social worker arrived behind schedule. Worried I'd be in trouble, I felt relieved as they arrived. My social worker said if I agreed to take my meds and go to therapy, I could go home. So, I'm done with that place. I'm free. I can't believe it. I'm so happy. Jesus set me free, Kaitlin." She squealed.

"I'm glad you aren't getting committed. I was scared for you." I was glad she'd found help."

"Talk to you soon. By the way, I transferred to the college next to yours, KD. We should get to see each other a lot more now."

~ Eighteen ~

I was one year into college in 2005 and didn't know if I should drop out or keep struggling to travel to school.

I had called the local hospital, and they encouraged me to apply once I got certified as a nursing assistant; I kept attending school, despite my inability to drive and the strain that put on Sean as my chauffeur. Back then, I told myself it would be better soon.

I stirred from sleep as Sean shifted in the bed beside me. "Everything okay?" I asked.

"I can't do this anymore," Sean said, as he leaned on his pillow.

Half-awake, I groaned. "What do you mean? You can't do what anymore?" I sat and looked into his eyes. Did he mean being intimate?

"This. You and me." He shrugged me away, then climbed out of bed.

"Wait. You can't leave me. We're supposed to get married someday." I wasn't sleepy anymore. Tears formed in my eyes. "What did I do wrong?"

"Nothing. I just know it's over."

"Over? Sean, I can't love anyone but you." I rose, then clung to his arm. "How can you leave me?"

"I'll take you anywhere you want to go." He left the room.

I slumped onto the floor, leaning against the bed, burying my face in my hands. How could this be happening to me? What would I do without Sean? He was all I had. What had I done to make him stop loving me? My eyes burned, and the tears wouldn't stop. Where was I supposed to go if I wasn't with him?

I wiped my wet cheeks, then ran to the bathroom and splashed cold water on my face. Maybe this whole thing was a bad dream I'd awoken from.

I called Wren. Maybe she knew where I could live. I hoped I wouldn't have to live with Mom and Mitchell again, but maybe it would be better now that I was older. I shrugged, then took a deep, shuddering breath.

Sean dropped me off in the college parking lot, and I didn't know if I'd ever see him again. My heart sank at the thought of how empty my life would be without his presence. The whole world was crashing around me. We were supposed to get married. Not break up.

I stayed in Wren's dorm room until I could get my room at the college. After I got settled into the dorms, Wren made a confession: "I prayed to God a few weeks ago that you'd return to Him. You seemed depressed, and I wanted what was best for you. I didn't know Sean would break up with you," Wren told me. "I'm sorry. It's my fault for asking God." She hunched her shoulders.

"It's not your fault," I said. It was God's fault, I told myself. He'd been the one who had said yes to her prayer. "I wish I knew what I had done wrong." I cried and wrapped my arms around her.

"It's going to be okay, Kaitlin, I promise." She patted my back. I knew she understood how I felt; she had just been through a nasty breakup.

"Thanks." I sniffled.

Sean never gave me a reason to end our relationship. At night, when all was quiet, I'd think about Sean and wonder how he was doing.

During the following semester, Wren sat next to a girl named Gwen, in Anthropology, and they became fast friends. Their professor forced them to write papers like 'Why God isn't Real.' Together, they encouraged one another to stand firm in their Christianity. Wren told me I needed to meet her new friend and that I'd like her.

Wren discovered Gwen's boyfriend was Sean. Once Wren told me this new piece of information, then I didn't like her friend, after all. Anger filled my heart. Sean had moved on? How could he? He was supposed to come back to me and realize his mistake.

A knock came at my door during the afternoon and being hungover, I hadn't dressed in my clean clothes yet. I answered the door to find Wren and someone I didn't recognize standing beside her. The girl had brown hair, fine and straight. She was pretty, in a girl-next-door way. I stared at her. Who was she? I glanced at Wren, and it suddenly dawned on me. This must be Sean's girlfriend, Wren's new friend. Good grief, Wren. When she mentioned me meeting Gwen, I never thought I would. I thought it was hypothetical. Why was his girlfriend here? What strange thought could convince Wren to bring that girl here? For Pete's sake, I was still wearing my pajamas.

"This is my sister, Kaitlin," Wren said. "Kaitlin, this is Gwen, Sean's girlfriend."

My face turned red. I glanced at Gwen again, then sucked in a breath. I had imagined the girl he'd be with to be a supermodel with a perfect figure. I never thought I'd meet her. As we stood in silence, I stared at her, trying to decipher what she had that I didn't.

The awkward moment lasted an eternity. I looked out the window at the dumpster and parking lot. Was Sean right outside waiting for her? Like he used to wait for me. No, she probably drove herself.

Wren cleared her throat. "I wanted you to meet each other. I like both of you; I know you'll get along."

What could I possibly say to this girl? I took a deep breath. "It's nice to meet you," I said, knowing I should say something and try to be polite. Now, if I could convince her to give me my boyfriend back, then everything would be right again. I crossed my arms.

"You too," she said. She cleared her throat, and she glanced around my room, looking as uncomfortable as I felt.

Wren said, "I know it's strange for you, but I felt like God wanted me to introduce you."

I loved Wren. She must want something good to come out of this encounter. I swallowed my pride and tried to be open-minded. "Can I add you to my messenger account?" I asked. If Sean loved her, she must be okay. If Wren thought we should try to be friendly, it couldn't hurt. "Then we can talk more if you want."

"Sure, my account name is saved eighty-eight."

"Mine's invisibly broken." I could try to be her friend. I wanted Sean to be happy. If it was with her and not me, then so be it. There was nothing I could do to change that. Inwardly, my heart sank.

He wasn't coming back for me.

One morning, as I sat in my dorm room, my messenger account went off on my computer, showing me, I had a new message.

It was from Gwen. It had been a month since I'd met her.

Sean is a Christian now, the message said.

He is? I asked, I was astonished. He'd claimed to be agnostic.

Yes, you planted a seed, and I watered it. God made it grow.

I responded, Thank you for telling me. I'm happy for him.

I had done nothing but hurt his chances of finding God. She was a sweet girl, giving me credit for planting a seed. I didn't even have God anymore, but I was glad Sean had Him. I sniffled. Sean had found his happily ever after, but I wished he hadn't taken mine away.

I was happy for Sean and his amazing relationships, but the emptiness inside made me hollow, like there was nothing left for me in this life. Why did Sean leave me? He'd loved me once, hadn't he? I longed to numb the pain of my broken heart. It was as if my first dad, Anthony, was leaving me all over again. Resurfacing rejection brought me further into depression.

Alcohol was the only thing that numbed my pain. When I drank with my friends, it was the only time I didn't care about Sean leaving me. I drank more and more.

After I drank regularly, I met a new guy and he asked me over to his place. Having gotten out of a relationship himself, he wanted nothing serious. I didn't care. I wasn't replacing Sean and I didn't care if the new guy and I had a real relationship or a title. It wasn't like I wanted to marry him. No one could replace Sean and there was no point in trying to.

The new guy and I drank, and one poor decision led to more. When I followed God, I never thought I'd fall into temptation, but those days had ended. Being intimate meant nothing to me anymore. It gave me no joy. I wanted Sean back.

I saw my new fling more over the next few months, and for a moment when we were together and drinking, I would pretend he loved me. Once, he even said, "That's why I love ya," but the way he said it, I knew it was a lie. If he had loved me, he would have said, "I love you," and there would have been a softness to his voice and brightness in his eyes. This "love" or whatever it was, was an afterthought. It was like he said what he thought he had in exchange for the piece of myself, I was giving away for nothing. For a while, the lie worked and the substitute for real love sufficed. Until the alcohol wore off and he left. And then I'd remember Sean.

It was morning and I wasn't feeling well so I missed class. I hugged the toilet in the dorm bathrooms and sobbed as last night's dinner emptied into the toilet. Did I have food poisoning? My stomach clenched and throbbed. Dry heaves came next. I held onto my stomach, hoping it would end soon as more of yesterday's meal lodged into the toilet.

I was alone, and an emptiness filled my heart, like I'd never smile again. Tears brimmed my eyes. There was no one to take care of me.

Staring at the tile floor, I blew my nose. Slowly, the nausea dissipated. I stood, bracing myself, my hands on my legs. Leaving the bathrooms, I returned to my dorm room and wiped the tears from my eyes. Thinking I'd better go to the doctor, I called Mom.

"Hello?" Mom's voice echoed through the phone.

"Mom, can you pick me up? I should see a doctor. This morning, I threw up. I have the flu or food poisoning."

"You aren't pregnant, are you?"

I paused for a moment, placing my hand on my stomach as I thought about the past month. "It's possible." I hoped not, because it could be this guy I'd been seeing, or someone else's. Too much time had passed for the baby to be Sean's. I hadn't kept track of my cycles, but it was possible, I guessed. Could I be pregnant?

Mom picked me up and took me to the hospital. I shivered in the car as the sun glared off the snow. Resting my hands on my legs, I rubbed them to warm.

The hospital had changed little since I'd been in it to visit Mitchell.

After checking in at the triage desk, a nurse led me to a room, then handed me a plastic cup to pee in. Mom stayed in the room while I headed down the hall. My legs were shaking as I entered the restroom. It was a routine test, yet the results could change my life forever. I wiped my hair out of my eyes. How would I raise a child on my own? What if I had twins like Mom? She had only been nineteen, then.

I returned to the hospital room after taking the test, then sat with Mom.

"If you have a baby, Kaitlin, I'll help you," Mom said, wrapping her arms around me as I sat on the cold, paper-covered exam table.

"Thanks, Mom." I gave her a half-smile. Her hug made me feel warmer.

Someone knocked on the door.

"Come in," Mom said, then she sat in a chair next to the door.

A man wearing a white lab coat walked into the room. He held a folder with my name typed on the tab.

Mom grabbed my hand.

"Not sure what you hoped for, but you are not pregnant," the doctor said.

Relief washed over me. I did not know how I would have taken care of a baby. I didn't even have a job. I knew I could've made it work, but it would have been hard.

"It's likely food poisoning. If you don't want to get pregnant, I suggest more reliable contraception. Get rest and lots of fluids and you'll be as good as new in a few days." He left the room.

I hugged Mom.

"Let's get you back to the dorms," Mom said, then wrapped her arm around me and walked me to the car.

~ Nineteen ~

Had I been pregnant during college, Mom would've helped me raise my child. Her words showed me how much she cared about me, and that she loved me despite my failures. It reminds me of Jesus and how much he loves me, despite my sin.

Sean works at a pregnancy center now, helping others who faced my situation find encouragement and support to raise their babies.

Sean's wife, Gwen, helped me while I went through a miscarriage. I was hurting and she prayed for me, showing only compassion. I am someone she could have easily hated, instead.

During college, I couldn't have known what the future held. Back then, I felt more helpless than ever, and if I believed in God at all, I wasn't sure He cared about me anymore.

Thankfully, God didn't leave me in that dark place.

Wren and I visited with Wren's friend, a girl who lived down the hall in the dormitories.

Wren's friend fixed her hair in the mirror, curls bouncing every-where. "You want to go to Chi Alpha with me? It's like a campus church." She moved away from the mirror, then plopped on one of the dorm beds.

I looked at Wren and shrugged. I didn't know what that was, but I hadn't been to church since high school.

"Where is it?" Wren asked. Neither of us drove; hopefully, it was within walking distance.

"It's in the building where we eat lunch, but it's on the top floor." She smiled. "It would be great to have you come with me."

I knew it well, it was where I used to eat lunch with Sean during Upward Bound. A pang of longing whispered through my heart. I missed him.

"It starts at six. We can walk over together. I'll meet you at your room," Wren's friend said, her eyes sparkling.

"Sure, sounds fun," I said. I guessed it couldn't hurt to try something fun and meet new people.

"All right, see you after a bit." Wren and I returned to our dorm rooms. Our rooms were across the hall from each other. Maybe we could find something to eat before Chi Alpha.

I was chatting with Wren when her friend came, and the three of us walked to the church place. We entered the building. Inside a large auditorium, the Christian radio station played over the loud-speaker, and a man with a beard and orange-red hair approached the three of us. He resembled John the Baptist, at least how I'd always imagined he'd look.

"Hi. I'm Aaron and that's my beautiful wife, Martha, over there." He pointed at the stage area where a lady stood. He shook my hand. "We're leaders for Chi Alpha Ministries. My wife is leading worship tonight. She's great, just started doing worship. You'll love her."

He gave us each a pat on the back. "I need to say hello to more people. See you all soon."

Aaron must be fearless. I'd always felt intimidated meeting new people, let alone speaking to them about Jesus.

"How are you, man?" Aaron said, somewhere behind me.

"Want to sit down? Wren's friend asked us.

"Sure," Wren said.

"Let's sit over there." Wren pointed toward the back row. Wren and her friend, and I sat.

Martha, Aaron's wife, sat on the floor off to the side of the stage area. She bowed her head as she sat next to a girl whose back shuddered. Martha wiped what I assumed must be a tear from the girl's eye.

Someone turned off the radio and then Martha stood. She walked over to a large keyboard with a microphone attached. "Let's get started," she said through the loudspeaker.

A few college students started playing the guitar behind her.

Martha sang, her voice filling the room. She had an earthy voice deep like a valley, and full of life, like a spring of water. Yet, she was vulnerable. Everyone crowded toward the front of the room, except a few who worshiped at the back. While the music played, the students swayed side to side, some with their hands in the air. Others sat, heads down, and hands folded. I stayed in my seat, preferring to watch. It reminded me of better days, sitting in Steve's living room and singing with the other kids from school. I didn't know how I'd been so brave back then; I couldn't imagine singing in front of all these people.

After five worship songs, Aaron grabbed his microphone. "This is a story from the book of John." Aaron sat on a folding chair to be at eye level with the group. He read, "'Teacher, this woman was caught in the act of adultery. In the Law, Moses commanded us to stone such women. Now, what do you say?' They were using this question as a trap in order to have a basis for accusing him." Aaron said, "The leaders often tried to trap Jesus.

"In the Bible, it says, Jesus bent down and started to write on the ground with his finger. When they kept on questioning him, he straightened and said to them, 'Let any one of you who is without sin be the first to throw a stone at her.' Again he stooped down and wrote on the ground.

"At this, those who heard began to go away one at a time, the oldest first, until only Jesus was left with the woman still standing there. Jesus straightened up, and asked her, 'Woman, where are they? Has no one condemned you?'

"'No one, sir,' she said.

"'Then neither do I condemn you,' Jesus declared. 'Go now and leave your life of sin.'"

My hands clammed and I wrung them out. This woman was like me. She wore shame like a scarlet letter, pasted across her chest as I did. I bowed my head, thinking about the story. Would I be able to stop sinning? If Jesus could forgive her, maybe there was hope for me, too. I imagined Jesus drawing a line through the sand; I imagined He did it for me.

The sermon was over. Wren, her friend, and I headed back to the dorms. Did God think I was savable or had my choices doomed me to the new life I couldn't escape? Did He care about me, despite all my mistakes? I hoped so because hope was all I had.

Wren paced her dorm room while I sat in one of her chairs by the window. We'd been doing our homework, and it was time for a break. We had nothing to eat except rice and gravy and I could not eat that for the third day in a row. There wasn't much else to do now that we finished our classes for the week. "What do you want to do now, Wren? I'm hungry."

"Let's go see my friend Matthew. He's a music major, and he lives right down the hall." Wren grabbed her guitar, and we headed down the dormitory hall. "He said we could play guitar together today."

"Wish I could play an instrument, too."

"No worries. You can sing with us." We reached the other end of the dormitories. Wren stopped walking and then knocked on Matthew's door.

A tall young man opened the door. "Come on in." Wren and I sat on the plaid couch that looked like it belonged in the '80s with a table in front of it. Matthew pulled out his guitar, then pulled out sheet music and set it on the coffee table. The smell of popcorn and men's soap filled the room.

Wren glanced at the paper Matthew had set down.

"I like this one." Matthew sat next to her on the couch and the two of them began strumming and then singing.

I recognized the song but didn't know it by heart, so I sang the chorus with them. Wren and Matthew played in perfect unison. They played a few more songs.

Matthew rose from the couch, setting his guitar back onto its stand. "Are you hungry? I have a ton of leftover macaroni and cheese. Nothing extravagant." Matthew walked toward his dorm refrigerator. "My mom made me an extra-large batch."

"Thanks. I'll take some," I said, relieved to be offered food.

Wren said, nudging my arm. "Told you we'd find something to eat."

I beamed at her. "Guess you were right."

Matthew microwaved the leftovers and handed us each a bowl. Then warmed a bowl for himself, too.

It was the best macaroni I'd ever eaten.

After we left, Wren admitted to me she had feelings for Matthew. I couldn't help being thrilled for her. Anyone that fed me when I was hungry was great in my book.

A week after the first Chi Alpha meeting, Aaron, the Chi Alpha leader, walked among the campus students in the lunchroom at the college. He stopped and talk to a few people, then moved on to the next table. He embraced everyone he encountered like he loved everyone. After he'd made his way to us, he sat at the table with Wren and me. "Hey, girls. Did I talk to you about SALT yet?"

"Uh, like the condiment?" I asked, unsure of what he meant.

He chuckled. "Sorry, I must not have. It's a youth conference for college-aged Christians. You can choose from an assortment of classes to take from journaling to evangelizing. Plus, there are key-note speakers, worship groups, and games. Would you both like to go? It'll be a lot of fun."

"Yeah, sounds like a good time. How much will it cost?" Wren asked.

"It's one hundred and twenty dollars. But if the money is all that's stopping you from coming, you're covered. We have donors that can help." His wide eyes crinkled as he smiled.

"Yeah, if I had the money, I'd go."

"All right let's do this. The trip takes place in January." A grin covered his face. He put his arms around our shoulders and squeezed. "See you soon? We will get those details worked out. God's going to take care of you girls."

"Thank you so much." I'd never been to a Christian conference. What would it be like? His belief and confidence that God could do anything reminded me of my youth pastor, Steve.

The Chi Alpha group, including Wren and me, traveled in a van to the Christian conference Aaron had invited us to. On the first day of the conference, a missionary spoke. He had experienced mirac-ulous escapes in war territories in Cambodia. His mission company brought refugees technology and equipment. He told us stories about how he had narrowly escaped armed guards because in the area he preached, Christianity was illegal to practice. His beliefs were punishable by imprisonment, but his entourage made it safely through a border without being caught.

A second speaker entered the stage after the first one left. He was a thin man with glasses. "Hello everyone, I'm happy to be here. Today, I'm going to tell you how I came to be a Christian. To start, I was a man whose past heartache altered my self-worth, and my self-image. My mother died when I was four. After her death, my father abandoned me. What followed was sexual abuse from rela-tives, which started at three."

The crowd quieted, clinging to every word.

My stomach clenched. How awful for him, and at the hands of his family, even worse.

I swallowed the lump forming in my throat. My family had fallen apart at a young age too, but I'd been older than the speaker.

"In college, Christians approached me, but I felt judged and the things they said were hurtful. Around that time, my Atheist friends called and said they'd become Christians and that they'd pray for me. I laughed at them because they had clearly lost their minds." The speaker sat on a stool on the stage, then chuckled.

"One day I read the Bible. As I learned, God revealed to me how much he loved me. God's grace, his unconditional love, love that I had so hungered for, that's what changed me. His love gave me the courage to face my pain."

He stood again, pacing the stage, then took a drink of water before continuing, "God didn't force me to change. It was hard to trust God's heart, at first, because I thought God would be like my dad and hurt me," his voice faltered.

The speaker's words stirred my soul. I wanted to have a father that loved me. Even though this man was different than me, some of our struggles were the same. I hadn't been sexually abused but it hurt thinking about my dad and how he loved me one day and then the next, he didn't. He had abandoned me, and I didn't know what I had done wrong. Was there any hope that someday someone would love me? I prayed, *Lord, the past hurts so much. I want to be loved. Please love me. Don't leave.*

I folded my hands and lowered my head, as an ache I had forgotten rose to the surface. Why did my first dad, Anthony, leave me?

I found Martha with Aaron outside the conference room after the speakers had finished. I approached them and glanced at the floor. "Can you pray with me, Martha?"

"Sure, I'd love to." She patted my arm.

"See you ladies in a bit," Aaron said, kissing Martha before leaving.

Martha and I sat crossed-legged on the floor in the wide hall of the hotel. I confessed to her how I fell short: how I'd put Sean before God, how I'd slept with him, then had a one-night stand, followed by a fling. I felt like I was drowning and couldn't get out of the water.

"It's okay, Kaitlin. We all need God's grace. None of us are perfect. Trust me, I've been where you are. Let me pray for you, hun."

Martha and I bowed our heads. I found comfort in knowing that Martha wasn't judging me. She didn't tell me I was a bad person, or that I was foolish. She didn't shun me for struggling.

I brushed my hair out of my eyes. I hadn't wanted to give in to temptation, but once I had, I couldn't control it. Only God could help me.

"Please, Lord, help Kaitlin overcome these strongholds in her life. Help her heal from her pain. I pray you wash this sin away that's keeping her separated from You. I pray she will grow to know Your heart toward her. Amen."

As the day wore on, I thought more about the baptism the conference offered. Mom said they baptized me as a baby, so I had never thought I needed to, but I felt like God wanted me to do it.

My shame was a chain, and the feelings only added to my depression. I remembered what Aaron said in his sermon about Jesus drawing a line in the sand. I had been casting stones at myself, stones I deserved. I wanted Jesus to dive into the waters with me. I needed Him to lift me up. Make me new.

I entered the enormous, humid swimming area. The chlorine scent filled my nose. Before me, steps led into the turquoise waters of the hotel's pool, like the place Sierra's dad had taught me to swim in.

Aaron and a bald preacher stood in the water. At least fifty people from the conference gathered around the pool. Some I knew, and some were strangers.

Towels sat on a shelf behind me. I grabbed one and set it aside to dry off after the baptism.

A few people entered the water before me, each one called by name.

After they had baptized seven people, Aaron announced, "Kaitlin Thomson." Aaron motioned me closer. I moved toward the pool. My hands shook, and my stomach was in a knot. I walked down three or four steps. The coolness shocked my senses, and I shivered. Ten steps forward and I reached the two men, who were in the waist-deep water.

Aaron said quietly, "Kiddo, so glad you're here."

"Thanks." I smiled nervously.

"Do you accept the sacrifice made for you?" the bald guy asked, so everyone in the room could hear.

"I do," I said, nodding as my chin chattered.

"Do you confess that you have sinned?" the bald man asked.

"I do." God knew I had. More times than I wanted to count.

"Do you confess in front of these witnesses you believe in Jesus Christ?" Aaron asked.

"I do." I sucked in a deep breath, mentally preparing to be submerged.

"Now we baptize you; in the name of the Father, the Son, and the Holy Spirit," the bald man said.

Arms caught my back as I dropped backward under the calm waters of the pool. Rising again, I became assured of my new life, my shame wiped clean.

~ Twenty ~

The SALT conference was the turning point in forgiving Anthony. For years, the memories were too painful to face, and the weight was more than I could bear. When I was young, I didn't realize I was carrying that pain and rejection into every relationship I had, expecting every man in my life to fix what was broken.

Aside from my father issues, were my sin issues. Before my baptism, my shortcomings stood stark against the beauty of God's purity. I felt so unworthy of love.

At SALT, it was as if God pulled me away from being Anthony's daughter and made me into a daughter of Jesus. That change in identity started healing me. I was no longer rejected, I was loved. I was no longer abandoned, I was found. I was no longer living in shame, but clean.

One day this year, I reached out to Anthony and asked his permission to write about him in my memoir. I hadn't spoken to him in years.

I prayed, *God if you want him in my book, he'll have to give me permission. Please make that happen.* If he said no, I needed to throw away the beginning of my book. I expected Anthony to say no but thought he deserved to know.

I waited by the phone for hours, wondering what his response would be. The next day, he texted, *You deserve to tell your story.*

He wished me well in my writing.

Recently the fears I've faced (asking permission from my ex and from Anthony to write about them) have been overwhelming. After working on a book for over a year, I had to face the lion-strength fear and be as brave as I could.

I walked into the Lion's den, expecting the destruction of my book efforts.

Instead, I learned that God was keeping the lion's mouths shut. All I needed was faith.

Mom said, "You should get a job, Kaitlin."

I had just dropped out of college because I ran out of money and couldn't afford my dorm room or drive. Mom sat beside me as we sipped on coffee in the living room of the house by the swamp.

"The gas station is hiring. If you get a job, you could get on your feet and find a place when you're ready."

I glanced at Mitchell, sitting at his computer, playing a game.

"You're probably right." I didn't want to live with Mom and Mitchell forever. Even if Mitchell was nicer now than during high school. We hadn't been arguing, but I wasn't sure if my good fortune would last.

In the afternoon, Mom took me to fill out an application. After Mom helped me enter all the right dates because her memory was better than mine. Afterward, she dropped me off at my new friend's house. I'd met him on social media the previous week, and he didn't live far from my house. His name was Eric. He lived on the same road Sierra's dad lived on. It shocked me that I had never met Eric before then because we lived in a such a small town. Even Sierra knew him, and she said he was nice. I hoped our meeting would go well. He had called me cute online, and I wanted to get to know him better. Not for a relationship, but for friendship.

The sky was clear, and the temperature was good for sweatshirts. I knocked on the door, and doubts filled my thoughts. Biting my lip,

I wondered, what was I doing here? Had I made a mistake meeting a stranger like this? My heart pounded. He was polite online; he knew many of the same people that I did. Not driving, I hadn't seen any of my college friends.

The door swung inward. "I'm Eric." His eyes met mine, they were full of pain, like Mitchell's. "Come on in. My roommates are here too, but they're in the basement. I'll introduce you if they come. Sorry, the place is a mess."

Following behind him, I passed a kitchen with empty pop cans and pizza boxes on the countertops. He kept walking, so I followed him into a room with a brown couch and a few reclining chairs. He sat on one chair. The room was like a bachelor pad, posters hung on the walls of the video game Halo.

"You can sit on the couch, and we can talk."

I sat across from him on the couch.

"So, are you seeing anyone?" He grabbed an XBOX controller off the coffee table.

He was direct, I became uneasy, not sure I wanted to tell him about Sean or anyone else but I decided honest answers were best.

"I was, a while ago. But I'm trying to have a relationship with God right now. So, no, no boyfriend. I got hurt pretty bad a while ago, and I'm still recovering."

He looked at me from where he sat, in the brown chair. "Yeah, I don't have a girlfriend. When I was younger, my girlfriend got shot by a drug dealer. The guy thought she had drugs and when she refused to give him any . . ."

His eyes reminded me of Mitchell's when his anger rose. Maybe he was like Mitchell, likely to lash out when provoked. I hadn't meant to upset him.

Filled with sympathy, I stood and sat on the floor next to him. "I'm so sorry. That must have been hard."

He started playing his game. "I still think about her. I wish I could change the past."

"Me too."

As he played his game, I continued sitting and watching.

Between respawns, he asked me, "So. You're back on the rez to stay?"

"Yeah. I've lived here so much of my life and my parents live here, so why not?"

"I saw you once at college, that's why I wondered. I think we have a mutual friend, Jack; he saw your pic on the internet and told me he knows you."

"Oh, that's cool. He's my sister Sierra's friend."

"Were you going to college there?" He killed some other character, then laughed. "What are your plans for the future?"

"No. I went to the tech school for nursing but dropped out. I've always wanted to take mission trips to Africa and Russia."

"Cool," he said. "That's talking to people about God?"

"Yeah."

"Cool." Someone killed Eric's character, he cussed, then a minute later, he respawned. "I'm a chef over at the casino. Haven't traveled much, but that sounds fun."

He played a while longer, then he threw in a pizza for us. After we ate, I called Mom and she picked me up.

Eric and I continued talking over the internet messenger and we understood each other in many ways: we'd both experienced losses, him with his ex-girlfriend and me with Sean. He didn't seem to judge me, and he wasn't cruel. Even if he did look angry sometimes. His dad had left him when he was young, too.

I was making sandwiches at my new job one afternoon when a family friend stopped at the sub shop. He stood on the other side of the counter. He was wearing his cop uniform, so he must have been on patrol duty that morning. Two years ago, Wren and I babysat his baby for him and his wife at their house.

"How are you?" he asked, his voice warm and inviting.

"Pretty good."

"When did you start working here?" He put his hands on the plexiglass separating us. "I haven't seen you in a while. Not since you and your boyfriend, Sean bought that car from me."

"I moved home recently."

"I'm glad I ran into you. I need a babysitter next week. Can you watch the girls? I have two now."

"I can do that." I finished wrapping the sub I'd been making. "I don't drive though."

"I'll pick you up." He grinned. "Since I'm a cop, maybe I'll have to teach you how."

"That would be great. See you next week." I couldn't believe I might learn how to drive. If a cop taught me, there's no way I wouldn't pass a test.

The family friend picked me up to babysit his two daughters the following week. Once we arrived at his house, he led the way upstairs. Empty liquor bottles sat on the counter. I shrugged. Lots of people drank, even officers. The kids trailed in behind me, excited to hang out with me.

"Want to see my back deck? You'll love it." He gestured for me to follow him through the living room.

"Sure." My stomach tightened. Why did he care what I thought about his deck? It's not like it was my house. He wasn't acting like himself. Usually, he was in his own world and didn't pay mind to me. He was treating me like he liked me, but that couldn't be right. I shrugged. He was Mom's friend and married to my sister's friend. I was imagining things.

Had he been drinking that morning before he'd picked me up? Maybe that's why he wasn't himself.

We walked out onto a wooden deck with tall rails and an electric grill. Wasn't I supposed to be babysitting? When would he be leaving?

"Don't you love it?"

I nodded.

"I knew you would." His tone was smooth.

The hair rose on my arms, and I wished I could escape. I brushed my hands over the goosebumps. The whole situation was strange. Like he had been thinking about me, imagining me in his house, hoping I'd enjoy it before I'd stepped foot there. I followed him back inside; where else could I go? I couldn't drive away. He lived in the middle of nowhere among tall pines and miles of dirt road. My heart pounded in my chest. Why had I been so stupid? I took a deep breath. Lord help me, I thought to myself.

He sat in his black La-Z-Boy chair. "Sit on my lap."

I didn't know what to do. What would he do if I refused? Would he hurt me? He was a lot stronger than me. As I did what he wanted, my body trembled. Shame filled me; this was wrong.

He put his arm around my waist.

Silently, I prayed, Lord please save me; I don't know what to do. I couldn't breathe.

His daughters came into the room, staring at me, their brown eyes full of confusion. Probably wondering why a girl was sitting on their daddy's lap. The youngest one's expressive eyes reminded me of myself when I was younger, back when I had first learned Sierra's dad had cheated on Mom.

"I always wondered what it would be like to kiss you. Can I?" he asked, his eyes wide, as he brushed loose hair behind my ear.

Disgust swelled in the pit of my stomach. How could he do this? How could he do this to his beautiful daughter, who was staring at us? I rose and moved away from him. "No." I moved back further. I put my hands on my hips.

His daughter's eyes had given me courage. For a moment, it felt like I was looking into the eyes of myself at her age and all the world faded around me.

"You can't kiss me." My heart pounded against my ribs, and my palms sweat.

"Why not?"

"You're married. Isn't that enough of a reason?" the words sounded strange coming out of my mouth; I couldn't believe I'd been brave enough to say them. If I didn't say them, who else would? My face burned. Who did he think he was? He wanted me to help him cheat on his wife. I pursed my lips, I would never be that person. Never.

"Okay." He stood and walked toward a closed door. "I'm going to rest a minute, sleep off this hangover. Can you watch my kids in the sandbox?"

"Yeah, no problem," I said quietly. I knelt in front of the two girls. "Want to go play outside and let your daddy rest?"

The older one shrugged, staring at her toes.

The younger one nodded, excitedly.

I extended my hands, and they grabbed hold. We walked together to the sandbox in the front yard. Sitting and playing with them. I prayed their father would change his ways and that his daughters wouldn't remember. What happened to my parents would never happen to them, not because of me.

An hour later, our family friend stood on the back porch. "Ready to go home?" he yelled.

"Yup!" I yelled back. "Come on, girls, let's get going."

I grabbed their hands and we walked to the truck. We all climbed in and headed to my house.

"I read that article you wrote for the newspaper about God and marriage. You did a great job."

Had he even read it? About how we should save intimacy for marriage? This guy had some nerve. I chewed my lip, trying to keep myself from yelling at him. He had completely missed the point. The pines blurred as we passed them along the dirt road. "Thanks, I worked hard on it."

He pulled into Mom's and Mitchell's driveway and parked, handing me twenty bucks for 'babysitting.'

I opened the truck door. "Bye." I swung the door shut before he had time to respond.

At my house, I rushed inside as quickly as my legs would carry me without running. Breathe, I told myself. Breathe. I shut myself inside my house and never looked back.

I called Eric. My heart raced from the encounter with a family friend. "Can you come to get me? Something happened with my cop friend, and I need someone to talk to."

"Sure. Be right there."

Soon he showed up and drove us to his house. I told him what happened.

"Come sit by me," Eric said. His hard, brown eyes softened. He grabbed my hand. "Don't be afraid anymore. I'll never let anyone hurt you."

At least I could trust Eric.

It was summer when Sierra and I moved, deciding to rent a house together in town, across the street from where I worked. We got to live there for cheap and my boss was the owner.

Wren's college was finished for the year, so she moved in, too and the three of us were under the same roof for the first time in years.

The living room made our voices echo as we wandered through it. The floorboards creaked as Sierra, Wren, and I walked between the upstairs' bedrooms, and through the hallway. The lathe and plaster walls needed repainting, but as we walked through, we discovered we'd each get our own room.

Sierra picked the largest room at one end of the upstairs and I chose the one on the other end. The landlord gave us a great deal, one hundred dollars per person, per month. It was close to Eric's house, about a mile-and-a-half away; it was good that it was an easy walking distance since I didn't drive.

The first night we lived there, an ear-piercing scream echoed through the house, coming from Sierra's room. Wren and I rushed into her room. She stood by a cracked window and her hands were covered in blood.

I dashed to the bathroom and grabbed a towel, then ran back to Sierra and wrapped her hands. I grabbed my phone and called an ambulance.

"Oh, it's nothing," Sierra said, her voice shaking. "The window slipped when I tried to open it."

What a rotten thing to happen on our first day in our new place. Should I complain to the landlord? I didn't know if it was his fault or not; the house was old.

"There's so much blood." Wren's face looked pale. "I'll call Mom."

Wren and I helped Sierra outside, so the ambulance could reach her more easily. The hospital was a half-mile away, but none of us had a car. First responders arrived a minute later and wrapped her hands in more appropriate cloth and tried to calm us down. The ambulance arrived and then left with Sierra.

A few minutes later, Mom came over. Wren and I rode with Mom to the hospital. Sierra got stitches in her hands after they flushed out the glass.

Sierra told me a few days later that she had gotten mad at her boyfriend and punched the window. When she told me, it didn't surprise me. A few months earlier, she had tried to hit Mitchell in the swamp house, and I pulled her away.

Wren got ready for work. She worked at a cafe diagonal from our house. Her tips from her job were enough to keep the three of us sisters eating in between both Wren's and my paychecks. Sierra had a part-time job but didn't make much extra after her share of rent and utilities.

After Eric got home from work, I visited him at his house. Sometimes he'd visit me at work, too.

A few hours after my shift started, I pulled a pizza out of the oven. Sweat beaded my forehead. There was no air conditioning.

"Hey, girl," a man said.

For a moment, my heart stopped. Please don't be the cop, I thought to myself. I peeked out from behind the oven station. Eric stood on the other side of the counter.

"Hi." My cheeks flushed from the heat and from seeing him. I cut the pepperoni pizza into triangles and then boxed it. "I'm about due for a break. Want to smoke?"

"I have some extra." He smiled at me. His pearly teeth were bright against his dark skin; they gleamed.

The two of us headed outside the gas station and smoked on the sidewalk.

"I've been thinking, we should record some songs together. My dad and I played in a blues bar. Did I tell you that?" He blew out a puff of smoke, his thick lips forming a circle.

"No, you didn't. That's so cool." I flicked the ashes off my cigarette.

"Yeah, we were amazing. I might have signed a contract if I didn't move from Nashville." He wrapped his arm around me. "I better head home. I'll be busy for a couple of days; the boys and I have an online tournament. After that, we should get together."

"Sounds great. See you, then."

He kissed my cheek, then left.

I sat in my room reading my Bible after work. I heard clomping downstairs and the old screen door slamming. My heart thudded in my chest. Was someone breaking in? We didn't own anything worth stealing. I wished I had something to defend myself. A minute later, someone climbed the creaking stairs. Should I holler for Wren? I stood, but then couldn't move. Who would visit this late? Maybe one of Sierra's friends was coming over. She was a night owl. I hoped it was one of them anyway.

Eric stumbled into the room and flopped onto my bed.

"Why are you here?" I gasped, catching my breath, my heart pounded inside my chest. He said he'd be too busy to see me. "Is everything okay? Are you hurt?"

He gulped. "No. Where am I? I need my dad. I don't know where he went." He sobbed, wrapping his arms around me, falling against me, limp.

He didn't smell like alcohol, but he smelled like he'd brushed his teeth. The sickly-sweet scent of his cologne was so thick I couldn't be sure if he was sober.

I thought he had been playing video games with his boys. I patted his forearm. "You'll be okay. You can sleep here. Get some rest." I tilted my head, looking at him carefully, then bit my lip. I cared about him and didn't want him to be unhappy. How he was acting didn't make any sense. Arriving at my house, unannounced, in the middle of the night, wasn't okay.

Eric laid down again and fell asleep, snoring as he lay in my bed. That night, I lay on the floor next to my bed, wondering what in the world he was doing at my house. I didn't want to wake him because I didn't know if he was drunk or delusional.

The next morning, he asked me how he had gotten to my house.

"I have no idea. You might have walked." I shrugged. "You were talking about your dad and then you fell asleep."

"Weird." He climbed out of my bed and grabbed his belongings. "See you later?" His demeanor was too casual for such an odd situation.

"Sure. Not in the middle of the night though, okay?" My fingers grazed his arm.

He laughed, then kissed me on the forehead and left.

I arrived at Eric's house. I hadn't seen or heard from him, so I stopped by to see if he was okay. If we were okay. I knocked on the door and Eric's roommate let me in. A blonde girl cried on the couch, she was a few years younger than me, I recognized her from high school. Her eyes were pools of sorrow. Eric had his arm around her, speaking in hushed tones to her. That was why I hadn't heard from him because he was too busy with this girl.

I stopped in my tracks and then turned to the door. "I need to leave," I said quietly to no one in particular. "I don't know what this is." I turned the handle. "I'll see you later."

The girl stood, moving away from Eric. "I stopped by because my boyfriend is such a jerk. I knew Eric would understand; he's a great guy; it's not what you think." She stared at him, her eyes burrowing into his. I'd seen that look before, it was hunger, she wanted to be with my boyfriend.

Maybe she already was.

Goosebumps rose on my arms. After not seeing or hearing from him all week, I came to visit him, and some girl is sitting on his couch and crying on his arm. My blood boiled. "I'll . . . see you later, Eric. I don't have time for this. I need to get to work." I headed outside of the house he and his roommates were renting.

Outside, the rain was coming down in sheets. I wrapped my arms around myself and lifted my sweatshirt hood over my head. I would need to walk quickly or run before I was soaked through. I quickened the pace, heading toward the house where I lived with Sierra and Wren. The heat from the pavement made the rain steam as it landed. I'd been such a fool to believe that Eric wanted me. He was like Sean. And Anthony. And Smith. I stomped through a puddle, not paying attention to where I was going.

Behind me, loud crashing echoed, heavy footsteps getting closer. Was someone going to rob me? I didn't have any money on me. Walking alone on the rez might not have been the best idea. A shiver crept down my spine; I quickened my pace, then peaked behind me.

Eric was jogging down the street headed right for me.

I stopped, letting out a breath.

When he saw that I'd seen him, he stopped coming so quickly. Panting, he grasped at his heart, then put his hands on his knees. He wasn't in the best shape, so I turned around and jogged over to him, hoping he wasn't hurt. "Are you okay?"

He grabbed my face and kissed me without answering. His warm mouth suffocated mine. "Please don't leave me. That girl is a friend. You didn't think—?" He paused, grabbing my hands. "I promised I'd never hurt you and I meant it."

Wren and I had the day off. She sat next to me on the couch in the living room of our rental house. "I think I'm going to go visit my friend Matthew." He was more than her friend, but it wasn't official.

"He's finally finished with basic training, and I miss him. He says I can stay a while."

I didn't blame her for wanting to go, this town wasn't the nicest place to live. "I forgot he left. How will you get there? Is Mom going to drive you?" I asked.

"No. I don't think she'd drive me that far. There's a bus I can ride, and it'll take me to South Carolina."

"Are you sure it's safe?" I frowned, I didn't want anything to happen to Wren, and riding on a bus sounded sketchy.

"It'll be fine. My boss gave me some mace." She laughed. "If all else fails, I'll spray anyone who gets too close." She was feisty, I'd give her that much.

Wren called me a short time after going to South Carolina to tell me that she married Matthew in a private ceremony at the ocean. I was glad she'd ridden off into the sunset with someone who loved her and made her happy. Someday it would be my turn, I hoped it wouldn't take long.

~ Twenty-One ~

Wanting what others have, led me down roads better off not traveled in 2007. It's not that I was unhappy, but the desire to be married was driving my actions. I was tired of waiting for Mr. Perfectly Right to come along. (By the way, spoiler alert: He is a myth.) Instead, I'd recommend waiting for the one God puts into your life for marriage, someone who shares your beliefs and values.

In my search for the "right" man, I made so many mistakes. I desperately wanted to follow God but when it came to men, the pressures were killing my identity in Christ. I wanted so desperately to be loved by a man, despite the enormous amount of love God offered me.

That year, Sierra, Eric, and I moved to an apartment building one town over. We had lived together for a few months, and I hoped things would get better, but they hadn't.

The Halo game blared through the living room of our apartment. Eric threw his headset against the entertainment center. Cussing, he lit a cigarette, even though he had finished one. He turned to look at me, disgust covered his face. "Babe, grab me a coke. I'm going to beat this tool."

Why couldn't he get it himself? I wasn't someone he could boss around all the time. I scoffed, then walked to the fridge and returned a minute later with his coke. All he wanted was for me to be his personal waitress. If I left the house, would he even notice? Probably when he needed another soda. I felt invisible in his world of video games and electronics. Someday he'd love me, I told myself.

Eric cleared his throat. "I forgot to tell you, I got fired for punching my boss. Looks like you'll need to get a job." Eric put his headset back on and respawned in the Halo game, given another chance to shoot his enemies.

Why couldn't he get another job? Why did I need to be the one? I didn't ask. Maybe if I got a job, he'd have to get off his butt and grab his own soda. With that satisfaction, I hopped online and filled out a few applications.

I walked into Burger King, my first real day on the job. The place smelled like fried onion rings. The grease made a sizzling sound as a girl dropped a basket of fries into oil.

"Fries down," she hollered.

Metal dishes banged as the person washing dishes dropped a few pans onto the floor. Two girls, a few years younger than me, scurried behind the counter filling orders.

Standing at the back wall, I punched my timecard for the second time. Yesterday at training was my first time punching the clock. My pulse raced as I walked toward the front of the service area. The uniform's "mom jeans" dug into my skin; I tugged on the waist for the third time since dressing. No one's butt looked good in those pants, I told myself for reassurance; I'd fit right in.

I stared at the register's screen, trying to remember the instructions the boss explained yesterday. The ball cap with a Burger King logo made my forehead itch. I waited for the customer, a chubby man with a polo shirt, to approach me and order. He had been my test driver at the DMV a few years earlier and I'd almost sworn at him that day because he refused to pass me. Ugh. It wasn't a great start to my first shift. I hoped he didn't remember me.

At last, he ordered. I stumbled through his instructions, clicking on the screen, and scrolling through the options. My fingers clutched the microphone, trembling. I'd never liked talking in front of people. "Chicken fried, ugh . . ." Feeling like an idiot, heat rushed to my cheeks; I didn't know what it was called exactly. I scratched at my forehead again. The screen said *salad*. I groaned. Pressing the *talk* button, I said, "Sorry, I'd like the crispy chicken sandwich—whatever that's called—not the salad." I hoped they'd know what I meant. "I'll fix it and get your change."

The DMV tester mumbled something and then moved to the pick-up side of the counter.

I backed away, took a deep breath, and wrung out my fingers. I turned to find my boss to see if he could help.

The boss sauntered by. "I don't pay you to stand there, sweetheart. Move."

I gulped the forming lump in my throat and wiped away the beaded sweat under the brim of my hat. I was not his sweetheart.

Before I could ask for my boss' help, a guy nudged my arm. "Name's Tommy," his voice was cheerful. "Don't worry about him; he's mostly harmless. I'll fix your order. Let me take the next one." He typed onto my computer's touch screen, then fixed the order, handing me the change.

I gave the DMV driver the right change and then breathed a sigh of relief. At least that blunder was fixed.

The guy named Tommy walked away, and I glanced too long. I was wrong about the jeans; they looked good on him. He wiped the counter two, three, and four times. He smiled at me. The counter looked clean to me, so why was he still wiping it?

When Tommy's arms flexed, I swooned. No, I told myself, don't look at him, you have a boyfriend. Eric was at home, waiting for me, and I couldn't think about Tommy; it wasn't right.

During my second week at work, Tommy and I worked as window order takers. We wore headsets and shared conversations through the microphones during drive-thru breaks.

Tommy confessed, "the pricing system at Burger King is rigged. If you order everything individually, it's cheaper."

"Really?" I asked, surprised at the confession.

I would have to try that on my next fifty percent off Burger King meal that we got for being employees.

My boss, who wore the other headset, buzzed by. "Keep it professional, and don't teach her that stuff; it makes us lose money."

Tommy walked over and leaned close. "Customers are always right. Give them a good deal."

I giggled at his rebellious behavior toward our franchise, a real rebel, I told myself. He always made me laugh and his eyes brightened every time he saw me or was it my imagination? I didn't know. Standing near the fry bin, I glanced at the next ticket waiting to be filled, then made eye contact with Tommy as he finished typing in a window order.

Tommy called out to me, "Let me get that drink for you. You can get the fries for my order."

"Sounds good," I said. I liked working with someone who worked well with me.

I approached the window and Tommy, with the bag of food in my hand. I gave the order to the customer outside of the window. The warm summer air filled my lungs.

Tommy stared at me, smiling, his dreamy eyes gleaming. "Long arms. Wow. You're getting good at this."

"Thanks."

I filled the next drink order at the same time as Tommy, mine for the front counter and his for the window. Our forearms crisscrossed and a shiver swept through my spine.

Our boss strutted over to Tommy and me. "Less talking, more working."

I flinched, spilling Sprite on Tommy's forearm. My shoulders tensed as I searched his face for irritation or anger, remembering that he mentioned not liking things that were sticky or dirty.

"No big deal." Tommy laughed and my tension eased. "I need to wash my hands anyway; I'll get my arms too." He nudged me, then headed toward the restroom.

I watched him leave and counted the minutes until he came back. Meanwhile, I returned to my workstation.

I clocked out at the end of the shift and scanned the schedule looking for Tommy's name. My boss always corrected me, and my supervisors didn't seem to like me, either. They'd let me work during the rushes, then sent me home. At most, I worked four hours shifts, so I didn't qualify for a break. I told myself if I was going to keep working at Burger King, for such measly pay, and for short shifts, then I'd be working with Tommy. I put in a request to change my hours.

After a few weeks, the boss moved Tommy to cooking duty, probably to separate us. No matter how much I explained that I wanted to be on fry duty because I didn't like people; I was always stuck in the "front of the house." During one of my conversations with Tommy, he said don't feel bad, the attractive people worked up-front; but Tommy was in the back, and he was better looking than I was. All the girls liked him, giggling every time he talked to one of them. After one shift, two of the girls confessed to having crushes on him. I told them I had a boyfriend at home, but Tommy seemed nice. I didn't tell them how sometimes I got lost in his eyes or wondered what he was like outside of work. I didn't tell them the only reason I still worked there, was to see him. What would it be like to date Tommy? I pushed the thought from my mind for the third time that day.

At home after work that night, I wondered at Tommy's assertion that I was attractive. When he said the attractive people worked up-front did he mean me? Maybe I was being presumptuous or maybe it was true; I hadn't been called attractive for a long time. I'd been in the relationship with Eric for a while, so I hadn't thought about anyone else. Until Tommy.

At the end of the next Burger King shift, the grease sizzled behind me as I dialed Eric's number. I asked Eric if he could pick me up. "Why can't you walk home, it's only two miles?"

My cheeks flushed; the agitation made my blood boil. If he didn't care about me, maybe Tommy would. "Fine," I said. "Whatever." I hung up the phone.

I peeked around to where Tommy was dumping fry baskets, sweat beaded his brow. I smiled at him through the gap in the fry warmer. "Think you could give me a ride home when you're done? My boyfriend, Eric, can't. Guess he's too busy playing video games or something."

"Love to. I'm off in half an hour if you don't mind waiting."

That night, Tommy dropped me off by my front door.

When I walked into our apartment, Eric was staring at the TV screen playing Halo again. He never asked how I'd gotten home, and I didn't tell him. I sat beside him on the couch, as he yelled into the headset.

As if realizing I was there, he asked, "Hello, babe. Home already?"

It was my day off and Eric sat next to me on the couch in our apartment. Sierra was upstairs hanging out with one of her friends and so we had the living room to ourselves.

"Babe," Eric said, concern filling his eyes. "I got to talk to you, let me pause the game."

I wasn't sure what was going on, but something was off with Eric.

He never asked me to sit close to him, and he was distant. "What is it? Are you okay?" Was he breaking up with me? I guess it wouldn't surprise me too much.

"I'm going to go live with my mom until she gets settled in her place." He put his hand on my leg.

"Don't worry about it, it's temporary."

I turned to look at him; he seemed sincere. Maybe he wouldn't leave me as I'd thought. "I'll see if my sister can pay the rent on her own. If I move out then help her here and there, I'm sure she'd be okay."

His eyes grew harder, losing their sheen appearance. "No. You're misunderstanding. There's one extra room at my mom's place, so my sister and I will share. I won't stay there long, and then I'll come back here. I'll visit all the time."

I wanted to hit him. It was just another reason to disappear as everyone else had. "Fine."

He kissed me on the cheek, then after grabbing the rest of his stuff, he left with his mom.

I paced the living room of my apartment. It smelled like ramen; it was all Sierra ate. Except when she ate hotdogs which were worse. My stomach growled. I opened the freezer and pulled out a pizza pocket. I started the microwave. The hot pocket finished cooking, so I removed my meal, carrying the plate to the living room.

I sat on the couch and texted Eric: Where are you? I thought you were stopping by soon.

No response.

I ate, then checked my phone again. Still no response. He was supposed to visit yesterday, but he never came. Was he mad at me or something? If he wanted to be with me, why wasn't he returning my calls? Was he with someone else?

I placed my plate in the sink, then smoked a cigarette. Still, he hadn't texted.

I called my female friend from Burger King. She used to go to Chi Alpha with me in college. At work, earlier that day, she had mentioned going bar hopping or doing something together tonight.

"Still want to do something tonight?" I asked.

"I need to do some late-night shopping at Walmart. We go there, then back to my house and hang out, watch some movies, maybe go to the bar."

"That sounds great," I said.

"Want me to invite Tommy?" she asked. "You like him, don't you?"

Was it wrong to hang out with him, as a friend? It wasn't like Eric was ever around. "I don't know if I like, like him. He's nice. You can invite him," I said. I wasn't going to wait around for Eric, who didn't have the time of day for me.

Changing into nice clothes, I smiled at myself in the mirror. I'd have fun, with or without Eric. I couldn't sit around waiting for someone who didn't love me. I blew a kiss in the mirror, then went downstairs. Eric always treated me like I didn't matter, and I would rather be with people who thought I was important.

After late-night shopping, the three of us, my two friends and I, went over to my female friend's house and she cooked us some Chinese food. We played music and talked, and then we called it a night. Tommy went home and I stayed with my friend for a sleep-over. She had offered to bring me to work the next day since she worked too.

At work a few days later, I checked the schedule to see which days I was scheduled. Scanning the paper, I saw all my three-hour shifts, from ten AM to one PM all week. Not a decent shift in sight. I rolled my eyes; they had scheduled me for the lunch rush. Again. It made me feel like they were using me, without wanting to trust me with a real shift.

When I got home, I told myself I'd apply for a job at Walmart. I couldn't live on four-hour shifts. I had worked hard and always been on time. Lots of people didn't show up for work, but I always did. I searched for Tommy's hours, and he started at three or four in the afternoon, always a few hours after my shifts ended. I washed my hands. I'd never see him now.

It was a few weeks later, and I got hired for a new job at Walmart. For a month, I worked at both Burger King and Walmart. Working out a schedule between two jobs was its own job so I left Burger King.

Wren was home from South Carolina for a visit with her husband, Matthew. I hadn't seen her in months. Her cute, five-months-pregnant belly was as hard as a rock when I put my hand on it. I couldn't believe she was going to have a baby. If only I could be that happy. Wren, Sierra, and I sat in the living room of my apartment.

"What's happening with me and Eric?" I asked Wren and Sierra as I paced through my living room as if they knew more than me. I wondered if they thought he was cheating on me, too. Maybe I was paranoid. Maybe he just wanted to break up with me but didn't know how.

Wren sat on the couch. "I don't know. I'm sorry he's being a jerk. What's up with this Tommy guy? I thought Eric was your boyfriend?"

"I don't know." I gulped. "Eric cared about me last week, now he isn't returning my calls. Instead of staying at my place most nights, like he used to, now he stays at his mom's house." It didn't feel like we were together, so what was the point of trying? "He wants to play video games and live in la-la land. He's too busy playing games to want me."

"Why don't you come and stay with us in South Carolina? Get some ocean air and take a break from Eric?"

"Can I?" I had never seen the ocean—not since I was old enough to remember. When I visited our aunt in the south with Grandma, we never saw the ocean. "The beach sounds great." This would be an opportunity to figure out if I wanted to be with Eric or not. I wanted to get married and start a family, and Eric had taken so much of my time already.

I was nearing the end of my late-evening shift at Walmart, and soon I would need to call Wren and see if she could pick me up from work. I could walk, but it was dark outside, and I was afraid of the dark.

Tommy walked inside the store; I couldn't believe he was there. My heart fluttered at seeing him; I had missed him. Did he come to see me? No. That couldn't be true. I smiled in his direction and waved.

He must have seen me because he headed toward me. He reached my checkout line. "How are you?" He fiddled with the loop on his pants. "Didn't realize you'd be here; I'm grabbing a movie." He smiled. "We've all missed you at Burger King. I've been thinking it might be time for me to find a different job."

"I don't miss Burger King. Maybe the people." Did he miss me like I missed him? I leaned forward against my register, getting closer to Tommy. "They're hiring here." It would be perfect; we'd see each other all the time, again.

"Yeah, I would because you're here, but I don't think it's for me."

Did he want to be around me? The compliment made me smile and I tried to hold back a giggle. I gestured at the clock on the wall. "I get off work fifteen if you want to hang out."

"That sounds good, I'd like that. I'll meet you upfront." He smiled and then walked in the direction of the movies.

I met Tommy at the front of the store after work. I was so excited to see him after the past few weeks. "Can I make you something to eat at my place? My sisters are both home, so you can meet them if you want to."

"Sure. I'd like that."

We wandered through the store. I didn't care what we ate; I just wanted to be with him. I grabbed a box of instant couscous and Triscuit crackers, hoping it was good enough to feed him something easy. The refrigerated section was freezing. Goosebumps rose on my arms; I rubbed them down.

"Are you cold?" Tommy asked as we reached the refrigerated section. "I have a sweater in my car you can borrow."

I clutched a package of Pepper Jack cheese. "Yeah, let's get out of here."

At the checkout, Tommy offered to pay, but I didn't let him.

I opened the door to my apartment for Tommy to come in, laughing at a joke he'd said so hard I lost balance. Wren and Sierra sat on the recliners with a look of confusion.

"Tommy, this is my twin sister, Wren, and my sis, Sierra," I said.

Sierra said, "Oh . . . your friend?" She winked. "Are you sure this isn't your boyfriend, KD?"

My face flushed, and I turned to Tommy. "Don't mind them."

Inside my apartment, in the kitchen, I sliced cheese and boiled water for the couscous. I threw in some microwave burritos for good measure. Tommy teased me about what I called cooking but said it was delicious. We sat at the small table devouring our late-night snack. The two of us finished eating and then we sat on the couch to start Tommy's DVD.

Someone fumbled with the door outside.

I looked at Tommy.

"It's probably my sister's friend."

Before I could answer it, the door swung open, and Eric appeared.

Eric scoffed as his gaze landed on Tommy. "What's this guy doing here?"

I rose from the couch, putting my hands on my hips. "None of your business. What are you doing here? I haven't heard from you, and then you show up out of the blue!?"

"Come outside with me, I need to talk to you for a minute," Eric said, his eyes wide, and glazed. Was he breaking up with me? He'd been gone so much I assumed he'd found someone else and didn't want me anymore. It was a relief to think I was finally free from him and his games.

I turned to Tommy. "I'm sorry, excuse me for a minute. I'll be right back."

He nodded at me, giving me a small smile, then turned his attention to the movie.

I followed Eric outside, my heart racing, pounding against my ribs. Would he think I'd been cheating on him? I liked Tommy because he was always nice to me, but I hadn't done anything physical with him. I had thought about it but hadn't given in to the desire.

Eric pulled me into an embrace and kissed me passionately.

I pushed him off me. "What are you doing? I haven't heard from you for a month; you don't answer my calls. You're probably seeing someone else. What, did you get dumped or something?"

"There's no one but you." He scoffed. "But whatever."

"I . . . I don't believe you. I'm trying to hang out with my new friend and you're being very rude."

He backed away from me. "There's no way that guy is just your friend. I see how you look at him." He lifted his hands in the air, then shrugged. "You used to look at me like that." He kicked at something invisible on the ground.

"If you were here more, he wouldn't be. He is my friend. Just my friend and you're being mean to him. He gave me a ride home, that's all and then I invited him over for a movie." I rolled my eyes at Eric, then walked back inside. He had the nerves to tell me what I should do with my life when he couldn't bother to be present. Where were his video games now?

Tommy stood as I came in, DVD in hand. He leaned close and whispered, "I'd better get home. I'll see you later."

It sent a shiver down my spine, having him so close.

He stole a glance at Eric, then headed toward the door. I looked at Tommy, confusion in my eyes. I hadn't meant to hurt him. Maybe I could go with him if he wanted my company. It seemed like he did.

I turned to Eric who now stood inside the apartment. "I'm leaving too," the words tumbling out before I could stop them. "You can't treat my friends like that."

Eric stood there, mouth agape. "You're my girlfriend, not his."

"I am not your girlfriend! You left me!" I sprinted after Tommy. "Wait for me!" I slammed the door shut, separating myself from Eric.

Tommy and I climbed into his car.

"Why's he acting like that?" Tommy asked.

I shrugged. "He left a few weeks ago and I haven't heard from him since." I pulled out my smokes, then put them away, because it would be rude to smoke in Tommy's car since he didn't smoke. "Figures he'd show tonight. He thinks I'm cheating on him with you."

Tommy buckled his seatbelt. "He seems like a jerk; we both know you haven't cheated on him." He gave me a sympathetic smile. "Want to do something fun? I'll show you where I go to think."

"Thought you'd never ask." I hoped Eric wouldn't follow us, but once we were out of sight of the apartment, I knew he wouldn't. He didn't care about me that much. He only wanted me now because someone else did.

Tommy drove to a nearby college and parked near the water. Boats were attached to docks, beneath a clear sky.

"Are you sure we can be here?" I teetered as I lifted my leg off the dock and into a boat anchored to it. The warm air caressed my face as I looked out at the dark waters.

"Why not? We aren't hurting anything. It probably belongs to the University."

I smiled; he was probably right. I doubted the campus police checked the boats often and we weren't drunk or anything. The boat jostled as we flumped in pleather captain seats, sitting side by side. Waves lapped against the boat, making the boat have a gentle rocking motion. "It's beautiful." I wanted to grab his hand but didn't.

Tommy leaned close and pointed above us. "See that? That's the Big Dipper and the Summer Triangle."

I loved the stars because they reminded me of God. Sitting underneath them reminded me how small I was and how big God was. "You believe in God, Tommy?"

"I don't think I ever will. Do you?" he asked.

"Ever since I was little." It seemed silly to me that Tommy didn't believe in God, but that he was fascinated with stars. Didn't he know that God made them? I imagined a meteor shooting across the sky and wondered if the universe had brought us together. No, it didn't work that way. I shook my head in the dark.

That night, Tommy didn't talk about his ex-girlfriend, the one he always talked about when he drove me home. He told me she'd broken up with him because he was clingy. I wished someone would cling to me. Not when it was convenient, but all the time. It seemed like everyone changed their minds about me. Did Tommy even like me? It was probably my imagination. I shifted in my captain's seat and buttoned my sweater.

Would he miss me if I went away as his ex had? I didn't ask.

Tommy and I walked to the dorms and talked until there was nothing else to say and silence sufficed. Inside the lobby, where there were TVs and comfortable couches, I rested my head on his shoulder and fell asleep.

Tommy texted me the afternoon after we'd been at the boat docks. He asked if I wanted to hang out and watch a movie. I opened my laptop and changed my status to single on social media, just in case Eric was confused about where we stood. He spent more time online than he ever did with me, so I knew he'd see it.

The following night, Tommy invited me over for a movie at his place. Inside his apartment were perfectly cleaned tiles and no dirty dishes in the sink. It smelled like Pinesol inside. We sat down on the living room floor because he didn't have a couch and watched the movie, we had tried to watch at my house the night Eric barged in. We paused the movie halfway through to talk. For some reason, we couldn't get into the movie. Probably because I was too distracted with Tommy being so near.

"I was supposed to have a date tonight," he said.

"Oh." I guessed this meant that this wasn't a date, and we were just friends. My heart sank a little, but I reminded myself that it wasn't like we were exclusive. "So, what happened?"

"She canceled on me. Said something came up." He pressed his lips together in a tight line.

"I'm sorry, I'm sure it's nothing you did." I hoped I'd be able to cheer him up. I patted his shoulder. "I'm sure she'll reschedule, you're a great guy."

"You really think so?"

"Of course."

"Well, I had planned to make one of my favorite meals for her, but I was wondering, since she canceled, are you hungry?" He gave me a look like he was trying to entice me. "It's snow pea stir-fry."

It sounded fancier than the couscous and Triscuit crackers I had made him. He really went all-out for his dates. I wished he had asked me on a date instead of her.

For the next week, Tommy and I spent parts of every day together. In between visiting with him, I visited with Wren. I told Tommy I had to leave for a while and that I was going to South Carolina to live with my sister. I quit Walmart and left. I told Tommy I didn't know how long I'd stay.

~ Twenty-Two ~

Being alone and abandoned were my greatest fears. At the time, I didn't know if I wanted Eric or Tommy, only that I wanted someone. If I had waited for my current husband, things might have worked out differently, some for the better, and some for the worse.

For days, I visited the different sights in South Carolina and wondered what a future with Tommy would look like or if we even had a future. He should've come with me to South Carolina. Stuck his toes in the sand with me. I pictured him relaxing to the sound of the crashing waves with me by his side. Having him nearby would've been so nice. Pulling out my phone, I texted him a picture of the ocean, with a message, *Wish you were here*. He responded, *Me too*.

I walked along the shore, listening to my MP3 player Eric bought me the Christmas before. Images of the past few weeks flashed through my mind. Tommy had made me snow pea stir fry from scratch with carefully sliced pork that tasted even better than restaurants made. And the night we walked around town talking. Or the time he let me kiss him after Eric and I broke up.

Those were the best memories, but then the other memories came. Tommy was quirky sometimes, like how he measured his cereal to make sure his portions were just so. And how he'd scrub things over and over until his hands looked raw. Would he measure my worth on some scale like he measured his cereal? Would I feel like I didn't measure up? Eric didn't care how much I ate, and he certainly didn't measure his food. Life might be more comfortable with him than with Tommy. I shook my head. How was I supposed to choose?

I needed to be in the moment and let go of the thoughts inside my head. Maybe neither one of them was right for me.

Tommy and I talked on the phone, me on one side of the country and him on the other. I hoped being beneath the same sky and phone calls were enough for us. Did he love me or want me to return? Or was he respecting my wishes, afraid I'd say no? I didn't ask. When his girlfriend left, she said he was clingy. Why wasn't he acting that way toward me? Maybe he didn't care about me as much as I thought.

At the military hospital, machines beeped beside Wren as she lay in the hospital bed, writhing in pain.

"The baby's head is crowning," the doctor said. "Get ready to push hard."

Excitement filled my heart; It was time to meet my niece and I couldn't wait.

Wren pushed.

"One more big push," the doctor yelled, her voice startling me.

"You can do it. You got this," I said, then patted her leg.

Wren let out a sob, then screamed as she pushed again.

A minute later, the doctor was holding a sweet baby.

After weighing and measuring, a nurse wrapped Wren's baby in a clean blanket and handed her to Wren. I couldn't believe how much I loved another human being, such a precious baby. From the second I first saw her, my heart swelled, growing larger to make room for my niece. I wanted a family of my own but didn't know if it would happen.

"I wish our real dad, Smith, could meet her." Wren gazed lovingly at the infant in her arms. "If I could find a way, maybe he'd want to meet her. I know it's crazy." She glanced at me; her eyebrows furrowed. "It's a dumb idea, isn't it?"

"Of course not. That's not dumb at all." I brushed a stray strand of hair behind her ear.

Wren's husband got the baby from Wren and then rocked her. "We are allowed to send a letter to anyone in the service." He kissed his daughter. "The service sends it, but we aren't allowed to know the address. It's the recipient's choice to respond or not. I don't want you to get your hopes up; he might not want to talk."

"He has the right to know his first grandchild was born," Wren said. She pushed the button on the bed to sit more upright.

"I'll talk to my superior," Matthew said.

The following week, Wren sent the letter telling him about the birth of his first grandchild.

We knew little about our biological dad. We knew what Mom had told us over the years, and what I had learned on my visit south to meet Smith's sister. There was no way to know whether to expect a call from him or not. For Wren's sake, I hoped he called.

Two weeks after being home from the hospital, Smith called Wren.

After she finished talking to him, Wren handed me the phone. My stomach tightened. What should I say to the man who would have been my dad under different circumstances? I walked outside and sat on Wren's porch swing. "Hello?"

"This is Smith. My friends call me Smitty. How are you?"

I wondered why he didn't use his first name, but I didn't ask. "Good, I came to stay with Wren for a while, mainly for a vacation and to meet my first niece. We've been having a lot of fun. We even did karaoke once at the dive bar. We've both been working at an exotic bird store."

"I'm in Germany, so I can't visit you, but I wanted to reach out since I got your sister's letter. I'm sure that wasn't what you wanted to hear."

"Germany, wow." I swung on the porch swing. "It's okay." I hadn't been expecting too much. "What do you like to do?" I hoped we had things in common.

"I like parasailing, skydiving, those sorts of things. Stuff to get the adrenaline pumping, but I'm high ranking, so I work a lot. Work first, then play. I have two kids, a boy, and a girl. I haven't told them about you girls. Not yet. I'm waiting until the time is right."

He hadn't told his kids about us. Wasn't that a big deal? We weren't exactly young anymore, he had twenty years to tell them. I pursed my lips. "That's okay, it's your decision," I said. Something in his voice told me, he'd never tell them. "So, what happened with you and Mom?"

"I joined the military when I was young. Your mom and I saw each other for a while, but it didn't work out for whatever reason. It's been so long. Anyway, I've been in the military since. Even made my way up to Master Chief."

I was glad he was so accomplished, but it wasn't something I valued.

"That's neat." I didn't know much about the military, but I remembered Wren telling me it was high ranking. I shivered, wishing I had brought a jacket outside with me. It was November and despite not being as cold as Minnesota, it was chilly.

"I'll call you when I get back to the states," he said.

"Thanks for calling Wren. I know it meant a lot to her, to us." I hung up the phone. I doubted he'd ever call again.

Holding my head low, I returned inside the house. I was already used to life without him, so nothing would change there.

"How'd it go with Dad?" I asked Wren.

"Eh, I don't know."

"Yeah." I frowned. "Not sure our relationship with him will amount to much."

"Probably not."

I hugged her. "At least we have each other."

The night after I talked to Smith, I sat on the porch swing outside Wren's military house when Wren handed me the phone. Had Smith called again? Was it Tommy? I had talked to him after Smith had called, but maybe he wanted to talk again. I held the phone to my ear. "Hello?"

"It's me, Eric."

It caught me off guard; I hadn't heard Eric's voice in so long, I forgot how he sounded. Why was he calling me? Couldn't he leave me alone? "Hey."

"Please come back," his voice sounded low and scratchy. "I can't live without you. You're the one I want; I broke up with my girlfriend for you."

"For me?" I was confused. I hadn't asked him to break up with anyone. "Your girlfriend?" I'd been gone a few months and he had already replaced me. I took a deep breath and realized I had replaced him, too. The feelings I used to have for him rushed back to my mind. He used to care about me, listen, and encourage me to keep trying. My lungs tightened and I felt sad at the love we had lost. I didn't know what happened to that man, maybe he was buried inside.

"Yeah. I broke up with her. She's not important. Listen, if you come back, I bought a ring."

I couldn't believe it. Something in his voice moved me—desperation? He loved me enough to buy me a ring when we weren't even together? Was he sure I'd say 'yes'? I was both irritated and excited.

"Okay." I sighed. "I'll think about it." Maybe I'd be able to have my own family, after all. Maybe he would change and have time for me. No, he'd never give up his games for me. "You know, Eric, I'm not sure that's a good idea." I bit my lip. What about Tommy? This would hurt him. I slumped onto the ground.

"I will marry you like you always wanted."

Maybe seeing me with someone else had opened his eyes to how he'd treated me. Maybe he would love me now.

The next day, I called Tommy and broke the news that Eric wanted me back and that I had to try to fix it because he loved me. I hoped Tommy would tell me not to, that he loved me too much to give me up. I wanted him to say, come back but he didn't. My heart hurt at his lack of passion. Eric seemed passionate to have me back.

In response to my confession, Tommy said, "I knew you'd go back to him." I could tell it hurt from the tone of his voice. "I should've known this would happen," he continued. He didn't hang up but stayed on the line. Silent.

It felt like a breakup to me, even though we'd never been anything official.

"I'm so sorry. It's nothing you did." Part of me didn't want to believe my time with Tommy was ending, because he made me happy, but I couldn't be with both him and Eric. It wouldn't be right.

"So, this is goodbye, I guess," he said.

"Goodbye, Tommy. Miss you." I hung up the phone and feelings of loss flooded me.

I left Wren's house and returned to Minnesota, unsure if my choice to give Eric a second chance was the right one or not. I'd left the forty-degree weather in South Carolina and returned to freezing Minnesota.

I made my way through the cool tunnel leading from the plane to the inside of the Minneapolis Airport, then descended on the escalator, leading to the baggage claim area. The airport was quiet on a Sunday morning and Eric was easy to spot. When I reached him, he threw his arms around me and embraced me.

"I missed you so much," he said.

It felt shallow and artificial somehow, but I pushed the thought away. I pulled back and half-smiled. "Missed you, too."

During my trip, I had hardly thought of Eric at all, so I knew I was lying. I missed who he used to be, and I hoped he would change back. It surprised me that he'd even noticed I'd left with how distracting his video games were. Would he ask me to marry him like he said he would?

We got into the truck. He lit a smoke.

I didn't ask for one. Wren and I had quit together on my vacation.

Snowflakes fell outside, making it hard to see the road. I peered out the window of the truck. Eric held my hand. "Are you doing okay?"

"I can't believe I'm back in Minnesota with all this snow. It really is pretty."

"And annoying." Eric laughed.

"I suppose." I returned my gaze to the outside of the window.

After two hours of traveling in the car, we hadn't gotten far. More snow rolled in, so we booked a hotel for the night. My mind and my body were both exhausted. I didn't know what the future held, and my thoughts raced between a future with Eric and a future without him. Was coming back a mistake? I tried to shake away the feeling.

"Let's go have a smoke," Eric said, his words drew me out of my thoughts.

"You know, I quit right?"

"That's okay, come with me, anyway. I won't make you smoke, but I'd like your company."

"When you put it that way, sure, I'll come along." We grabbed our coats and headed to the back entrance of the hotel.

Outside of the hotel, it was surprisingly calm. Next to the sidewalk, the snow was piled high in two-foot banks on both sides. Eric lost his balance and fell into the snowbank.

"Are you okay?" I asked, grabbing his arm to try to help him.

He laughed, then moved to one knee. "Will you marry me?"

My mouth dropped, I couldn't believe he was ready to have a real life together, at last. "Yes." I hugged him. "Think you better give me one of those smokes, too."

After we arrived back in Minnesota, Eric and I went to Walmart in the evening, and standing there, with eyes wide and spiky hair combed, was Tommy perusing the discounted videos. The ones we used to look through together.

When I saw him, my heart filled with a thousand regrets I wished he knew. As my eyes met his the expression in his eyes was full of unspoken words. He stared at me a moment longer then glanced away. Eric and I walked passed him on our way to the video games.

It took every ounce of my strength not to turn around and be with him.

A few weeks later, my friend from Burger King called me to tell me that Tommy had moved. I hoped he found a job he liked better than Burger King. They didn't deserve him, and neither had I.

~ Twenty-Three ~

I can't help but see both positive and negative consequences of my actions. God can take something negative like our mistakes or our heartache and use it for good. I've seen it over and over in my life.

There were positive things that came from my choice between Tommy and Eric. Had I chosen differently, it might have cost Mitchell his life. For that, I owe gratitude to Eric.

One year into Eric and my marriage, I flew to an airport in Rhode Island to visit Wren and her family. Eric had no interest in coming. Wren's husband, Matthew was still in the military doing shore duty. Her house, a one-level brick building, looked like every other house on the street. Typical military housing. A swing seat sat inside a screened-in porch. The air was cool, the climate was like Minnesota.

We headed inside the house. The walls were empty except for a trombone painting leaning against a wall in the living room. I put my suitcase in the spare room and played with my niece on the couch. I couldn't wait until I could have kids of my own someday if Eric wanted to.

Wren was cooking hush puppies in the kitchen for me to try since I'd never eaten them before.

I peeked around the corner and talked to Matthew, "Do you mind if I check my email and Facebook? I want to check in with Eric and see how he's doing."

"Go right ahead," Matthew said.

I logged onto my Facebook account. My husband's ex had been posting on his Facebook right about the time I left on my trip. Why would she talk to him? My heart pounded in my chest and a sick feeling grew in my stomach. What was he doing?

I had his password, so I logged onto his Facebook. If Eric was innocent, there was no harm in peeking. He'd have nothing to hide, right? No, he was a good man.

A message popped up from his ex. I clicked on it. As I feared, there were messages between my husband and his pregnant and married, ex-girlfriend. Engaged, but lonely, she'd written.

It's okay, he wrote. You're a great girl, don't be down on yourself.

He was being a good friend trying to cheer her. That was fine. I read more.

She wrote, I miss your touch.

He responded, I wish I could put my hands all over your body.

My heart sank, my breath was ragged, and my stomach weakened like I might vomit. This was my husband, not hers. Hot tears rolled down my face. How could he do this to me? Why had he married me if he didn't love me and still loved her? It didn't make sense.

Wren walked into the room. "Are you okay, Kaitlin?"

I started, startled by my sister's presence. "I don't know. Eric—he's cheating on me. I can't believe it. It's that girl, the one he was seeing when I visited you in South Carolina."

"Are you, sure?" Her eyebrows creased as she moved closer to the computer.

"It's on his Facebook. Here, read this." I scrolled through the messages.

Wren leaned over me, reading over my shoulder.

My hands shook as I looked at the keyboard.

"Oh, no. I'm sorry, Kaitlin. You can stay here however long you need."

"Thanks." I stood and hugged her tightly. "I don't know what to do." I didn't know if I should stay in Rhode Island with Wren or return home and try to fix it. Did he even want to fix it? I was scared to tell him that I knew.

Soon, I brushed the fear aside and called my unfaithful husband.

The next week when it was time to go home, I reasoned through my decision. Fixing my marriage had to be possible. I had to try. If I didn't make an effort, I would regret it, I told myself.

Wren took me to the airport. She walked me to the door and then hugged me.

Tears welled in my eyes and hers.

"See you soon, Kaitlin. I love you. Remember, you can always come back."

"Thanks." I sniffled. "I love you too." It was too bad our trip had to be ruined by Eric and his unfaithfulness.

Arriving home, I pouted in my bedroom, blaming myself for the mess I found myself in. If I hadn't left him for Tommy, maybe Eric wouldn't have cheated on me. Eric still believed I cheated on him with Tommy; maybe it was revenge.

Either way, everyone abandoned me in the end, so maybe that was it; I was unlovable. Maybe I hadn't given him attention lately. I'd been too busy reading my fantasy novels and visiting Wren. My face flushed; it was my fault. I threw my stack of books against the wall in our bedroom. When he couldn't get attention from me, he got it from his ex.

Our marriage would never be the same, it couldn't be, could it? Most marriages can't survive infidelity, I'd read that on Google, but I hoped I'd be an exception. I wasn't going to walk away without a fight.

I sat on my bed; my fists clenched. Mom and Sierra's dad had lost everything because of infidelity, and they'd had a kid together and a business. If they hadn't survived cheating, how was I going to? I screamed into my pillow then pounded my fists into my mattress. How could Eric betray me? I wiped my nose on my sleeve, then sniffled. I got out of my bed and stormed into the living room. I faced him, standing with my hands on my hips.

"Why did you do this to me?" I asked. I had to know, I needed an answer, or I'd never be able to fix it.

"Ugh. It's not a big deal." He rolled his eyes. "I tried to cheer her up. She was depressed." He lit a cigarette. "Want one?"

"Sure." I took one from his outstretched hand.

"If you hate me, then leave." His eyes hardened.

"Is that what you want?" I whispered, tears pooling in my eyes.

"I don't know," he said, staring at the floor with his hollow beady eyes.

Determination to persevere, despite my feelings, filled me. "I won't leave you. Even if you don't care about me. I made a promise to God to love you. I need to understand why you did this." I lit my cigarette.

"I didn't do anything. I do care about you. She lives in another state. I don't love her." He rose and wrapped his arms around me. "I love you."

He didn't even say he was sorry. I took a deep breath. How would God want me to behave? He'd forgiven so much of the things I'd done wrong, maybe Eric deserved another chance. I swallowed the lump in my throat. "Let's try to work this out."

It was a midsummer day. Eric and I went with Mom and Mitchell to look at a cabin Mitchell's sister owned. It was in the town I grew up in, on the reservation. Hopefully moving here was the beginning of a new start for Eric and me.

In a single-file line, I followed Josephine, Mitchell's sister, inside, her dark curls dangled across the nape of her neck. Mitchell followed me inside. Under my feet were cracked linoleum floors.

"So, this is it, huh?" Eric asked, climbing the steps to our new cabin, trailing me.

"Looks great." I bit my lip. It was okay.

The dining room and kitchen were one room like the single-wide trailer from my childhood. I walked through it as a breeze carried a smell into the room, like wet earth and mothballs.

"Looks like you'll need to clean it, Kaitlin," Eric said.

I scoffed like he was one to talk. He only cleaned his computer area.

"Not bad, Josephine. You got a good deal, but this needs a lot of work," Mitchell said. I stopped exploring, to better hear what Mitchell would say.

Josephine's expression changed to one of confusion. "What does it need?" Josephine asked Mitchell.

"This cabin is not winterized, for one."

"What's that mean?" I asked, afraid of what that meant.

"Means, it has no insulation." He knocked on the outer wall. "Once winter hits, better have it fixed or trust me, you won't want to be here." He pulled a cigarette from his shirt pocket and lit it.

"I'll see what I can do," Josephine said.

"Want to help us get it winterized?" I asked Mitchell, kind of joking and serious.

"You can't afford me." A half-cocked smile formed on Mitchell's face.

"Yeah, probably not." I shrugged. I'm sure Josephine would come up with something.

I walked to the kitchen window on the opposite wall from the door. Against the far wall was a deep two-welled sink and an older faucet arched overtop. I walked to it. The letters C and H decorated the knobs. I turned the C knob, but no water came out.

Someone moved beside me. "The water isn't hooked yet, but I'll get it done soon," Josephine said. "Rent is five hundred. I'll be next door if you need me." She left.

Eric walked toward me. "It doesn't have any Wi-Fi, either." Eric cleared his throat. "How long before we get the internet?"

I rolled my eyes and pretended not to hear him. All he cared about was video games. He couldn't live in the actual world like the rest of us.

"All right. I'm going to head home, too. See you later, Kaitlin," Mitchell said.

"See you."

I walked through the second door. Beyond it was a cozy-sized room with two rickety windows above a full-size bed. A draft seeped in from the window. Mitchell must be right about the insulation. We'd freeze if we didn't finish before winter. If we were lucky, we'd have three months to get it done.

"I guess it'll work," Eric said. He sat on the bed close to me and then lit his cigarette.

"Got an extra one for me?" I asked.

He rolled his eyes and handed me one.

The day after we looked at Josephine's cabin, Eric and I moved in. Mom and Mitchell lived next door to our cabin in another cabin. They had lost the swamp house last year to the mortgage company. The lack of water in the cabin reminded me of living in the swamp house, and even though those days were difficult because of Mitchell's PTSD and our poverty, I missed the past. Things were harder but simpler. I didn't have a husband to please; life was full of possibilities. I hoped this cabin would get fixed like our swamp house had, maybe it could fix my broken marriage. I couldn't give up hope, but it would take a miracle to fix it.

Otherwise, we'd have to move again. I took a deep breath and decided to get to work cleaning. The place smelled stale; it would be a lot of work. Thankfully, my job at the gas station was only part-time.

I awoke to the whoosh-whoosh noise the following day, as cars drove over the overnight puddles on the paved highway. I opened the windows, so the wind would clear the smell of the musk. Outside, lights shone through the trees surrounding the cabin. It gave me a peaceful feeling.

I sat at the table. Eric left for work, and I was alone. Mitchell walked by the window, then knocking came at the door.

"Come in."

"Someone's got to help you get this place fixed, or it won't be livable," Mitchell said, as he walked past me. He sat on a folding chair across from me. Mitchell handed me a cup of coffee he'd carried over.

"Thanks. Eric is at work now." I took a drink. "He doesn't know how to do that kind of stuff, I guess." I shrugged.

"Yeah." Mitchell walked over to the sink. "We better do the plumbing first. You need water."

"That'd be nice. Josephine said we can pay you to fix it. If we buy supplies, then we take it out of the rent."

He scribbled something onto a piece of yellow paper then handed it to me. "This is a list of supplies I need from the hardware store. Give it to your mom. She's home right now."

I walked twenty steps next door to Mom and Mitchell's cabin through a few trees. I knocked. Mom opened the door, holding a cup of coffee in her hand. Steam rose from the mug.

"Mind if I look around?" I asked.

"That's the living room." She pointed to the right and said, "That's our bedroom." Mom pointed to the middle room. "The third room is Mitchell's computer room."

Mom's cabin looked like mine except the carpet wasn't stained and she had three bedrooms instead of two.

"It's great, Mom." I wished we had gotten this one. It was much nicer.

"Kaitlin, did Mitchell send you over with a list?"

"Yup." I reached into my pocket, then handed her the folded yellow paper.

"We'd better go before he thinks we're taking too long." Mom put her arm around me. "He can be nice when he wants to be." She nudged me, smiling.

I giggled. "Yeah. I suppose he can."

Mom and I returned with a bag of supplies from the store. I found Mitchell crawling beneath my cabin. "What are you doing?"

"Be right up." Mitchell came out from under the house and grabbed the white plastic bag of plastic tubes I'd bought at the hardware store. He grabbed glue, then crawled under the house, where he stayed for a few hours.

A chill returned to the air, as the sky grew darker. Mitchell came into the cabin for a Mountain Dew, also on his supply list. He chugged it. Sweat beaded his brow. He removed his black hat with a veteran logo and wiped his hairline with the back of his hand. Thin gray wisps curled toward the top of his starting-to-thin hair. "Be back later to finish the plumbing."

I was surprised when Mitchell returned the next morning. Wasn't pushing the physical work a bit too much for him? I hoped he wouldn't overdo it. "Good morning, Kaitlin. I'm going to work underneath the house. Holler at me when it's lunchtime."

I finished cleaning the cabin while Mitchell worked. I glanced at the clock, and it was nearly lunch already. Mitchell came inside, without me having to tell him the time. "Can you grab me another Mountain Dew?"

"Yup."

"Thanks." He took a labored breath. "Go turn the faucet on."

I walked into the kitchen and turned the C knob. This time water flowed from the silver gooseneck spout. "Thanks, Mitchell!" I grinned at him.

"Oh, no problem. See you tomorrow. I'll be back to start working on those walls."

After we removed each board, Mitchell stood with hands on his hips facing the walls. "This is where the insulation goes." Mitchell pointed at the space between two-by-fours. We can do it tomorrow. I need a break. It's getting too hot. Go next door and grab me a Mountain Dew."

"Okay, be right back." A few minutes later, I returned with his soda.

We sat in silence as he sipped. After he finished, he crushed the aluminum can with his hands. "If you go into town, pick up insulation for the walls. You're going to need a lot."

"What kind do we need?" I grabbed my notebook.

"It's called R-fifteen."

I wrote it down. "Okay, I'll get it as soon as I can. Thanks for the help."

"Someone's got to do it. Ain't going to be Eric, that guy you married doesn't want to get his hands dirty. Guess it's going to be me." He smiled, then he put his hat on and left.

~ Twenty-Four ~

I am convinced that working on the cabin was Mitchell's way of showing he cared. Without his help, I don't know what I would have done. Ecclesiastes 3:1, 3B says there is a season for everything under the sun. A time to tear down, and a time to build.

At the time, I didn't know what I was building and what I was tearing down.

After Eric and I moved back, I got rehired at my old job making subs and pizzas in my childhood town.

It was eight o'clock, time to head home for the night. I swept the floor behind the counter, then ran water for the mop bucket. The phone rang. I wiped the sweat from my forehead and turned off the water.

My coworker answered the phone on his side of the store. We shared a line, but it was too late to accept last-minute orders; the oven was off for the night.

My coworker walked toward me then reached over the counter and handed me the phone.

Who would call this time of night? Hopefully, it wasn't a disgruntled customer; it must not be because my coworker seemed calm. In the past, he had defended me when an angry customer called. I held the phone to my ear. "Hello?"

"This is your Aunt Josephine."

"Is something wrong?" I wasn't sure why she'd call me at work. Was rent late? I didn't think so.

"We need to get to the hospital. Mitchell isn't doing well." She sniffled.

"I don't have a car. What do you mean, he isn't doing well?"

"I'll pick you up on my way there. Be ready. I'm leaving now. I'll explain more."

I hung up the phone. My mind went fuzzy. What had she said? Mitchell might die. My throat tightened, and a sob rose in my chest. Mitchell couldn't die. Not tonight. I'd seen him earlier today, and he was fine.

"Everything okay?" my coworker asked, leaning on the counter.

"Uh, no. I need to leave. Family emergency."

"Okay. I'll mop for you."

"Thanks," I mumbled.

A few minutes later, a car pulled in front of the gas station. I headed outside and found my aunt waiting for me. She explained that Mitchell might not make it. He'd been picked up by ambulance right before she called me.

The night air blew against my face. The parking lot had three cars and it felt eerie being so empty. Usually, the walk-in clinic was packed, but tonight the clinic was closed and only the emergency doors were open. My aunt and I walked into the emergency entrance side door.

Once inside, the security guard said, "Write your name on the line here."

I wrote my information, then handed the clipboard back.

Mom stood beside me. Mitchell's mom and sisters stood, leaning against the wall. Across from them was the hospital's emergency operating room.

As reality set in, time stopped. I hugged Mom, then sat on the floor crossed-legged and prayed, *Please God, don't take him away.* This was all my fault. If I hadn't pushed him so hard to fix the cabin, he wouldn't be here. *Please Lord, help him pull through. We aren't ready to lose him.* My chin trembled. I prayed, *Lord, He doesn't even know You yet. Please help him.*

A nurse exited the OR, everyone stared at her. "The patient is in ventricular tachycardia. His heart is beating faster than normal." He paused for a moment. "We consider between one hundred and one hundred and twenty normal. His heart rate is hitting two hundred or more beats per minute."

One of Mitchell's sisters whimpered, and Mom sobbed into her hands.

The machine inside the OR let out an eerie screech. My heart pounded in my chest. Did he die? A wave of nausea swept over me. The nurse rushed back into the OR.

"Code blue, code blue," the intercom went off. I put my face into my hands and prayed harder, as I plead with God.

Mom gasped.

Mitchell's mom hugged Josephine.

More staff rushed into Mitchell's room.

One minute went by. No news. It couldn't be the end; Mitchell was too much of a fighter. Two or three more minutes crept by. I feared a nurse would appear and tell us the time of death. As my hope wavered, I prayed. Six more minutes passed.

Mom's shoulders shook. I hugged Mom. Was this the end for Mitchell, God?

A nurse came into the hallway. "Who is the wife?"

My eyes went wide. Was Mitchell dead? Why else would they ask for his wife? Tears pooled in my eyes. No. I took a step away from Mom so she had space.

Mom raised her hand and sniffled. "I am."

The nurse moved to where Mom and I stood. "Your husband was clinically dead, but a minute ago, a rhythm reappeared on the monitor."

Mom let out a soft gasp, then covered her mouth with her hands.

"He's alive, but he isn't stable. We need to move him to a bigger facility." The nurse put her hand on mom's shoulder. "This hospital isn't equipped for these complications."

Mom nodded a few times, ever so slightly. "Keep him alive, please."

A doctor came out in blue scrubs. "Take turns and say something to him. It helps them know they aren't alone. In five minutes, we'll move him by ambulance."

Mom and Mitchell's family took turns going in. When it was my turn, I grabbed his hand. The rough texture of his weathered fingers felt strange, but if talking to him might help him pull through, then I had to try.

The doctor had taped his eyes shut. The moment was surreal like out of a movie.

I whispered, "Please live. We need you and we love you." I gulped the lump in my throat. Could he hear me? I'd never told him I loved him before. Tears streamed down my face. I took a deep breath and closed my eyes. *Lord, I prayed, please, help him. We need a miracle.*

We left the OR.

I rode with my mom to the next town's hospital, and Mitchell's family followed us. After that, the second hospital moved him by helicopter to Fargo. The staff in the third hospital said they weren't equipped to handle the situation, either. So, they sent him by ambulance to a specialty hospital in Minneapolis.

My aunt drove us all to the cities in her van. My other aunts chatted, except for one that slept. The radio played softly as my aunt drove faster than the legal limit. Mom leaned over and whispered, "If it wasn't for your husband, no one would've been there to call an ambulance."

"I thought you or Aunt Josephine called."

"No. I was alone with Mitchell when he had a seizure. He sank to the ground as I struggled to hold him. I couldn't leave him, not even for more than a minute. I'd learned that during nursing, but I didn't have minutes on my phone, so I opened the door and yelled. It was all I could do." She whimpered.

I grabbed her hand. "He'll be okay, Mom. You heard the nurse. He's tough."

"You're right." She smiled and patted my leg. "After I yelled, Eric must have heard me because he ran over and called nine-one-one. Without him, Mitchell would be dead."

Mom, Wren, Sierra, and I slept in waiting rooms when we couldn't afford hotels or when we wanted to be close to Mitchell when he was in surgery.

During the first week at the hospital, Mitchell had multiple surgeries. Each surgery took several hours. The types of surgeries seemed very complicated, involving cutting nerves involved in the sweating process and startle responses nerves. I didn't pretend to understand it all. He had a skilled team working on him and I spent a lot of time praying for him.

Finally, after a few weeks, stable and healing, they sent Mitchell home.

I read a statistic online that individuals who suffer cardiac arrest outside of a medical setting rarely survive. I thank God, Mitchell lived that day. It was a miracle.

He told me when he flatlined, he saw a dock with a door at the end. He asked me if there was more after this life. I said I believed there was.

~ Twenty-Five ~

At many points in my life, God had been like a father to me when I didn't have one. There were times when God was more like a spouse, knowing me and holding me through difficult challenges, particularly when my spouse wasn't.

Eric and I sat in the living room watching a movie. The main character, a teenage girl, dumped her boyfriend because she liked someone else.

"What a hooker," Eric said, then scoffed.

The girl had the decency to break up with her boyfriend before having another relationship. Unlike Eric. "Why do you talk about women like that?" My jaw clenched. Women deserved more respect than that.

"I'm kidding. Why do you take everything so personally?" He stood facing me, with his hands on his hips.

I took a deep breath to try to calm myself before continuing, "Since I've got your attention and you aren't watching the movie anymore, I wanted to talk to you about something mentioned at church today."

"Why do I care about your church?" He approached the television, turned the movie off, and turned on his XBOX console.

Of course, he didn't care about my church, it wasn't like he'd ever gone with me. I was the only married attendee who didn't come with their spouse. "The things that matter to me should matter to you."

He stared at me; his eyes were hollow like he hated me.

I ignored his anger, and said, "Anyway, I've been thinking, I want to go on a mission trip next year." I needed a break from this place, from him.

"You can't take a mission's trip." His nostrils flared, then he put on his headset.

"What? Why not?"

"If you do, don't bother coming back. I won't wait for you. You could get hurt. I'm not open to that kind of pain." He plopped back onto the couch.

I threw my hands up. "What kind of pain? I could die here too." He didn't care if I was here, so why would he care if I died out there?

"I don't know. Don't come back. Choose that or me."

Huffing, I stormed out of the room. If I wasn't here, he probably wouldn't even notice anyway. I'd given up so much of my life for Eric and what did I get in return? Nothing but grief. I walked to our bedroom to get space, closing the door behind me. If God asked me to go on a trip, I would give Eric up. I didn't care how much Eric fought my dreams. Someday I'd do something worth remembering. There was more to living than playing video games. I stayed in my room until I heard knocking on the door, so I went to answer it. I entered the living room where Eric was still playing his game.

"Come in," Eric hollered.

His cousins came in.

"Hey, guys," Eric said over his shoulder, then shut his game off.

Sure, he'd shut it off for them, but what if I asked? That would be too much.

"Ready to have some fun?" He approached them, shaking their hands. "I was going to have the wife make us dinner. Come and sit. Hey, Kaitlin. Bring in the twelve packs of pop, will you?"

Eric had me make spaghetti for his cousins then they watched a horror movie. I played on my computer while they watched; I hated horror movies. After his cousins left, I approached Eric. Hopefully, he had cooled off since our argument earlier about mission trips. He'd been pleasant the whole time his cousins visited, maybe he'd hear me out. Maybe if I let him do something he wanted, he'd be more open to my wishes. "Do you want to see that concert in town this weekend?" I asked. Maybe doing something together would rekindle our relationship.

He shrugged. "Not this weekend. The guys are coming over. Plus, there's a new game coming out."

"Another one?" I slumped onto the couch. It was no use trying.

He exhaled his cigarette smoke. "I need to get online to start this game. We'll talk later, babe." He put on his headset. He may as well have been a hundred miles away. "Get off here, little kid! You don't know how to play!" he yelled at the television. "Why don't you go cry to your momma?"

What kind of jerk picked on kids? I went to bed. What was the point in trying to communicate with him? He only cared about his games. I went to bed, knowing Eric wouldn't join me.

I rolled over in the blankets, the clock said eleven. Eric hadn't come to bed, so I peeked into the living room to see if he was there. He hadn't moved since I'd gone to bed two hours earlier.

I went to the kitchen to make some coffee. Maybe I'd stay with him for a while and hang out like old times.

Eric's eyes met mine, as I crossed his path. He held out his arm for me to stop then took off his headset. "I'm headed to the bar. My cousins will be here in a minute to pick me up."

"You know they don't like me." I frowned, hoping he'd change his mind. "Let me get changed I'll go with you."

"I'm going by myself, so you won't have to deal with them. Go to bed. I'll be back in a few hours."

My chest tightened. He was cheating on me again. What other reason would he want to go out and leave me at home? I felt so trapped; I was such a fool to think he could change. I stood there, staring at him. I wanted to yell or scream at him, tell him that I wouldn't let him go because he was my husband and he needed to act like it; but no words came out.

"I am coming home to you, so why does it matter where I go? I need to blow off steam."

"You didn't even ask if I wanted to go," I said under my breath, too quiet for him to hear or he pretended he didn't hear.

He went to our room and returned wearing different clothing. The smell of his nauseating cologne lingered in the air as he brushed past me toward the door.

I felt so unseen.

Headlights reflected on the kitchen wall and a moment later, Eric left.

I walked, my head lowered, to my room and laid on my bed, pulling a pillow to my chest. I closed my eyes and prayed, *Please, Lord; I don't know how to save this marriage. He doesn't want me or love me. Why am I not good enough? Why does rejection hurt so much? I wish I could prove he was cheating, so I could leave. I don't know how much more I can take.*

From off my nightstand, I pulled out my Bible, feeling the thin pages in my fingers. In the reference section, I looked up betrayal. Maybe reading what the Bible said would help. I opened the passage and read about Jesus' friends betraying him with a kiss, and then I turned to a verse in Psalms about David being betrayed. At least God and the Psalmist understood what I was going through.

I awoke with a start. Had Eric come home yet? I reached over and his side was empty. He wasn't in bed. I rubbed my eyes and headed toward the living room. One thirty A.M. the clock said, and Eric still wasn't home. I sat in the living room and waited for him. He arrived home half an hour later.

I smelled beer and cigarettes on his clothes. "Are you cheating on me?" I asked.

"How can you ask me that? Will you ever let me live this down?"

"I'm trying to forget. I am. Coming in late at night isn't helping your cause." I held out my hands to touch him.

He pulled away from me. "You need to leave me if you can't let it go," he said, his eyes were cold and empty.

"I won't leave. Most married couples are having children by now."

He rolled his eyes. "We've been over this. I thought neither one of us wanted kids."

I crossed my arms. "I don't know if I want kids, but I might, someday."

"I don't. Maybe we need a break from each other. Why don't you live with your sister for a while? I know you miss her. Spend a couple of days there."

"Fine. I think I will," I said sarcastically. I turned on my heel and left him there. Wren had moved back to Minnesota after Matthew got discharged from the military. Her new house was now a three-hour drive. Since I didn't drive, I hadn't seen her in a few months. Maybe if I was gone, Eric would see what he was missing.

The sunlight shone through the windows; it bathed Wren's kitchen in the soft morning light. I drank my steaming coffee. A few days became weeks and I had been at Wren's for a month now. Eric hadn't mentioned a divorce but hadn't offered to come and get me, either.

The distance was supposed to help him want me back. See what he was missing. Why hadn't it worked? He must be cheating; why else would he stay so distant? I would prove his infidelity. Why else would he treat me this way? I swallowed a sip of coffee and tried to swallow the lump in my throat. Pulling a chair to the computer, I opened the messages he had received from his coworker on Facebook. In the message, he told his friend he had hit on a girl at the bar. She had turned him down. Good for her.

I called him. "Who are these messages about? Why are you picking up some girl from the bar?" I slammed my hands on the counter. "Tell, me. I have a right to know."

The page reloaded, and the messages disappeared.

"Someone at work used my account. He talked to his girlfriend on my messenger. I don't even know my password because he changed it.".

I took another sip of coffee. "The messages are gone now. That is odd—unless you erased them." My face burned as hot tears ran down my cheeks. I couldn't believe the nerve of him. He was my husband, not a single man picking up chicks at the bar. I was stupid for believing him.

"Think what you want—I sent nothing. I don't even know what it said." He made me feel like I was a crazy person, and I hated the way it made me feel. "I need to get back to work." He hung up.

Spring had turned to summer, and nothing with Eric had improved. I was ready to quit running from my problems. I packed my stuff and asked Wren if she could drive me home the next day.

I moved home to live with Eric, to try to work things out.

After work one evening, Eric came home, and we'd eaten spaghetti for dinner, again. It was his favorite, so I tried not to complain, but it was my least favorite food.

"Doll, guess what?" A wide smile covered his face, and his eyes brightened. "I'm attending boxing class two nights a week."

"Oh, wow. Good for you. You won't get hurt, will you?"

"No. I don't fight for a while. I need to learn some techniques first. Look what my trainer taught me today." Eric bounced between his feet, punching into the air.

Maybe this would be what I'd waited for. Maybe Eric's old charismatic personality was back. He used to be so happy and today, it was like that personality was back.

"That's great. Well, I'll miss you, but I hope you have fun."

Eric had been attending boxing for a month, and in my mind, something didn't add up. He said he'd been practicing at a gym at work, but I didn't think his work had a gym. Maybe I was imagining things. I stared at him suspiciously after he changed and stood in the living room, getting ready to leave for another practice. His belly fat and flabby arms hadn't changed. He didn't seem sore or skinnier.

"I won't be back too late," Eric said. I wanted to follow him, but I couldn't drive. My heart sank. I hated feeling like I couldn't trust him.

He walked to the door and rested his hand on the doorknob. "I'll be gone this weekend."

"Why?" What did he possibly need to do? He acted like he didn't want me to be around. I didn't like being excluded. "Can I come with you?"

"Sorry, I have to go alone. My dad is in treatment in Fargo. I'll need to visit on weekends until he gets out."

He was lying. I knew it. He never spoke to his dad, not since last winter, when he figured out his dad was using drugs again. I rolled my eyes. Who was he kidding? His dad didn't live in North Dakota. "What's the name of the place he's staying at?" I asked.

"Ugh. I don't know. Let me guess, you think I'm cheating on you. Well, I'm not. You need to stop. I'm not doing anything wrong. If you can't get over it. . ." He paused. "I'll see you later."

Mom said when Anthony was cheating on her, she knew. Maybe I wasn't crazy, or maybe I was. He had to be cheating. After he left, I started researching treatment facilities in Fargo.

After searching for the treatment places, I realized, there was no way to prove he was lying. I couldn't access his phone to find anything concrete.

I grew increasingly desperate each week trying to confirm my suspicions. I felt like I had lost my mind, as broke into his computer, and searched through the search history. He was looking at girls in bikinis, but nothing worse. No solid proof of infidelity. For all I knew, my roommate could have done that.

In the middle of the night, Eric snored beside me. I couldn't sleep with the obnoxious noise. How could he sleep with a dirty conscious? I couldn't contain my anger any longer. He had promised to love me when he married me. I pushed my cold feet against his back and shoved him as hard as I could. He crashed onto the floor, dropping from the bed. In my tired delirium, I stifled a laugh.

He stared at me like I'd killed his puppy. He slowly backed away toward our bedroom door. "I'll sleep on the couch tonight." His hard eyes stared into mine.

It served him right, coming in late every night when he should be home with me. For once, maybe he'd regret treating me like I didn't matter. I prayed and my anger eased. God felt so near like I could hold out my arm and touch Him. Slumping onto the floor, I imagined God holding me in His arms, as I buried my face in my knees. It would be okay, no matter what. God wouldn't leave me, even if Eric did.

A few mornings after the bar night, I reached under our mattress as Eric slept beside me. Feeling around, I grasped Eric's phone in my hand. I tiptoed out of the room. Then ran to the bathroom. I'd finally discovered his hiding place. Please, let the messages still be there. I locked the bathroom door.

My heart pounded against my ribs and the sick feeling in the pit of my stomach returned. I opened the newest messages. Several texts came from a young man named Adam, who, I guessed, was not a man. The texts mentioned their night spent together and how fondly she remembered the things they did during that time. It took place during the weekend he'd visited his father. My cheeks burned; my fingers trembled. I texted her, the other woman.

My fingers shook as I responded to the homewrecker: *You can have him. I'm done with him.*

Eric barged into the bathroom. "What are you doing!?"

"I finally know the truth. I'm not crazy." I handed him the phone.

He stood, wearing a dumbfounded expression on his face. "I was going to tell you."

"Yeah, right." I brushed past him and returned to my room to pack my belongings. I called Mom, and she dropped off boxes for me a few hours later.

While I was sorting through the books, Eric answered his phone. It was probably his dumb girlfriend calling. He sank onto the floor and sobbed into his hands.

"What's wrong?" I asked, kneeling by him, surprised at his outburst.

"Grandma's gone," he choked out.

"I'm so sorry." I hugged him, he smelled like his sickly-sweet cologne. "Can I pray for you?" He had hurt me, but I couldn't abandon him. His grandma had been feeling ill the past week, but her death was unexpected. She was such a sweet lady.

"Dear Lord, please help him. Please continue to be with him in his life like you've always been with me. Please be with him in this hard season of losing his grandma. Remind him You are with him. Amen." I unclasped my hands. "Should I stay? Are you okay?"

"Go," his tone was edgy. He put his face into his hands. Then more softly he added, "I'll be okay, really."

His girlfriend would help him through his loss, so he would be okay. The thought both comforted and irritated me.

I was proud of myself for praying, but I knew the strength and love hadn't come from me. It reminded me of how Jesus loved Judas all that time, even though He knew Judas would hurt him.

I finished packing and moved in with Mom and Mitchell.

After things settled, I discovered that Adam, from the dirty text messages, was the girl from the bar.

~ Twenty-Six ~

It was crushing to know Eric had been with his girlfriend for months. Despite the pain, I felt relieved from the burden I had carried for so long.

After Eric and my divorce was almost finalized, I had a full-time job and things were improving. I was living with Mom and Mitchell back in the town I grew up in. I felt like I was finally on the right path toward my future.

On the way home after work, Mom and I bought Mitchell some McDonald's food. I handed the bag to Mitchell.

He peered inside the paper bag. "You should have gotten two sandwiches. One's probably not going to fill me up, but thanks anyway." He scrunched his face and ate his burger.

I wasn't sure why I tried. I never bought him what he wanted. Sighing, I sat down next to him and ate my fries. I had to face it, Mitchell would probably always be grumpy, and I shouldn't take it personally.

After eating, Mitchell grabbed his laptop and began clicking keys. "Good sandwich," he said.

I smiled. Even if he didn't say it, I knew he was happy I'd remembered him. "What are you working on?" I asked, moving to sit next to him.

"It's a story I've been wanting to write for some time now. It's about the war."

"I didn't know you enjoyed writing." I stood up and walked to get a cup of coffee. "Hey, you want a cup of joe?"

He moved his hand onto his stomach before removing it. "No, I'm good for now. If I drink too much, my stomach hurts."

I returned with my cup and sat beside him again.

"You were good at English in school. Want to read what I have?"

"Sure, if you don't mind sharing."

"When you're done reading that, put away that pile of stuff behind you. You sure like to heap things in corners, don't you?" He smirked. "Kind of messy."

"Sorry about that. I'll put it away as soon as I'm finished."

He put the computer in front of me and then went to the kitchen.

During the war, Mitchell served as a mechanic in the Army. He and two soldiers were alone, miles from the others, when their convoy broke en route. Hopeless in the unforgiving heat of the desert, he and his companions possessed few supplies. Mitchell ventured off, looking for any help he could find. The others stayed behind in case anyone found them.

In the distance, he noticed a glimmer—a piece of metal or glass reflecting the brilliant sun. He hoped it might be something that could help them.

He hiked across the desert, toward the light. Sweat streaked into his eyes, and the sun burned his skin. He put his hand to his forehead, trying to block the sun from his eyes. As the desert sun pounded against his exposed flesh, his throat grew drier. He shook his canteen. There wasn't much in it.

After miles of trekking, he arrived at the source of the reflection. The light had come from another broken vehicle, likely a reflection from the mirrors. He opened the back; the vehicle was full of supplies. Supplies that might save their lives. Pep in his step, he hopped inside the vehicle.

Turning the ignition, nothing happened. He jumped out and checked the fluids. The fluids were low, but that was to be expected. He would need time to get the convoy running, but his companions needed supplies or they'd die in the desert. Wanting to protect his comrades, he loaded as much as he could carry, then traveled back to his companions.

After returning, he gave his companions the supplies, then took some time to rest. Before nightfall, he squatted to the ground and traced an SOS in the sand, big enough for a helicopter to see.

The next morning, before the sun was high, he trekked through the sand and dry heat. Wind blew sand into his eyes as he traveled back to the broken vehicle for a second time. Once he arrived, he worked to fix it. The blistering sun burned his neck, oil caked his fingernails. After hours of tinkering, the vehicle started. The roar of the engine was the best sound. He laughed in joy. They would be saved.

He headed toward his convoy. In the distance, he saw flickering lights. It might be gunfire. In case it was enemy forces, he quickened his pace. He hoped no one noticed him as he drove back to his friends. Wiping sweat away from his brow, he hoped his friends weren't hurt.

He needed to be careful, because even if they were friendly, the desert sun brought out the Native American in his complexion, and his dark skin could put him in danger if the American troops mistook him for an Arab. The first time it happened, weeks earlier, friendly guns aimed at him until he proved he was an American. It was not an experience he wanted to repeat.

He returned to the others and was relieved they were safe. They told him someone had seen his SOS and had left to get them help. It must have been the lights he had seen earlier and hoped weren't gunfire.

He and his crew, now with supplies because of Mitchell, waited for help to return. Once the help came back, he and his crew

242 ~ KAITLIN DAWN THOMSON

followed them to their platoon in the vehicle Mitchell fixed. They had spent seven days missing in the desert. The Army later awarded him a medal of valor, determining that Mitchell's actions had been heroic because he saved two soldiers and himself. All this time, he was a hero. How didn't I know?

I returned the laptop. "Your story is amazing. I didn't know you were a hero."

Mitchell smiled, then looked at the floor. "Anyone else would've done the same. Want to help me stack some firewood?"

"I can do that." I didn't want him doing it himself. Sometimes it seemed like he forgot his heart wasn't functioning well.

"You better change your pants first. They're dragging on the floor."

I looked down at the frayed ends of my mud-caked jeans. "I guess they are." It reminded me of my favorite pants when I was a teenager. They were athletic-style Adidas sweatpants. He had said the same thing before they went missing. Then, one day, after I had long forgotten about them, Mom told me Mitchell had burned them while I was at work. I raised an eyebrow at him, curious if he would burn these pants, too. I shoved them down into the bottom of my dirty clothes pile, hoping he wouldn't find them. After I changed, we headed out into the yard and stacked firewood together.

~ Twenty-Seven ~

2008 was the first time Mitchell told me about his experiences in the Army. I'm ashamed to say that I never asked how he'd gotten the military awards that hung on the wall behind the couch. I'd never asked what happened in the Gulf war. Maybe I'd been too afraid of his answer. Not considering other people's thoughts and feelings was wrong of me. We could have had a good relationship years ago. How much suffering could I have prevented if I hadn't been so focused on my pain and my problems? I'll never know.

The sun shone through the tops of the trees as Mom drove me to church. The yellow, orange, and crimson leaves filled the trees. Autumn was more vivid this year. Maybe because I was no longer with Eric and I finally felt free.

"Kaitlin, guess what?" Mom looked at me from the driver's seat.

"What's up, Mom?"

A grin spread across her face. "Mitchell's been meeting with Jude."

"I'm surprised he'd be willing to talk to him." Jude was a part-time preacher who worked with us at the gas station.

"Me too. Well, at night, he's been reading his Bible, too. I know how happy it would make you to know he's thinking about God."

"That's amazing, Mom." Maybe all these years of Mitchell's struggles would become rejoicing. They say that one sinner repenting causes joy in heaven. I hoped he would come to know God like a friend as I had.

After church, my friend invited me to her parent's house for lunch. She'd been the one to bring me to her church in the first place when we worked together in 2007. It meant a lot to me that she wanted me around despite my divorce. She hadn't been judgmental at all; no one had. I rode in her car to their house. It was tucked into the woods, next to a dirt road, halfway between the church and Mom and Mitchell's house. Stucco siding and dark shutters made the house resemble the French countryside. Chickens ran in a fenced area to the side of the house.

The branches of their fruit trees drooped, weighted from the apples on the branches. My friend and I climbed out of her car and walked toward the home. I followed my friend inside and down a long hall that opened into a kitchen and a connected living room. I stood leaning against the wall as everyone waited for lunch to begin.

Pat, a guy from church who'd always been nice to me, moved to stand beside me. "You want help to hold up the wall?" He planted his feet on the floor, glancing at me with soft, blue eyes.

"Yes, sure." I blushed and hoped he didn't see it.

"I've been wanting to ask. Do you want me to teach you to drive? It might help you."

"Would you? I might crash." My brother-in-law had started teaching me, but I hadn't gotten confident enough to pass the test. Then, I had moved back in with Eric and the practice stopped.

"You won't crash. I promise. It'll be fine. And if you do, I have insurance." He shrugged and then chuckled. "My sister already hit a deer with my truck."

I laughed. "Well, at least that makes me feel better. Let's do it." I needed to force myself to be brave.

"It's time to eat," my friend's mom said. She had her hair pulled back like curtains, fastened with bobby pins. After looking at her husband, she asked, "Dear, can you pray?"

Her husband bowed his head. "Dear Lord, thank you for our friends and family who are here today. Please bless this food for our bodies. Amen."

"Amen," I said.

We played games all afternoon. Before I left, Pat gave me his number so we could arrange a time to drive together.

Do you still want to teach me to drive? I texted Pat. I hoped it wasn't too soon to ask, but I didn't want to wait until he forgot his offer. Mitchell was ready for me to be independent.

Sure. How's tomorrow work? He responded.

Great.

The next day, Pat picked me up at Mom and Mitchell's in his Chevy truck. I hopped inside and he drove for the first ten or fifteen minutes of our time together. When would he have me drive? I wasn't in a hurry to fail.

"Ready to drive?" he asked me, as he pulled onto a less busy road.

My hands trembled as I imagined the truck being under my control. "I'm nervous. Can we pray before we drive?"

"Sure." He pulled off the road onto a dirt side street.

We bowed our heads, and I prayed. "Dear Jesus, thank you for my time with Pat today. Please keep us safe since I'm driving today. Amen." My chest swelled with warmth. It was nice to be around a man who shared my faith. Eric had told me he never understood me or my God.

Pat climbed out of the truck, and we switched sides. I scooted into the driver's seat, then adjusted the seat. Pat was a lot taller than I was.

Pat buckled up. "All right, I'm ready. Let's get lost. You can drive anywhere you want to."

During the first half an hour of our trip, I got lost after taking back roads. I drove slowly.

As a car passed, I tensed, clutching the wheel.

As if sensing my tension, Pat said, "Don't worry. Let them go around. You take your time. We aren't rushin', we're American. Ha-ha, get it? We aren't Russian."

I laughed at his silly joke, relaxing my grip on the wheel.

I pulled over to stop and take a break. A tall building with new siding sat in front of a body of clear blue water. My heart pounded. I glanced at a restaurant bar. It was the place that served the "best tacos in the world." I could hardly believe it. Somehow, I'd traveled down memory lane by accident.

"This is where my parents took me to eat when we were kids." I stared at the restaurant. The owners must have updated the building; it looked nice now with new siding. "I haven't been here in years."

"I've never been. I grew up a few hours away in a town called Aitkin."

My mouth dropped. "I've been there." I glanced at Pat. "One time at four in the morning, my sister, my friend Sean, and I ran out of gas there. We had to flag down a cop to get home. The officer unlocked a gas station and filled up our tank." I laughed. What were the chances? "My friend didn't have a license. Thankfully, the cop never asked."

"That's funny. Most people haven't heard of Aitkin."

"I hadn't either. We took a wrong turn." I pulled onto the road and drove on a scenic highway, near where Wren had stayed during her time in foster care. The road was winding and narrow, lined with acres and acres of forest. We drove for another half an hour.

We reached a gas station along the highway "Hey, let's stop at that gas station over there." He pointed toward a building. "It's time for some food."

We went in and grabbed some lunch, then we headed back to my house.

Pat picked me up at my parent's house in his truck. It had been a week since the first time that we had driven together.

"Thanks for hanging out with me today," I said. "I had plans before this, but they fell through."

"What do you mean?" he sounded concerned.

I sighed. It was hard sharing things about my ex with Pat. "A friend of mine is getting married today. When she found out about my divorce, she asked me not to be her bridesmaid anymore, because my ex is a groomsman."

"That's no good. I'm going to help make it up to you." His blue eyes met mine. He seemed so happy. "What can I do?"

"I could use some new dishes for when I find an apartment." It was nice to have someone care about me. Over the past few years, I had gotten used to Eric's anger and apathy.

"Let's do some antique store shopping."

We went to an antique shop where I found a tiny cast iron pan big enough to cook an egg. It was the first piece of cast iron cookware I'd ever owned. Mitchell owned a few; it was the one dish he forbade me to wash. He'd mainly used them on our camping trips throughout the years. Now I had my very own.

We walked a few blocks to Goodwill and found silverware and a pottery bowl. I found little to help me with a new apartment, but Pat made me smile and we had fun shopping.

We stopped at a coffee shop for lattes after shopping and sipped them on a black leather couch facing a fireplace.

"So, what made you decide to live here?" I uncrossed my legs and faced him.

"College. That's when I came here, and I fell in love with it. This was where I wanted to live. I found a job and moved. It took a while to get on my feet."

"Well, I'm glad you did." I took another sip of my latte and hoped I wasn't blushing. He was obviously a hard-working man who didn't give up easily if he had moved all by himself and supported himself. The thought made me feel more secure somehow.

"Want to practice driving some more? I think it'll make your life a lot easier," he said.

"Sure." It would make Mitchell happy, that was for sure. He and Mom had been driving me back and forth to work and the miles were racking up.

We left the coffee shop, but as we walked outside, it rained. Would I be able to drive well in the rain? "Maybe I'll let you drive. I'm not sure I'll do it right."

"It'll be okay. You may as well learn how to drive in the rain. It won't always be sunny when you need to go somewhere. You'll do great." He didn't want to prepare me only for easy driving but difficult as well. It reassured me. He didn't seem like a person who would give up on someone else when things got hard. I was tired of people leaving when things got challenging.

As the day wore on, I realized that I wanted to be more than his friend, which caught me unawares. What if he didn't want more? What if people within the church expected me to never remarry? They had been like a second family for me since I'd first attended five years ago. I hoped they wouldn't judge me for making so many poor decisions. I didn't want one choice to ruin all chances I had at happiness.

Pat called me in the afternoon. Outside of my parent's place, I paced around the yard while we chatted. We talked about when we could practice driving again.

"Before we pick a time, I've been thinking and decided that we should talk. I don't believe in dating, so let's continue being friends, but I would like to see if this becomes more," Pat said.

I couldn't believe it. He had thought about being more than friends someday. "I wasn't sure if you'd ever like me. I messed up in the past."

"I want to get to know you better."

"Okay, me too." I smiled until my cheeks hurt, but would it just be another let-down? I didn't know what to think. He liked me. Eric had promised to love me and that didn't turn out. I took a deep breath. This was going to be a challenge. My mouth went dry, so I entered Mom and Mitchell's house for a drink of water.

Pat continued, "Let's see what the church thinks, they know us both really well. If they're okay with what happened with your divorce, then I don't have a problem with it, either."

"Great!" I felt some relief.

The people in the church had always been welcoming. Then, reality hit. I hadn't talked to the church about my divorce. I had avoided bringing it up. Would they shun me? Say I wasn't good enough for Pat?

I took a deep breath. Maybe it wouldn't work out after all. I knew how I felt about divorce, but I didn't know how the church would react. The Bible said if a non-believer didn't want to live with me or was unfaithful, then I could leave. Eric had committed adultery, so I knew where I stood, but would the church share my point of view? I was afraid to ask.

It was the beginning of December, and the snow fell in heavy flakes, almost pouring. Pat and I pulled into the church parking lot. Tonight, was the night when the church would determine my future. My hands clammed. Would my church understand? Pat and I walked in together. The leaders separated us into men and women for a special Sunday night prayer time.

My heart pounded in my chest. Before the meeting, I promised God I'd honor Him, no matter the outcome. I wanted this decision in His hands and not mine. My way always led to disasters. I took a deep breath; it was time.

We went around the group of women, saying what we wanted to pray about. It was my turn and my heart raced. "I'm hoping you will accept Pat and me as a couple. You all know I'm divorced."

One lady giggled. "We thought you were dating. I think it's great."

A deep wave of relief washed over me. After everyone shared their prayer requests, we prayed.

Pat and I walked toward the middle of the Walmart store. He'd picked me up late in the morning and we planned to visit his parents after a few stops. I couldn't believe he was interested in me enough to take me to meet his parents. My stomach twisted into knots; what if they didn't like me?

Pat led us to the stationary section of Walmart.

"What did we need to get again?" I asked, confused about what he'd want in the office-supply area of the store.

"I want us to each buy a notebook."

"What for?" I loved writing, so notebooks were always welcomed, but it seemed like he wanted it for something specific.

He paused. "Sometimes, I want to say things to you, but I shouldn't because we aren't married. I want to write those things in these notebooks." He grabbed a black notebook off the shelf.

"Oh." I blushed and heat rushed to my cheeks. I felt that way many times, too. I wanted to be around him every moment I could, maybe I would write that down. Or that I loved his eyes and how he made me feel. Starting a future with Pat both terrified and excited me. He was nothing like Eric. I grabbed a pink notebook.

"If we get married, we'll exchange them," he said. "For now, when I want to say something but can't I'll say 'Psalm 23,' and then you'll know I want to write something in my book."

I beamed at him, I love that Bible passage. "Psalm 23," I said.

I felt warm inside thinking about being married to him filled me with joy. "You are so thoughtful." The books were a great idea, anything to make temptation easier. Then maybe, it would keep us from hurting each other. It amazed me how much he wanted to honor God in our relationship by avoiding temptation.

We bought the notebooks, then headed to his parent's house a few hours away. The message from Pat was clear: you are more to me than what you can physically offer me. My trust in his intentions grew.

Pat drove through a city on our way home after visiting his parents. It had been a pleasant visit and I enjoyed seeing where Pat grew up. We had shared our first hug and my heart still pounded a half-hour later.

"It's getting late." Pat pulled down another street. "Where should we eat?"

"Do you want to eat here?" I pointed at a pizza place.

"Let's drive until we see something else." He pulled into an Applebee's a few minutes later. "This place okay?"

I nodded. I wanted to be near Pat, so I would eat whatever he wanted.

We got out of the car and approached the glass doors. He opened the door for me.

A server stood near the entrance. "Table for two?" The restaurant smelled like burgers. My mouth watered.

"Yes, please," Pat said. Inside, dim pendant lights hung low over tall tables. Booths lined the border of the room.

"Right this way." The server grabbed menus and headed to the right. She motioned toward one of the tall tables. "Your server will be right with you." She handed each of us a menu.

Pat and I sat facing each other.

"Should we share something?" Pat opened the menu.

"How about chicken strips and mozzarella sticks?"

"How do you keep reading my mind?" He grinned at me.

After dinner, he let me drive home. My driving test was three days away and I needed the extra practice. Pat turned on the radio. 'Silent Night,' my favorite, played. It reminded me of lights and time with family a long time ago.

"Silent night, holy night," we sang together.

Blue and red lights flashed in my rearview mirror. "Oh, no." Not the lights I wanted to see during the holidays.

I pulled off the road. I'd never been pulled over by a cop before. What was I supposed to do? My heart pounded. Maybe I wasn't ready for my test, getting pulled over already.

An officer with slick brown hair in a low ponytail approached my side of the car with a clipboard. I rolled down my window.

She gave me a side-long glance. "License and registration," the officer said, not looking amused in the slightest.

Pat fumbled through the glove box.

"Just a second." My hands shook. What was taking him so long? I reached into my purse and found my learner's permit.

"Do you know how fast you were driving?" She looked at me as if she knew the answer.

"Forty-five?" I didn't want to lie, and that was the speed I last remembered going.

"Yes, forty-five. This is a thirty-limit zone. It changes to forty-five, but you have to wait until after the limit changes, not before."

My face turned red. I was such an idiot. "Sorry. I'm learning how to drive. My test is next week."

Pat handed the officer his papers, then grabbed my hand.

"I'm going to run your permit and his license." Holding my permit and Pat's license, she returned to her vehicle. Would I get into trouble? I didn't want it to prevent me from getting my license.

The officer came back to my window after five minutes. "I'll let you off with a warning this time." She handed me a slip printed on receipt-like paper. I tucked it into my purse.

I breathed a sigh of relief. There was no way I could afford a ticket. I'd finished single-handedly paying for a divorce.

"Make sure you're not speeding up too early. Drive safe. Have a good night."

"Thanks, officer," Pat said.

I drove the rest of the way home and I didn't speed. At last, I pulled into my parents' house. Pat got out, hugged me, and held on. My knees weakened. Butterflies of excitement fluttered in my stomach.

Grabbing my hand, he walked me to the door. "See you soon."

I smiled. He was the one I loved. I prayed, *Lord, please let me keep him.*

Pat had let me use his car for my driver's test and by some miracle, I passed. That night, Pat asked if I wanted to take a walk along the lake. It was a pleasant temperature for wintertime in Minnesota.

Stringed lights blinked on the trees next to the lake; their light reflected off the waters. Pat and I walked along the bike trail observing the sights. It was turning out to be another nice date night. A cup of coffee heated my chilled fingers. The brisk air bit the tip of my nose, but my heart was happy with Pat beside me. White petals of snow floated, landing in my hair.

Pat touched a flake, and it melted in his fingers. He put his arm around me. "I better keep you warm."

"Thanks." If he were near, I'd never be cold inside again. On the drive home, Pat looked at me with soft and kind eyes and said, "Psalm twenty-three."

"Psalm twenty-three," I said. Did that mean he loved me?

We continued getting to know each other through December, January, and February. Sometimes we went out to eat or for coffee. Sometimes Pat came over to Mom and Mitchell's. It was almost St. Patrick's Day, and I had invited him over for dinner. I hoped to impress him with my mediocre cooking.

I stood near the stove, biting my lip, watching Mitchell as he leaned close to the open oven. Sticking a thermometer inside of a piece of chicken breast, Mitchell checked the internal temperature. "You don't want to overcook it. It's best to check the temperature, then you'll know when it's done."

Mitchell was quite the chef since I'd moved back in with him and Mom. In the past, he didn't cook unless it was over a campfire. I couldn't cook unless the meal was from a box, and my ability to make macaroni wouldn't impress Pat, so I recruited Mitchell's help.

Mitchell asked, "Want to play a game of scrabble before your date gets here?"

"Sure, I know I'm going to lose, though."

He gave me a sympathetic smile. "It doesn't matter if you win or not. I know I'm hard to beat."

Mitchell was right. The entire time I'd known him, I had never won.

After dinner with Pat, Mom, and Mitchell. I washed the dishes in the kitchen, so Mitchell wouldn't have to. Whenever I did them, he thanked me, and I enjoyed keeping our relationship peaceful.

Once I had finished cleaning up, Pat and I watched a movie. Toward the middle of the movie, Pat dug into his pocket. I continued watching the movie. What was he searching for? Maybe a mint or something. What if . . . I took a deep breath . . . what if he wanted to marry me? He didn't like me enough to marry me, did he? My eyes met his. He pulled out a ring, a silver band with a beautiful shimmering diamond.

"Will you marry me?" he asked in an excited, yet quiet, voice.

I cupped my hands over my mouth. "Really?" I threw my arms around him, embracing him. "Of course, I will." I leaned away, then grinned at him. I squeezed him tightly. "You want to?"

"Of course, I do." He slipped on the silver band with a diamond on it.

A beautiful ring hugged my finger. I'd never let my Pat go. "Psalm twenty-three," I said. It was our code phrase for I love you.

"Psalm twenty-three." Pat squeezed me tight.

"Wait."

"Oh, no. What is it?" He looked worried.

"Nothing, it's just. . . Did you ask Mitchell's permission?"

"Of course. I asked him last week."

I threw my arms around him and squeezed. The whole thing felt old-fashioned and romantic.

The grass was fresh after the winter snow melted. Sierra spent a good portion of the morning attempting to curl my defiant hair. A necklace hung around my neck, three connected strings of pearls my grandma Nelly had given me. Long, dangling pendants hung in my ears. My friend from church tied orange roses and tiger lilies together in a bouquet. I clenched them in my hand. The colors were vibrant against the evergreen trees outside the church. My dress, a gown with white lace, flowed into a short train.

On a wooden slab bench, to the side of the altar, two members of the church played Pat's and my favorite hymns, one on the violin and one on the guitar. The church members had covered the ground with straw, with benches on both sides of an aisle I'd soon walk down. Each bridesmaid wore one color of the sunset, a variety of pinks, reds, yellows, and blues. The groomsmen wore orange. It was a brand-new start.

The bridal party walked arm in arm toward the wooden-stump altar. Sierra's daughter, Pat's sister's daughter, and Wren's daughter scattered flower petals across the path.

Everyone was in their place, the music paused. Silence. My heart pounded, jumping against my ribs.

Mitchell wore gray slacks, and a blue dress shirt with a black tie and laced his arm through mine. We walked from the church's back door to the end of the benches, waiting until the bridal song began. The grass felt squishy and cool beneath my bare feet.

Everyone stood and turned to face us.

"I hope I don't trip," I whispered to Mitchell.

"You won't fall." He chuckled. "It'll be fine. Just watch where you step."

I nodded.

The music began. The audience continued watching Mitchell and I as we drew closer to Pat.

Each step, walking next to Mitchell, brought me nearer to my future.

At last, we reached Pat.

"She's all yours," Mitchell said, then winked at Pat.

They shook hands. It made my heart happy.

Pat held my eyes captive as I moved beside him. I giggled and grabbed Pat's hands as the preacher spoke. My nerves intensified as we got further and further into the sermon. Today, we would share our first kiss. We had avoided being alone as often as possible to prevent the possibility of slipping up. It had been a challenge, but he wanted to marry me because he loved me, not for a false intimacy. I hoped I didn't let him down.

"You may now kiss the bride," the preacher said.

I looked at Pat, daring him to make the first move.

He paused. Then chewed on his bottom lip.

I waited for him to move closer.

The audience became a party to our secret that we had never kissed before.

They laughed, and we laughed. My face flushed.

"Oh, come on already," my grandma Irene said from somewhere behind me.

Pat looked at me, his eyebrows raised. His chest rose and fell, and he let out a loud sigh. He leaned forward. His warm lips met mine.

"You are now husband and wife," the preacher said.

Our marriage began with the laughter of the congregation. After the reception, Pat and I climbed into his Chevy truck and began our new life together as husband and wife.

~ Twenty-Eight ~

Five years into our marriage, Pat and I had two beautiful children via C-section: a girl and a boy, and we were expecting a third: another girl. After having two miscarriages, I see how blessed I was.

Wren found Smith, the man Mom thought was our dad, on Facebook in 2017. We hadn't heard from him since Wren and I were in South Carolina when she'd written to him about her oldest being born.

When Mom was younger, DNA testing wasn't accessible like it is today. Facebook didn't exist. While these advances make some things easier, they also complicate things. How many people have uncovered forbidden secrets? I've heard that Ancestry has added warning labels on their products.

I wrote to Smith on Facebook messenger, *I'm glad Wren found you; we've wanted to talk to you.*

He responded, *I told your sister I want to help you with your past, so ask me whatever you want.*

I thought of all the questions I could ask. How he and Mom met, how long they were together. Why didn't it work out?

I told him I was expecting my third child.

Congratulations, he messaged.

It wasn't but a few weeks after we found Smith that I called the doctor because I had bled.

A nurse escorted Pat and me to an exam room for an ultrasound. The nurse handed me a terry-cloth towel to cover my lower body. After I covered up, she squirted warm bluish gel on my stomach. She pressed the nodule onto my skin, then turned the television on so we could see.

Immediately, I saw a heartbeat on the television. I breathed a sigh of relief. Did I see something like another baby? Was it a gestational sac? I couldn't see a heartbeat, so it must not be a baby; what was it? It was the same size as my uterus or bigger. Would I have twins? No. It couldn't be.

The ultrasound tech clicked on her computer. Calmly, she said, "I've got to send this over to the doctor. He'll want a word with you."

My mind raced. What was wrong? Was it having to deal with that area the size of a second baby? I had seen my baby's heartbeat, so everything had to be okay, I hoped.

The doctor walked in, the same one who told me I was going to have a C-section with Rose. "There's good news and bad news. The good news is that your baby is healthy." He stood next to the screen. "You're bleeding is because your body is taking a long time to heal. It's called implantation. That's normal and will resolve soon.

"So, for the bad news. See here." He pointed at the screen toward the odd baby-sized spot. "That is a tumor on your left ovary. It's ten centimeters. You'll have to have surgery as soon as possible, preferably after fourteen weeks. I'll send the images over to your doctor and she'll schedule your next appointments.

"Do you have questions?" He glanced up from his clipboard.

"Is there anything I can do to make it shrink?" Was it my fault? I hadn't eaten everything I should have. I didn't drink enough water or exercise enough. Could that be what caused it?

"No, there's nothing."

"During pregnancy, is surgery safe?" My face tensed.

"Yes, with lots of success, in the second trimester. In the first trimester, surgery isn't safe because it can lead to miscarriage, and in the third, it isn't safe because surgery may cause premature labor. I want to contact a few of my colleagues. One is in South Dakota and one is in North Dakota. The one in South Dakota is a specialist in robotics surgery, a minimally invasive surgery. That's your best chance."

While I waited to speak to the specialists, I tried to stay busy. I prayed to God for guidance. As I tried to push the worries from my mind, I remembered it wasn't in my hands anymore.

On Saturday, Pat and I drove into town to the local farmer's market where I worked. We set up the canopy tent together, and I set out the baked goods I'd made the day before. Early customers wandered table to table, checking out the products.

A man approached my table. He wore thin glasses and a jean shirt. "Do you have anything gluten-free?" he asked.

"Yes, it's all gluten-free."

"That's great. My wife doesn't handle gluten well. I'll try this German almond cake." He grabbed the cake. "Hey. Is there something you need prayer for? I think God's asking me to pray for you."

"Actually, yes." I hesitated but wanted to accept any help I could for my baby's sake. "I'm pregnant and I have a tumor on my ovary. Surgery might hurt the baby; I don't know what to do."

He bowed his head and touched my shoulder. "Okay, let's pray."

My cheeks flushed. I'd never had a stranger ask to pray for me.

"Lord, I pray for strength in this situation, for healing and Your guidance, Lord. Thank you for her faith in You. Show her which path to take. Amen."

God saw my worries and sent someone to encourage me. *Thank you, Father.*

After the market, I texted Smith and told him they'd found a tumor on my ovary.

Everything will be okay. Don't worry, it sounds like your doctors know what they're doing. My wife had rough labors with our kids, too. It all worked out. He was encouraging when he wanted to be. *How's your mother doing these days? This situation with your tumor must stress her out.*

She's doing well. I rolled my eyes. What did my mother matter to him? He'd left her all those years ago and cheated on her and didn't care. *My stepdad hasn't been feeling well, though.*

Sorry to hear that. I forgot I was going to tell you something.

What's up? I responded.

I'm moving overseas again. Russia. He had been living in Florida for a few years now.

It was another subject change. I guessed he didn't want to talk about my stepdad being unwell. I sighed. *That's so cool.*

I was happy for him to explore a new place, but with him so far away, it further diminished my hope of meeting him. Why didn't he want to meet us before he left the country? He was always avoiding it. *Talk to you soon,* I texted.

I had hoped Smith would learn to love Wren and me over time, but neither of us felt like we belonged to him. I found no likeness in his face, his personality, or his belief systems.

One day, after he had moved, I worked up the nerve to ask him something I'd been wondering for some time. Because we'd been talking for so long, I felt braver. Smith answered his phone after three or four rings.

"Hey, I've been wanting to ask, but I've been a little nervous."

"What is it? You can ask anything," Smith said.

"What does your wife think about you getting to know us? Does she want to know us, too?"

He cleared his throat. "I haven't told her yet. She didn't ask, so it's not lying," he said. "I'm not sure I'm your father, but I don't want to suggest anything about your mother. You understand."

"Yeah." If he didn't think he was our dad, what would be the harm in him taking a DNA test? I was sure Wren had mentioned to him that the results were confidential when she mentioned that we were thinking about taking one. We talked a while longer about how he was liking his new location and then we hung up.

After the last market of July, I was cleaning up my baking mess from the day before and putting away my piled-up dishes.

Wren called in the evening to see how the farmer's market went. She then told me, "I ordered the DNA tests for us. I know Smith won't check his DNA, but maybe I can find a connection to someone else we're related to. It'll take a bit to get the results back." She paused, then laughed. "You know," Wren said. "If he isn't our dad, we're having a relationship with Mom's ex-boyfriend. Seems strange when you think about it like that, doesn't it?"

I chuckled. "That would be weird. Maybe it's good you got our DNA tested then."

"Yeah."

I was at home, getting the kids ready to go to my in-laws for my appointments in Fargo. The phone rang, and I ran to answer it.

"Hey, Kaitlin," Mom's voice was dry and scratchy.

Something must have happened. "What's wrong, Mom?"

"Mitchell had a heart attack. We were in the McDonald's drive-through and when he said something was wrong. He passed out, then hit the car in front of us."

"Oh, no. Is he okay? Was there a lot of damage?" I sat for a moment.

"Nope, no damage. Our bumpers hit. I yelled at them out the window to say sorry. Getting him to the hospital was my primary concern. I shoved Mitchell's body to the side then I headed to the ER a few blocks away. He's stable in the ICU."

"Hold on a second, Mom." I walked to the living room where Pat was and held the phone to my chest. "Mitchell had a heart attack." I frowned. "He's in the ICU in Fargo. Can we visit him before my appointment tomorrow?"

"I don't see any reason why not."

I put the phone back to my ear. "Okay, Mom. We'll be there tomorrow. Love you and tell Mitchell we're thinking of him."

"I will. See you tomorrow."

I hung up. "Let's try to get there early," I said to Pat.

He stood and wrapped his arms around me. "Are you going to be okay?"

"I hope Mitchell is okay and our appointment. I can't lose him and a baby."

Pat and I traveled to my appointment two hours away while the sky was still dark. The roads stretched through towns until we hit the interstate. I hoped Mitchell was stable. The miles dragged and my nerves built, worrying about Mitchell and my unborn child.

Inside the city, multiple black lanes spun through traffic circles. Mitchell's hospital, five minutes from my hospital, was our first stop.

A morning chill lingered in the air when we arrived, but I could tell it'd be a pleasant summer day. We walked into the hospital. The first room we entered was a huge circular lobby. The floors ascended, higher and higher, like a spiral staircase inside an atrium-shaped room.

We knocked on Mitchell's door. My heart raced. I hadn't seen Mitchell in the hospital in a long time. I hoped he was doing better than the last time.

"Come in," came Mom's voice.

I opened the door. Mitchell sat in bed, wearing a white hospital gown, his skin gray and pale. A machine beeped to the side of his hospital bed.

"Hi. How are you, Mitchell?" I gave him a sympathetic smile.

"Eh, I'm okay. They're making me do a stress test and they won't let me eat." He gritted his teeth.

"They won't let you eat?"

His chin quivered, and he cleared his throat. "No, I can't have coffee either. Man, I could use a cup of coffee." He grimaced, then glanced at the floor. "Some dumb test. I don't even need it." Pity for him swelled in my heart.

Mom stood and hugged me. "Are you ready for your appointment, Kaitlin?"

I felt silly worrying about my problems when Mitchell looked so sick. I said, "I'm nervous, but it's an ultrasound, nothing crazy. We will talk to a few doctors. It shouldn't be bad." I shrugged. Having an ultrasound wasn't as scary as a heart attack.

Mitchell changed the channel. "Thanks for coming. I hope they'll transfer me to the Veterans' hospital before I'm dead." He shifted on his bed and crossed his arms. "I want my doctor. I trust him. These doctors know nothing."

"I hope they get you there soon. I'll be praying for you, and ask God to help you get to the VA."

"Thanks," he said, as if not sure a prayer would help much.

Pat and I sat and talked with Mom and Mitchell for ten more minutes. Mitchell began resting his eyes, and I knew he needed us to go if he was going to get any sleep. "We should get going; my appointment is in an hour."

Mitchell stirred in his bed. "All right. Thanks for stopping. I hope I make it through this."

I gave him a half-smile. "You will. It'll be okay," I said, hoping I was right.

"Love you, guys," Mom said.

"Love you too. See you soon."

Pat and I headed to the elevator. I choked back tears. Was Mitchell going to die? His skin was so pallid, like the time he had almost died.

At my hospital, a few miles away, a nurse led Pat and me into a room with an ultrasound machine next to an examination bed. The nurse handed me a gown and asked me to change. She left the room.

I put on the gown.

The ultrasound tech entered a few minutes later. Her ponytail followed the movement of her head. "First, we'll check on the baby, see if he or she is okay." She turned on the machine, then rubbed the transducer across my belly. "Baby is doing well. Their heartbeat is strong. It's about one hundred and sixty. The bladder and kidneys are functioning well. The baby looks great. Let's check on that tumor now. Okay?" She clicked on her keyboard and mouse. Lights flashed on the screen of the machine.

"What are the lights for?" I asked.

"It shows the blood flow around the baby. Let's get the doctor here and he can read the results to you. Do you want to know what you're having?"

Pat's eyes met mine.

The question had caught me off guard. "Can we? I'm only thirteen weeks; isn't that too soon?"

"If the baby will let me, I can give you a reasonable guess," the ultrasound tech said. "This machine is more sensitive than the ones they use in the clinic."

Pat shrugged. "Okay, sure. That's great. Can you write it on a piece of paper so we can look later?"

"Sure, the baby isn't giving me the best look." She moved the device again, sliding it. "I think I know." The tech wrote something on a card, then stuck it in a black envelope. She handed it to Pat.

The doctor walked in, a tall, thin man wearing a white lab coat, in his mid-forties with salt and pepper hair. "I'm Doctor Ludlow, I'm a specialist in Maternal-Fetal Medicine. Let's see that baby." He sat on a swivel chair, grabbed the transducer, then rubbed it across my tummy as the tech had. "The baby looks good. Let's look at that tumor."

What would he say? Did I need surgery? I chewed my lip. If he didn't say I did, maybe I didn't.

"All right. The tumor is twelve centimeters." It had grown two centimeters that fast? At this rate, it would be the size of a basketball soon. Fear grew in my thoughts; the baby might run out of room.

"What do you recommend we do?" I asked, my voice shaking.

"I want to see what Dr. Augusta has to say about the tumor before we decide to remove it or not."

"Thanks." I sighed. Ugh, now there'd be more waiting. I hoped this doctor would be more opinionated, so I'd know what to do.

The Dr. looked at the ultrasound tech, beaming. "Did you tell them what they're having?"

"Yes, they didn't want me to tell them yet."

"Okay, great. Kaitlin, if you deliver early, you can deliver here in Fargo. Great to meet you."

"You too, thanks."

The doctor left.

We arrived at our second appointment to see the other specialist, the one from South Dakota. Pat sat on a chair, and I sat on the patient table next to him.

The nurse inserted my arm into the blood pressure cuff and took my vitals. "Blood pressure is a little high." She handed me a white hospital gown. "Put this on. The doctor will be right in."

"Okay, thanks," I mumbled.

Across the room from me, were pamphlets in neat rows on a rack. *You and menopause, Surgical Menopause, You and Your Hormones, Surgical Hysterectomy.* What if they tried to take away my womanhood? With no ovaries, would I feel like a woman? What if my baby didn't make it? Goosebumps covered my arms.

Two women walked in, one blonde and one brunette, both tall and thin. They could be models. Self-conscious now, I looked at my ever-growing belly and pulled my gown as close to my knees as I could.

"Hi, I'm Dr. Augusta, I'm the surgeon. This is my physician's assistant, Camile. I'll give you a pre-surgical exam today, then we won't have to do a pre-op later. It'll save us both time."

"Sure, sounds good." I rubbed my arms to warm up. She sounded so sure I'd have surgery, assuming I needed a pre-op physical. She hadn't explained her thoughts about surgery yet.

Dr. Augusta retrieved a stethoscope from around her neck and stuck it on my back. I arched my back as a shiver crept down my spine.

"Two deep breaths. Okay, exhale, inhale, exhale. Lung sounds are perfect." She looked at her chart. "Blood pressure isn't high enough to worry." She grabbed my ankle. "No edema. Everything looks as it should."

The doctor glanced at her clipboard. "So I see on your chart, that you have had one ovary previously removed?"

"Yes. With my first daughter, they found a tumor on it during my C-section."

"I see," the doctor said.

I couldn't wait any longer to ask, "Should I have this surgery, doctor?"

Her eyes hardened. She almost scoffed, but I could tell she was trying not to be mean. "Yes. You need this surgery. However, I won't do it after twenty weeks of gestation. You need to decide in the next few days. If the baby gets too big, it becomes impossible to work. We need it done soon. There's a chance, though I wouldn't count on it, to save part of your ovary. It will depend on how the tumor is attached. The sooner we get started, the better."

I nodded, thankful for straightforward answers, but scared too. If something went awry, a twenty-week-old baby couldn't survive outside of my body.

"Call my office to set an appointment. Questions?"

I shook my head.

Pat mentioned a family history of malignant hyperthermia which required a different type of anesthesia to be used. The doctor said she'd discuss it with her surgical team, but she didn't think it would be a problem.

She turned on her heel and exited through the door, followed by her assistant.

Pat rose and stood by me, then grabbed my hand and squeezed.

What if I had to choose between me and the baby? I couldn't lose my baby, but I didn't want my children to live without their mom, either. *Lord, please guide me to the right choice.* I sniffled.

"It'll be okay." Pat rubbed my hand.

"I hope so." On Pat's shoulder, I rested my head. "I love you."

I thought and prayed about the surgery for a few days, and I finally felt at peace with my choice. I was thankful for a doctor that told me the truth, without sugarcoating it. At least with the laparoscopic surgery, I may not lose my ovary and it was less invasive. I knew what to do now.

We checked into the Fargo hospital when I was nineteen weeks along for my surgery.

"We have to wheel you to surgery," the nurse said. "Your husband will wait for you in the recovery room."

Pat and I kissed.

The nurse pushed my wheelchair across the shiny linoleum floor. I swallowed the lump in my throat. The nurses brought me to a cold room with a foam wedge laying on an operating table.

"Scooch onto this table," the nurse told me.

The room was full of staff. I lay on the metal operating table, not knowing if I'd be pregnant after surgery. My knees knocked together, and my teeth chattered. I didn't know if I'd go through menopause in six months.

The nurse tilted me to one side and stuck the pillow wedge under my hip.

The anesthesiologist put in an IV and a single tear rolled down my cheek. The nurse wiped the tear away. "It'll be okay. I promise. Count back from ten."

"Ten, nine . . ." I drifted under the power of medicine.

A nurse stood at my side, leaning close to me. "Hey, you're awake. How are you feeling?"

I looked long and slow at her. "Is my baby, okay?"

"Your baby is doing great. Your vitals are good. We will get you to your husband in a few minutes," the nurse said.

Relief washed over me; The baby was okay. They hadn't mentioned my ovary, but it didn't matter as much as the tiny life inside me. I tried to sit up but had a hard time moving.

After a few minutes, they wheeled me to my husband.

I dozed, in and out of awareness for the next couple of hours, occasionally catching glimpses of Pat watching television.

The surgeon came in. She wore ordinary clothes underneath a long lab coat. "We saved a fourth of your ovary. We don't know if it'll function. The baby tolerated surgery. You can go home tomorrow. Questions?"

"None I can think of."

She walked out as I uttered, "Thanks."

~ Twenty-Nine ~

In 2018, Wren and I awaited our DNA results. Smith still hadn't mentioned meeting us in person or when he'd return to the states, if ever.

My two oldest kids splashed in the puddles in our driveway, and I carried baby Tilly. I squinted at the mounds of snow melting. The spring air was fresh against my face.

Wren called me. "Kaitlin," she said. "Our results came in, but no matter how hard I try, our ancestry doesn't fit Smith's. I'll keep searching until it makes sense."

"Do you think you'll know for sure?"

"Probably. New people test every day. We need the right person to test, that's all. Could be tomorrow, or next year." I adjusted Tilly on my hip.

"What do you mean Smith doesn't fit? Mom said it couldn't be anyone else." Why would Mom lie? I told her I wouldn't be mad if she'd tell me the truth. Justus jumped, sending water flying upward all around him.

"It's, well—I don't see how Smith could be our dad. I don't know what to do. His last name isn't here anywhere, despite being common. I'll keep digging and see what I can come up with."

"I'll pray you can figure it out. Wish I could help you more."

Wren called me a few months after the results had come in. She had been trying and trying to piece everything together, but it was proving difficult. I didn't know why Smith wouldn't test himself. We'd told him our sample was sent in. "In the next half hour, I'll figure out who our dad is. I'm so excited!" Wren said.

My mouth dropped. "So, you still don't think it's Smith? I figured he'd eventually fit into the equation."

"No, I don't think it's Smith at all. Our biological dad's first cousin popped up. I'll know in a short matter of time now, but Smith isn't our dad unless he's adopted or something. I'll call you back. Besides, whoever our dad is, he's Swedish."

"How do you know that?" I asked, fascinated.

"Mom's ancestors aren't from there and Smiths aren't either. Smith told me that his ancestors are English. We are coming up as close to ¼ Swedish descent."

"Wow. That is crazy. Call me as soon as you know anything else, okay?"

"I will," Wren said.

Was the DNA process inaccurate? When I told Mom we were testing, she wasn't sure our saliva could contain so much truth. I creased my eyebrows. Did she think DNA tests weren't accurate? Or was she embarrassed or something? Who could our father be if it wasn't Smith? Mom said there wasn't anyone else it could be. Was I supposed to believe Mom or science? I rested my face in my hands. Ancestry would find the truth, at least I hoped it would. What would Wren and I do then? What if our father was dead? No, it couldn't be. At least I hoped he wasn't. If he was alive, what if he didn't want anything to do with us? I wasn't sure I could handle that.

Wren called me back twenty minutes later. "Our dad is one of two brothers. One wasn't anywhere near us when Mom got pregnant, so I guess I found our dad."

"What's his name? Can I call Mom?" My heart thudded in my chest. "Is he alive?"

"Yes. He lives in Florida. Call Mom and let me know what she says. His name is Alan Alms. I'm going to call him. I found his number on Google."

"I can't believe we found him! I'm so nervous," I said.

"Me, too."

I hung up the phone and called Mom as fast as my fingers would push the buttons on my phone. What would Mom think of this discovery? My heart thudded in my chest. Would she recognize his name or deny knowing him? Could a DNA test be wrong? My cheeks flushed. All I wanted was the truth. I paced in the living room.

"Hello?" Mom asked.

"Mom. We figured out who our dad is, and it isn't Smith."

"What? That's—? Well, who is it?"

I paused for dramatic effect.

"Kaitlin? Who is it?" Mom begged.

"Did you know someone named Alan Alms?" I asked.

"Yes! He was one of my closest friends in the Airforce, we were miliary cops together. I didn't know he was your dad. I didn't think he could have kids. That's so crazy. He was a good guy. Have you called him yet?" She paused, then more sorrowfully added, "I am sorry for all of this."

"It's okay, Mom. Remember when I thought I was pregnant in college?" I paused. "If I had been pregnant, I wouldn't have known who the father was."

"That was different."

"Not really. And yes, Wren is calling him, I think."

We ended the call, and then the phone rang again.

"Hey, Kaitlin," Wren sounded out of breath. "I worked up the nerve to call Dad's cell phone. I left a message, asking for Alan, and seeing if he remembered Mom from the military. Now we wait and see if he calls back."

"I hope he does. Mom said he was her friend," I repeated Mom's reaction to Wren. "I don't know what I'll do if he calls me," I said. "Let me know how it goes."

"I will. Talk to you soon. I'll text Smith." I let out a breath.

"Okay. Let me know what he says," Wren said. I texted Smith and told him the news.

Smith texted, *Are you sure we can believe this Ancestry.com?*

I don't think it lied. Ancestry didn't know Mom dated this guy. I don't see how it could be wrong.

Okay.

I couldn't tell if Smith was relieved or upset about the Ancestry news. For the past few months, it seemed like he had gotten attached to us. I couldn't be sure.

Is it someone I know? Smith texted.

I'm not sure, I wrote back. I didn't know if I could tell him without upsetting Mom or our biological father and I didn't know if he'd remember Alan.

It had been a few hours since Wren left the message on Dad's phone; had she talked to him yet? I paced through the living room, my fingers tingling. I couldn't wait to know how this whole situation turned out. Would he want us? My phone rang, and I jumped at the noise.

"Kaitlin, I talked to Dad! I can't believe it's him. He's so excited. On the weekend, he's going to call you."

The weekend? That was five days from now. I sighed. How could I wait that long? My stomach became unsettled, but at least he wanted us; that was good, right? I didn't know how he could wait so long to call, though. Maybe he wanted nothing to do with us, or maybe he needed time to figure out how to reject us.

Wren said, "He had a feeling all along that he might be our dad. He's been waiting for us to call telling him his suspicions were true."

"Wow," I said, unsure of how to feel about any of this. Did he really want us? "I'm so nervous."

"He's easy to talk to, don't worry. It'll be fine. His personality is like ours."

"That's great." I felt better. If he was like Wren and me, maybe there wasn't anything to worry about.

All week, I waited.

Saturday, late in the afternoon, the phone rang.

"Hi," a man said, with a slight southern drawl.

"Hi." I fidgeted.

"How are you?" he asked.

"I can't believe I'm talking to you." I felt out of breath. Was he my dad? God had written the answer in our DNA. Ancestry.com wouldn't know about Mom and Dad and their relationship in the '80s. It had to be true.

"Me either. I can't believe you girls found me. After all this time, I wondered if I'd hear from you."

I ran my fingers through my tangled hair. "Did you think we were yours?"

"Deep down, I knew you were mine. I tried to find you, but I didn't know how. One day you were gone. I wished I knew where you'd moved. We didn't have social media. It was harder to find people." He paused and his voice lowered, "We've lost so much time."

"I know." At last, we'd found our father, but we were in our thirties, and he was in his fifties. I took a deep breath and refused to give up. We might still have lots of time. Besides, it had taken so long just to find him. I wasn't ready to give up so easily. "So, where did you grow up?"

"I grew up in New York, near Rochester."

"What were your parents like?"

"My mom and dad are both gone, but I'd rather talk about them some other time. It's a tough topic for me."

I frowned. Oh, no, I'd upset him. Maybe it had been the wrong thing to ask. Was he like Mitchell and prone to overreacting? Maybe the conversation would be better if I refocused it on something more positive. "Are you sure you're my dad?"

"I'm going to order my Ancestry test. I can't wait to see if my DNA matches."

"Oh." I sat down. I hadn't expected him to question the results. I hoped he didn't think we were trying to take advantage of him. "We thought some guy named Smith was our dad, and we've been talking to him for about a year now."

"I remember the name Smith. In the military, Smith and I did not get along. Threatened me if I didn't stay away from your mom, as I recall."

"Wow. I didn't know that." Tilly curled up in my lap.

"He needed a smack in the mouth." Alan laughed. "I hadn't seen your mom in a while. A buddy of mine told me she left; he didn't know where to. I didn't say goodbye or anything. It wasn't fair."

It seemed like he felt abandoned. "We left Mississippi and then moved again a few times. I was so little back then."

"When did you move to Minnesota?" he asked. "I thought you lived in the South."

"At the end of kindergarten, we stayed with our grandma, Anthony's mom, when we were six."

"Okay, so who is Anthony?"

I hoped I didn't confuse him too much with more names. I sighed. "He's my little sister's dad. He raised us until we were ten. We thought he was our dad, but Mom says she didn't meet him until we were toddlers."

"I remember one of the last conversations with your mom. It played in my mind over and over. I couldn't let it go. Throughout the years, I wondered if I was your dad," he said, sounding dejected.

"It's okay. You did what you could." It wasn't fair. I bit my lip. I didn't know how to ease his pain or mine. "You have us now." I hoped I could lift his spirits. "And beautiful grandchildren you can enjoy, too." I felt choked up, thinking about how he'd missed all my children's births. "Do you have any other kids?"

"No, we never did." He continued, "Let's give my wife some time to get used to this. In the meantime, we can wait for my results to come back."

My heart broke for them. I didn't know what I'd do without my kids. They changed my life in so many ways.

"Wren and I don't want to hurt your wife, that's the last thing we'd ever want." My heart became heavy thinking about the distance between us. Florida is a long way from Minnesota. Maybe it was too good to be true, after all. I walked to the kitchen and poured myself a cup of coffee. "I hope we can meet someday."

"Me, too. Before we realize it, another year will disappear."

"Yeah." Would this relationship ever work? My gaze fell to the floor. I couldn't go back in time and change it, even if I wanted to. I didn't know how this relationship was fixable, but my relationship with Mitchell had been terrible and we'd made it work. Maybe my pessimistic outlook was getting the better of me. I'm sure the relationship needed time to grow and then everything would be okay. I tried to reassure myself. It could work if Alan gave it a chance.

"It seems like you cared about us and Mom. Why did you and her break up?" I took a sip of coffee.

"Well," he paused a moment, "I'm not sure we broke up. I'm not sure we even dated."

There was a long, awkward pause. Maybe he didn't want to bad-mouth Mom, or he's embarrassed about their history. I walk to the coffeepot to fill up my cup.

He finally spoke, "We saw each other a few times. I'm not sure— is that dating? We were so young; I wanted to be around her every chance I could. I couldn't stand not being near her. I'm not sure she felt the same, but I didn't care. We hung out and talked for hours on end about everything under the sun."

"So, what happened?" I sat back down in the chair and glanced through the window overlooking my garden.

"When you were under a year old, I worked the night shift on base. Your mom approached me wearing a toga, of all things."

"A toga?" I creased my eyebrows, that was strange.

He laughed. "A toga. Yes, we were crazy kids back then. Once I was drunk in a water fountain on base, but that's a story for another day. Anyway, that night, your mother asked what I'd do if you were mine. I don't know why, but I didn't answer. Couldn't find the words."

"You probably thought we were Smith's children. That's what Mom thought."

"I'm not sure what I thought." He paused. "She asked me if I was dating anyone, and I told her I was dating a woman named Kim. I wanted your mother to stay with me and skip the toga party, but I said nothing." Alan exhaled loudly.

I didn't know what to say. It was an important moment; one I would've been too young to remember. My past regrets had always plagued me too. My brain was always wired to be hyper-focused on my mistakes. Maybe his brain worked the same as mine.

Alan added, "I wish I would have said something. Soon, the three of you were gone. It was all pretty messed up."

"You didn't know. I'm not mad at you or anything. I hope some-day we can make up for some lost time." I thought again about making the conversation more pleasant. "What do you do for fun?"

"I'm headed out tomorrow morning to go fishing. It's one of my favorite things to do. You should see the ocean. It's beautiful in the morning. I'll send you a picture."

"I love fishing! I haven't gone fishing in a long time, though." My dad loved fishing, too? I could see us sitting on a dock somewhere, casting, and talking about life. "Hopefully we'll meet someday."

After a few more weeks of talking with us, conversations with Smith and me became sparse, then non-existent. Wren was right. It seemed strange to spend more time getting to know Mom's ex-boyfriend; I felt at peace with the way things turned out. Of course, I know as the years go by, we might still touch base from time to time, as we always have.

After Alan's test results, he confirmed his parenthood to Wren and me. After the initial and expected shock wore off, Alan's wife, Anna, was excited to get to know us, too. She seemed so nice, and I looked forward to getting to know them both better. I called Wren, and we planned a trip to meet our dad and his wife during the third week in August. It would give him and his wife five months to mentally prepare. Wren called him and the dates of our plan worked for him, too. My heart thudded in my chest. What it would be like to meet our dad? There was only one way to find out.

On August fifteenth, I sat in the window seat on a large plane with Pat and Tilly. Wren was taking another plane that was closer to where she lived. As I glanced at the clouds, a circular rainbow surrounded the shadow of the airplane. Perhaps God sent me this rainbow, a promise of the future yet to come. I prayed, *please let this go well.*

The temperature was sauna-like. Wren, Pat, Tilly, and I climbed into the rental car. My lungs expanded wider to accommodate the southern air. It was perfect.

Pat climbed into the driver's seat, and I sat in the front passenger's spot. In the backseat, we buckled Tilly into her car seat and Wren sat next to her. It was finally time to start our adventure. I turned around facing Wren in the backseat and we smiled at each other. She pulled out her schoolwork for college, a thick textbook then started reading. She was attending school to finish her master's degree.

Pat pulled the car out of the rental parking lot and onto the road. Palm trees swayed on the side of the freeway beneath the ramp leaving the airport. It was an entire world away from Minnesota, maybe it would be a lot like South Carolina. I had loved South Carolina. To think, we had been only hours away when Wren had her oldest and wrote that letter to Smith. Too bad we'd sent it to the wrong man.

My heart raced each mile that the distance shortened between my sister and me and the man we'd never met, our father. It was an hour-long drive from Orlando to our hotel, and the ride wasn't fast enough.

Pat, Wren, Tilly, and I arrived at the hotel. We paused at the desk until a man arrived to check us in.

"We're here to meet our dad for the first time," Wren said as she leaned her elbows on the counter.

The hotel attendant raised his eyebrows at her. "Oh yes," he replied, "I met your dad. That man seemed mighty nervous." The attendant let out a light laugh, then pointed down the hall. "He's in the room on the right."

Wren and I giggled. Alan, our dad, was so close. Wren texted him, so he'd know we were only a few feet away.

Wren, Pat, and I walked through the hall. I giggled more as we inched along the corridor. My heart pounded. I couldn't believe after thirty years I would finally meet my dad.

Wren peeked into the visitor area first, then walked inside. Pat, Tilly, and I entered the room behind her. Three strangers smiled at us: our dad, his wife, Anna, and her mother, Libby.

Alan handed me purple flowers in an ornate bundle and Wren a pink bouquet. I held them to my face, breathing in the sweet scent of lilies. Wren and I embraced our long-lost father, one of us under each of his arms. A tear crept down his cheek. He was a few inches taller than us. His eyes met mine, familiar, yet new. They were the same as Wren's and mine.

"I'm so glad you're here," his southern drawl was slight and relaxed, then he squeezed us again.

The hotel attendant from the front desk peeked inside the room behind Alan. He smiled, let out a chuckle, and then walked away. He must have known how rare a moment like this was and couldn't help wanting to witness it.

We stayed up late talking by the poolside that night, discussing our favorite music from the '90s and Alan's favorites from before we were born. We'd gone to bed earlier than I'd wanted because Tilly needed sleep, but I think none of us wanted to sleep when there were memories to be made.

The next morning, we pulled onto a road leading to the ocean, then after driving thirty minutes, we parked in a beach-front lot. It was on our second of the three-day trip. Black tar ended where sand resembling flour covered the ground. Palm trees reached upward, and palmettos covered the landscape beneath. Beyond the parking lot was a wooden planked walkway. Pat, Dad, Wren, Anna, and I walked across the boards toward the ocean. A warm breeze blew off the waters; I tasted salt in the air. I descended five steps until I reached the beach. Pat, Dad, Wren, and I pulled off our shoes and stepped on fine sands. It was natural to be around him, a puzzle we'd always belonged to. I wished this moment would last, but it couldn't, so I held onto every detail for as long as I could.

The sand refreshingly rubbed against my feet, polishing away the roughness. I sauntered along the ocean's edge and picked seashells to take home with me for the kids. Wren and Dad walked together as I trailed with Pat and Tilly. The water came inland, lapping against my ankles. My legs swayed as the tide tugged, then the waves returned, and I balanced again.

Wren giggled, pointing. "Look at that silly bird."

Something about the long-legged bird was fascinating. His memory was terrible. When he ran into the ocean, he was carefree. He'd skitter across the sand, plucking bugs out. Then as another wave drifted onto the shore, he'd turn around, full of fear, and run away from the water. Then as if forgetting all about the wave, he'd run headlong into the ocean again, unprepared for what happened next.

I followed behind Dad and Wren, watching them skirting the water. Holding my phone, I took pictures of our footprints in the sand. Just like in the famous poem. Once, Smith gave Mom a clock with the poem *Footprints in the Sand*, on the face. During my divorce, I'd accidentally left it behind. Wren and I had our dad's feet. I smiled at the observation.

I reached to grab another seashell; its ridged pattern was rough against my fingers. Breathing in the humid ocean air, I allowed it to fill me. I snapped another picture knowing I'd look at these pictures someday and remember. This one time, we'd all been together, the three of us, reunited.

Like the waves, soon life would sweep us away, to our own homes. We would all move forward in time and somehow, we'd still be here, anchored to this moment. The brilliant sun, shimmering off the glass ocean, reflected a warm glow, and it made me think about how happy I was right then. It warmed my heart being near my father after all the time we'd spent apart. The next morning, we'd go home, and this would end.

Anna and Dad walked with us into the empty parking lot. The air felt heavy like it might rain. The palm trees swayed as I smelled the southern air, savoring it. I stared at the pavement. How did three days go so fast? We must have been having too much fun to notice. I took a deep breath, and my chest tightened. It was time to say goodbye.

Dad gave us hugs.

I didn't know what to say; I didn't want to let go. My throat tightened. When would I see him again? I frowned, knowing I would miss them, unsure if I'd see them again. Pat and Anna stood, hand in hand waiting on the sidewalk. It was hard to leave them behind, but I didn't have a choice. Wren and I trudged to the car, each step heavier than the last.

Dad and Anna waved.

We waved back, then climbed into the car.

Time passed like sand through my fingers, and no matter how hard I tried to squeeze it, it slid through. I had to let go of Florida and return to my kids. Minnesota's auburn, flame orange, and gold leaves would soon fall to the earth and crunch beneath my children's feet. Yet all the beauty that awaited me at home in 2019, didn't make it any easier to leave my dad.

Pat turned the ignition and reversed the car. We left, but a part of my heart stayed behind. I fought against the tears, but they came anyway.

~ Thirty ~

Ecclesiastes 3:1-11 says "There is a time for everything, and a season for every activity under the heavens: a time to be born and a time to die, a time to plant and a time to uproot, a time to kill and a time to heal, a time to tear down and a time to build, a time to weep and a time to laugh, a time to mourn and a time to dance, a time to scatter stones and a time to gather them, a time to embrace and a time to refrain from embracing, a time to search and a time to give up, a time to keep and a time to throw away, a time to tear and a time to mend, a time to be silent and a time to speak, a time to love and a time to hate, a time for war and a time for peace. What do workers gain from their toil? I have seen the burden God has laid on the human race. He has made everything beautiful in its time. He has also set eternity in the human heart, yet no one can fathom what God has done from beginning to end."

I walked through my yard; leaves crunched beneath my feet as I drew closer to the apple tree. Mitchell had discovered it in my yard a year ago. I'd never even noticed it there, and he, being a nature enthusiast, didn't miss it. That day, he walked to my front door. As I came out to greet him, he thanked me for the apple. I didn't have any idea what he was talking about, so he walked me over and showed me. I couldn't stop laughing at my stupidity that day. I had lived there for at least two years and didn't realize I had an apple tree growing fifty yards from my front door.

I grabbed an apple off the tree and took a bite. I loved fall harvest time. Preserving food was laborious, but I loved eating things out of the garden during the harsh winters. A chill ran through the breeze. The first frost drew closer each day. I placed the remaining vegetables into the kids' red wagon, whistling as I loaded the last vegetable in.

I told the kids, "Let's go inside and wash up."

Justus, my middle child, climbed in the wagon and I carried Tilly as I pulled it. Rose pushed the back of it until we reached the front of the house. I put the vegetables inside. The phone rang in the living room. I rinsed the dirt off my hands and sprinted to answer it.

"Hello?"

"Kaitlin. How are you?" Mom asked.

"I'm good. Do you need any tomatoes?" I laughed. I had buckets and buckets of them.

"Not now. I'm calling because Mitchell's on the list for a new heart."

"What? That's great, Mom." He'd talked about it for years, but Mom said he'd never felt worthy of taking someone else's heart. Survivor's guilt, Mom had called it.

"He's scheduled to speak to a specialized doctor next month."

"Let me know how it goes."

The date approached in September, for Mitchell's transplant meeting. Mom called me. "He changed his mind," Mom said, then her voice softened. "He says he's made peace with dying."

"I'm so sorry."

Mom cried into the phone. "I don't know what to do. You know, once he sets his mind to something, there's no changing it."

"Yeah." I heard some rustling in the background of Mom's phone.

"Mitchell needs me; I need to go."

I hung up the phone, and tears filled my eyes. I wanted to make her feel better, but I couldn't help her. If Mitchell decided not to get a transplant, then nothing could be done.

Pat and I were sitting on the couch, watching a Disney movie with the kids. My phone beeped. I swiped the screen to see what the notification was for. Mom messaged me on Facebook. We hadn't spoken since our last conversation earlier that month. *Mitchell's having stomach pain. The doctor said he needs more fiber. We are asking for another opinion. I pleaded for the doctor to help him, but that idiot didn't listen. Mitchell can't eat and he's in constant pain. There is no way it's a lack of fiber.*

I'm sorry, Mom. I'll pray for him.

I'll tell you when I know more, she responded.

It took Mitchell a month to get a colonoscopy, and I waited to hear more news from Mom. She called me the evening after his colonoscopy in October.

"How was Mitchell's procedure?" I asked. I walked to my room and shut the door so I could give more attention to my conversation with Mom.

"That's why I'm calling. They couldn't get in. His colon is blocked."

"What does that mean?" Was he okay? Nothing ever seemed to stop him before, but with his stomach blocked, he wouldn't absorb nutrients. That couldn't be good. No, he had to be okay. I had to keep being positive. Anything could happen. He'd be fine.

"A tumor prevented the camera from going in. The sample they took came back positive for cancer. It's stage three. Six months. That's all they gave him." She sobbed. "Kaitlin, I don't know what I'm going to do."

"Can't they do chemo?"

Her voice cracked, then she continued, "His heart's too weak." Mom took a labored breath. "Kaitlin, I'm going to head to bed. It's been a long day. They're going to do another exploratory surgery in a month. It'll be a long wait."

"K, Mom. Goodnight. Keep me updated. Love you." I hung up the phone and rested my face in my hands. Why was this happening? Was he going to die? He was fifty-four and had survived seven heart attacks and war. He'd pull through this, too. He had to.

Pat and I packed the truck with the kids. We traveled the two hours to Pat's great grandpa's farm for hunting season. I felt guilty doing something fun while Mitchell was suffering and maybe dying. I should be with Mitchell and Mom, helping. My cell phone rang during the drive. The caller ID said *Mom*. "Hi, Mom. How are you?"

"Mitchell had the exploratory surgery," her voice sounded raw. She sniffled.

"What's wrong, Mom?"

"The surgeon wanted to remove the tumor and see if cancer spread."

"So, what happened? You don't sound happy?"

"The colostomy bag part went well."

"But?"

"During the surgery, they discovered cancer in the lining of his stomach. They couldn't take the tumor out because it's everywhere in his stomach. The doctors changed his diagnosis to stage four Colo-rectal cancer. The doctor said he has less than three months." Mom's voice cracked. "That's February."

"I don't know what to say," my voice wavered. He'd defied the odds many times before now. Something like cancer wouldn't stop him. He was still running 5ks with Wren and me after he'd had several heart attacks.

"Mitchell thinks the surgery went well. The doctor never told him any different. How am I supposed to tell him he's dying? I can't do that. I can't tell him he's dying." She wept. "I'm not sure he'll make it until February."

"You can't think that. Mitchell is a fighter," I said, trying to re-assure her, but unsure myself. "I wonder why they didn't tell him. That's awful."

"I don't know what to do."

It was February, the month Mitchell's doctor predicted he would die. I finished homeschooling for the day and put Tilly down for her nap. The phone rang. I answered.

"Hello?"

"Hello, how are you?" a man asked.

"We're good. How are you?" I didn't recognize his voice.

"Doing the best I can, getting through it. Thank you for the birthday card."

I finally realized it was Mitchell. I rolled my eyes at my stupidity. I'd sent him a gift card for pizza because I never knew what to buy him and he'd told Mom he was sick of socks and chocolate. "You're welcome."

"Have your garden planned out?" he asked.

I walked to my shelf with my seed order for the year. I thumbed through my stack of seed packets; there were so many, perhaps I was too ambitious. "I never know how much I need until I plant, but I have a rough outline. I bought a lot this year."

"I heard this will be an early spring; are you going to plant in early May?"

"At least the cold weather crops, like kale and cabbage." There was a long pause. I wasn't used to talking to Mitchell on the phone; I had forgotten that in better health a few years ago, he had a beautiful garden that he had cared for.

He cleared his throat. "I called to thank you for the present and see how the kids are."

"The kids are good. As energetic as ever. It is nice to hear from you." I don't think he had ever called me before then. At least, not that I could remember.

"Please, say a strong prayer for me. Ask God for healing." Mitchell coughed.

"Oh." The request caught me off guard. I wasn't used to hearing him talk about God. "Of course. I'd love to pray for you. Ask any time."

"Thanks. Tary has got supper done here, so I'm going to let you go."

"Okay. Thanks for calling." I sank onto the couch.

"Take care," he said.

Was he acting differently and calling me because he knew he was dying? I covered my hand with my mouth. Would he be alive when the marigolds opened, the green buds peeling back? Would he be alive when I plucked the first green bean from my garden in July? My hands trembled. Mom said in February Mitchell might die. It was still four months before planting even began. *Lord, please, if it's Your will, heal him,* I prayed.

That night I tried to sleep, but only cried. It might be the last birthday present I'd ever buy Mitchell. Even if he hated presents, I still wanted to buy him one every year.

How many more conversations would we have? Only God knew.

Mom called me in April and told me Mitchell had started hospice care. Hospice meant mostly bed rest, and usually, a person didn't live long. I slumped onto the floor of my living room. I couldn't believe he'd taken a turn for the worst so quickly; even though the doctor believed it, I didn't.

After he got off of work, I talked to Pat, and he agreed that he'd stay with the kids so I could visit. On the way to Mom and Mitchell's house, A sense of melancholy, finality, and sorrow filled my heart. It was a day I longed to experience because I'd get to see him and still, I feared to endure it because it meant I was accepting the inevitable.

It was cold when I arrived in Fargo at Mom and Mitchell's apartment. They'd lived there a few years now. I walked on the sidewalk leading to a wooden gate door, up to four or five steps, and into Mom's apartment. The smell of cigarettes filled the air.

Mom greeted me, and I hugged her. Her eyes looked hollow and bloodshot like no tears remained. I glanced down the empty hallway, fearing to see Mitchell so sick. The room where he rested was at the end of the hall.

As I took off my stuff, Mom walked down the hall, without me, then she said, "She's here now."

I hoped I could distract him from his pain and encourage him out of desperation. I didn't know what to say but I had to face my fears of seeing him dying. He needed me. I loved him and needed him, too. He was part of me, and Wren, Sierra, and I were part of him. It didn't matter that he wasn't our biological father. Time had bound us together in its way. I walked quietly down the hall in case he was resting.

He laid on the bed, under a fleece blanket, his flesh pallid. His hands moved to his stomach. He groaned and winced. It reminded me of one of his post-heart attack hospital stays. He'd had many throughout the years. That year, he was in the hospital on his birthday so Wren, Sierra, and I had gone to the store to try to find him last-minute gift items: one was the Scrabble game, and the other was a fleece blanket like the one he used now. On his birthday, Wren and I had played Scrabble with him and never once won.

He winced again.

I averted my eyes. I didn't want him to know I'd noticed his pain. He'd always tried to hide it before, by leaving the room when his arm hurt. When I was younger, Mom told me that when he had his first heart attack the pain had started in his arm. Since then, he'd always rubbed his arm when his heart was bothering him.

"Say cheese, Kaitlin," Mitchell said. I smiled, then he took my picture. He printed the photo then handed it to me.

"This is neat," I said, gazing at my photo.

He frowned. "It's mine to keep. I'll print you another copy if you want one."

I handed it back. Pulling a white box out of the nightstand, he added my picture to his stack. I felt honored to be treasured, like gold he sought in the rivers of Yellowstone.

"Hey, Tary, grab that Gulf War military book from the other room."

"What?" Mom jumped as if startled.

Mitchell clutched his stomach and grumbled something I couldn't hear, but he gave Mom a harsh glance. She stood, then left. She returned a minute later with a book and handed it to Mitchell. Mom sat on the bed. Her bloodshot eyes met mine. Her chest shuddered, and she looked at the floor. No doubt she had been through a lot during the past few months. Mitchell wasn't the easiest person to get along with.

I hoped she was okay. Whatever he said had upset her. Back in high school, she'd told me he became hurtful when he felt sick. His actions weren't excusable, but it helped me think of him as human. Mom's long-suffering and faithfulness was beyond my ability to understand. I admired her strength, humility, and faith. She loved him at his worst when others would have, and should have, left. Mitchell was lucky to have her.

Mitchell thumbed through the book. What was he searching for? It must be important. He reached over and pointed to a map in the back section.

"This is where my platoon started. This spot on the edge is where our Humvee broke. And here,"—he pointed to another place—"this is where we reunited with our unit seven days later." He sighed. "On the right is where I encountered hazardous biochemicals."

Those must have been the chemicals he blamed for his heart failure.

"Tary, grab that yearbook I have on the shelf." Mitchell waved toward the bookshelf.

Mom darted across the room, retrieving Mitchell's book and gave it to him. He handed it to me. I opened it and looked at the pictures from his boot camp.

"I'd almost finished Ranger school. I must have been good at my job because they put me into that program, but I figured out that Ranger school meant I'd be a walking soldier." He lit a cigarette.

The smoke stung my eyes, but I didn't mention it.

"I didn't want to do that. I wanted to be a riding Army soldier. Was dropping out before graduation a mistake? Maybe I shouldn't have, then I wouldn't be dying." He clenched his fist against his stomach.

"All those surgeries I've had. It's not fair. What did I do to deserve it?" Mitchell rubbed his arm.

"It's not your fault," I whispered.

"I wanted to do so much, live until I was seventy, at least." He puffed on his cigarette. "I'm not finished with life yet." He lifted his nose in the air and cringed. "Can you smell that? It's awful. Those neighbors are cooking with onions again. Man, it stinks."

I couldn't smell anything raunchy.

Mom told us in Yellowstone how onions reminded him of dead bodies he had discovered in a foxhole in the war.

Mitchell turned on the television and chose an old war show. We remained silent and watched TV for a while together.

Mitchell broke the silence, "You know, during the war, my buddy and I were at a security checkpoint." He stared ahead as if his mind was elsewhere. "The passenger in the car in front of us reached the gate first." He sucked in a loud breath. "The gate guards shot him through the window. My buddy and I drove by. I couldn't believe it. There was so much blood." He put his hands over his face and took a deep breath. "Since then, I can't get that memory out of my head. It's burned there." He sighed. "That image will be gone soon, like. . ."

My voice disappeared as I searched for words. I couldn't find the strength to meet his eyes. There was nothing I could do to help, except pray. I looked away. I didn't want to think about him leaving us. It was too soon.

Watching him there, so close to dying, my heart pounded. It was like a terrible dream. I wasn't ready to say goodbye. "Thanks for letting me visit." I tried to smile but couldn't.

"I hope God eases this pain soon." His eyes watered. "I want peace. I've been praying." His voice softened. "I hope God hears me because I know my days are numbered." He cleared his throat. "I'm not ready to die. Your mom will be alone, and I'm worried about her. She has to take care of me while I'm like this and watch me die. I know she wants to help me, but she can't." He pulled his shirt up over his chin and sobbed. His thin jaw moved side to side like he was grinding his teeth.

I finally gathered the strength to speak, "I promise I'll annoy her every day. You know I can. I'm good at being annoying." I winked but there was a sob in my chest. "I'll help take care of her. Promise."

"Thanks," he mumbled.

"I won't say goodbye," I said. "I'll say, see you later. I know I will."

"Okay." He grinned, then pulled his shirt near his face again. "See you later," he said through his collar. He leaned back in his bed, then rested his eyes.

Tears ran down my cheeks. I turned the corner and walked toward the living room. I stopped for a moment and then went into the spare room. With all my strength, I focused on breathing in and out. This couldn't be the end. What if I never saw him again?

Sierra arrived, we chatted for a while in the living room since Mitchell was resting, and then I went home. The sorrow of Mitchell's health issues suffocated me. I tried to breathe in and exhale slowly. My heartache rose to the surface like a fishing bobber. I'd cast back out again and try to catch something else. Like a fish on a hook, would I ever escape sadness?

After I arrived home, I wrote every word Mitchell said so I could remember it accurately. It was a present to my future self, a beautiful melancholy moment frozen in time.

I distracted myself with reading some days while Mitchell was in hospice, and other days I worked on writing. Each day I tried to distract myself by waiting for that call. The one where I'd learn Mitchell died. As I tried to push away the thought, the memory of Mitchell, sitting in bed, clenching his stomach, flashed in my mind. Tears welled in my eyes. The aching heaviness came in waves. In the core of my soul, rose the question of why his life was cut short. He'd been in pain, for almost as long as I knew him. Why him? I'd never know.

During some of my reading, I read a Bible story about the Israelites arriving at the Promised Land, also known as Jericho. The Israelites planned to invade Jericho so they could live there. During their time in the desert, the Israelites lived mostly on manna, a bread from heaven, because there was no food. I realized that after they entered the land God gave them, they wouldn't need manna anymore. I imagined the story like I was there. . .

An image of long, golden grass swaying entered my mind. Manna had fallen from a dull sky. People scooped it into their open palms, receiving God's gift. I imagined one Israelite sitting and cooking manna, the bread of heaven, over a blazing campfire. It reminded me of how Mitchell cooked potatoes in Yellowstone. As I read, I felt like God was telling me, *Remember when the doctors gave Mitchell five years when he had his first heart attack? Since that day, I've been feeding Mitchell life like manna from heaven, enough every day to survive, to keep him alive.*

Tears ran down my cheeks. It was a beautiful image that filled me with hope.

Like in the story, soon Mitchell wouldn't need manna anymore. Every day, he was getting closer to Jesus. In the Bible story, the walls that were impossible to penetrate, grew weaker every day as the Lord's army marched around the city. After seven days of marching, the stones crumbled to the earth. The Israelites had spent forty years in the desert, struggling and suffering, and eating manna, many unable to rise above their rebellion against God.

Still, each day they made their way closer to the Promised Land. It reminded me of how Mitchell had spent thirty years being sick and was now getting closer to heaven. These images gave me such peace when I had little.

It was the end of April and spring came, and Mitchell was still alive. I wasn't sure he'd make it that long, but he did. If anyone could outlive a doctor's estimation, it was Mitchell. I planted asparagus roots into the sandy soil in my garden and hoped they would grow, knowing I couldn't pick any for at least two or three years or risk the plant dying.

I wiped the dirt from my hands against the grass. The smooth blades cooled my fingers. How patient God must be with us. Grass grows in weeks but sometimes our faith takes years.

I stood. "It smells like it'll rain," I told Pat.

He stood nearby in the garden. He shook his head and looked at the sky. "It's not in the forecast."

It would rain, anyway. I had memorized the smell, and the feeling it gave me. My entire life, anytime I'd been heartbroken, it almost always rained, even in November.

I walked to the mailbox to relax and breathe. I prayed, Lord, *please help Mom and Mitchell lean into You. Comfort Mitchell and help him feel Your presence and Your peace. Amen.* I inhaled the scent of the rain and damp soil and swallowed the lump in my throat. Sprinkles fell from the sky, landing on my face.

Walking back inside, I wiped the water from my glasses, then pulled out my phone. I sent Mitchell a message and told him I was writing a book about how much we love him. It could be my last chance to tell him how I felt. *We are so blessed that you became a part of our family*; I wrote.

I hope I taught you the important stuff, he replied.

You did. You did a great job. I sniffled and tears pooled in my eyes, and a pain radiated through my heart.

He had taught me how to love challenging people. He loved us the best he could, and in his way. His determination taught me to never give up. When I was younger, all I wanted was to be loved, but Mitchell had turned my head toward loving others. Loving others was one of the most important skills we will ever learn.

In the book of Matthew, Jesus himself tells us the most important commandments are to love God and love our neighbor as ourselves. In First Peter 4:8, it says: "Above all, love each other deeply, because love covers over a multitude of sins."

Mitchell texted. *My pain was a lot better today. Those pills are finally helping.*

That's great, Mitchell. I'm so glad. Heat radiated through my chest. God had heard my prayer. My throat tightened.

Early in the morning, I headed to Mom and Mitchell's house in Fargo to visit again. During this visit, I brought Mitchell one of his favorite treats, maple donuts. He didn't like gifts, but I had to give him something. Not wanting to mess my surprise up, I bought each kind the bakery had, five different types, and I bought two of each. On my previous visit, Mitchell had wanted a maple-glazed donut, but Mom couldn't find one. He had been very upset. The donuts smelled like a pastry shop, as I carried the box to the back of the house where Mitchell was.

As I entered the room, Mitchell was laying in his bed resting next to Mom watching television.

"Hi. I have a present for you," I told Mitchell.

"Oh, yeah?" he asked. His eyes went wide as I opened the large bakery box, then held it so he could peer inside. "You got all of this just for me?"

"It was the least I could do."

His chin quivered, and a tear ran down his cheek, then he cleared his throat. He reached into the box, then grabbed two donuts and leaned against his pillow, a smile on his face.

I sniffled, blinking back tears, so happy I'd brought him a single ounce of joy during his suffering. That smile of his was a present to me.

Mitchell dozed in and out of sleep most of the day. I'd noticed that he had skipped taking his morphine, probably to stay lucid. I was flattered, but I didn't like seeing him in pain, either.

It was now two o'clock, the red numbers on the alarm clock stared at me, a reminder that time moved no matter what. We continued watching the TV.

"Sierra will be here soon, KD," Mom said.

"Oh good. It'll be nice to see her." I half-smiled at Mom. I welcomed anything to make this day less sad and was glad Mom would have her here. Sierra gave a light tap on the door frame. Halfway through the show, Mitchell was watching, Sierra arrived with her twelve-year-old daughter. "Hey, KD," Sierra said.

"Hey. Glad you made it before I have to leave." I rose and hugged her.

Sierra's daughter climbed into bed and sat between Mom and Mitchell, probably wanting to be closer to her grandpa. They'd always been close since she was a baby.

Sierra was holding a polish sausage on a fork. She bit off a piece.

Mitchell stirred, groaning, then his gaze fell on Sierra. "What are you eating?" he mumbled.

"It's a brat."

"It smells so good. Do you have any extra?" He straightened up a little in bed.

Sierra handed Mitchell the fork with the rest. It amazed me how selfless she was giving him her brat.

He ate it, chewing slowly. "Wow, that's good."

It warmed me inside seeing how thoughtful Sierra was and I knew every bite of food Mitchell took was a few more hours of energy. His manna. He had eaten so little that day.

"How are you doing today?" Sierra asked Mitchell.

"Resting mostly. Been visiting with Kaitlin watching some TV."

"That's good. Sorry, we were late here." Sierra grabbed a donut from the box.

"I'm glad you came," Mitchell said. A few minutes later, Mitchell dozed off again.

I talked with Sierra and Mom for a while, but knew I'd have to leave if I didn't want to drive home in the dark.

Mitchell was sleeping when I stood to leave. I didn't want to wake him just to say goodbye. My throat constricted as I stood in the doorway, taking one more glance before leaving. My heart told me I wouldn't see him again, on this side of Heaven, but I still couldn't say goodbye.

A few days after my last visit, on May fifth at 8 PM, Mitchell took his final breath with Mom near his side. The phone call came as Pat headed toward the house, kids riding with him on the four-wheeler.

On a wooden nightstand, a few feet from Mitchell's bed, his Bible pages held a bookmark. He'd been reading in Psalms. The Bible that the preacher from the gas station gave him.

The day after Mitchell died, I read a story in the Bible about when Jesus walked on water. After reading it, I closed my eyes and imagined Mitchell standing in a fishing boat as he scanned the horizon, searching for his way home. He squinted, and a tiny glimmer in the distance caught his eye, like the vehicle he had found in the desert. Waves lapped against his boat, crashing, then ebbing away, teetering the vessel. The motion pulled his attention away from the light. He looked up. Storm clouds rolled in, and the wind whistled. As Mitchell gazed at the sky, a frown stretching across his face. He sat and grabbed the oars. He found the glimmer again, and rowed toward it, trying to escape the storm. Sweat beaded on his forehead. Seeing something new on the water, he stopped.

A man walked on the water toward him, his tunic rippled in the wind like a flag. A look of recognition flashed across Mitchell's face as he realized the man, was Jesus.

Jesus said (as he said in the book of Matthew), "*Take courage! It is I. Don't be afraid.*"

Mitchell stared at the rough waters and His eyebrows creased until, at last, Mitchell pulled his worried gaze away. His eyes met his savior's. Mitchell answered Jesus, like the apostle Peter did in the Bible, "*Lord, if it is you, tell me to come to you on the water.*"

Jesus said, "*Come.*" He held out his nail-pierced hand, and Mitchell grabbed it.

With Jesus' help, he climbed out of the boat, and together they walked on the waters into eternity.

I was going to see Mitchell again someday.

For weeks after, I dreamt of Mitchell. Most times, he'd wave at me, the way he always did, hand in the air, palm open.

~ Thirty-One ~

Winter turned to spring, and spring to summer, and my dad, Alan, visited Wren and me in June. It was weird to call him dad because it was a word I had struggled with for so long.

As I've grown older, God has changed how I see the word dad. It doesn't hurt anymore to hear it. Because when I hear it: I hear my children call my husband "dad," I think of my relationship with Mitchell and how God healed it. I remember eating the best tacos in the world with Anthony and now, it doesn't hurt anymore remembering. If it wasn't for Wren and God making it possible, I'd have never found my dad, Alan. Dad isn't a word I need to fear or dread. It means restoration. Hope. Purpose.

Embers crackled in the fire pit in the center of our back deck during my dad, Alan's visit. I was happy he would take the time and money to travel across the country to see us. He could have walked away or ignored his phone the day Wren called to tell him he was our father. He could have given up, but he didn't.

The kids wanted to roast marshmallows. Campfires are one of our favorite things. They reminded me of the nights around the campfire with Mitchell, the good nights, and the nights during youth group in college when we'd sing worship songs.

So Pat, Dad, the kids, and I headed to the front porch to start a bonfire in the fire pit.

The flames of the fire were low, perfect for marshmallows. Fireflies' lights flickered in the grass beyond the porch and occasionally smoke from the fire drifted into my eyes. Bales of hay sat on the field. The sun was low but bright, purple and pink clouds stretched across the sky. There were two more hours of light before the darkness would come and stars would fill the sky.

Pat grabbed the roasting sticks from the garage and brought them to us. Tilly, my youngest, flitted around the porch. To block her from rushing into the fire, I wrapped my arms around her and pulled her away. God was like that, rescuing me back from danger.

Dad put a marshmallow onto his stick, then held it over the coals. Leaning forward, he said, "This is going to be a perfect one. Just wait and see." He rotated it over and over, bringing it to a happy golden brown. The marshmallow looked great, but to me, the night was perfect because my dad was there.

"Grandpa, can you teach me how to roast a marshmallow?" my oldest, Rosie, asked.

"Of, course," Dad said, pulling his marshmallow off the roasting stick and squishing it between chocolate and graham crackers. "Here you go, bud." He handed his perfect s'more to my middle child, Justus. Dad put a fresh marshmallow on the stick.

"Okay, Rosie. Hold the stick like this." My dad put the stick into her hands. "Keep it here and turn it slowly. Try not to get too close to the coals, or it'll catch fire." Rosie's face was full of joy as she lightly browned her marshmallow. Staring at the fire, her eyes were wide with wonder. It seemed like yesterday, I was beaming at Anthony, and the world was full of possibilities. Now, I was watching my dad interact with his grandchildren and it filled me with happiness. The future was full of possibilities again.

As Rosie ate her marshmallow, Dad ran into the house and returned with his iPad a few minutes later. He turned on an Allman Brothers song and set the iPad on the railing.

"Dance party!" Rosie yelled.

The kids and their grandpa danced on the porch, and I watched, knowing it would be one of those beautiful moments I'd always remember.

Pat and I put the kids to bed and after the kids fell asleep, Pat, Dad, and I sat on the couch and watched a Canadian sitcom until no one could keep their eyes open anymore. I didn't want the day to end.

The End

ABOUT THE AUTHOR

Kaitlin Thomson is a writer from the upper Midwest. She loves her family, Jesus, and gardening. In her free time, and when not chasing after young children, she also loves to read. You can find more of her writing on Femelle Soul's online publication, Flash Flood Fiction, and on Little Old Ladies Comedy website.

Please leave me a review on Amazon or Goodreads. Your feedback greatly helps authors. Thank you so much for reading my memoir and for walking along this journey with me.

www.ingramcontent.com/pod-product-compliance
Lightning Source LLC
Chambersburg PA
CBHW071141130626
46553CB00004B/1472